CRITICAL ASSUMPTIONS

CRITICAL ASSUMPTIONS

K. K. RUTHVEN

Professor of English, University of Canterbury
New Zealand

CAMBRIDGE UNIVERSITY PRESS

CAMBRIDGE

LONDON · NEW YORK · MELBOURNE

Published by the Syndics of the Cambridge University Press
The Pitt Building, Trumpington Street, Cambridge CB2 IRP
Bentley House, 200 Euston Road, London NW1 2DB
32 East 57th Street, New York, NY 10022, USA
296 Beaconsfield Parade, Middle Park, Melbourne 3206, Australia

First published 1979

Printed in Great Britain at the University Press, Cambridge

Library of Congress Cataloguing in Publication Data
Ruthven, Kenneth Knowles
Critical assumptions.
Includes bibliographical references and index.
1. Criticism. I. Title.
PN81.R8   801'.95   78-57760
ISBN 0 521 22257 5

To Rachel

Contents

Preface

This book is based on seminars conducted with postgraduate students whose first degree was in English. All were competent at the art of writing essays on literary topics, but few had had the opportunity to examine very carefully the critical principles they had picked up from a variety of teachers. I imagine that students elsewhere have the same experience.

To try to understand why we say what we say about books is a worthwhile ambition, if only on account of the taste it creates for inquiring into our reasons for saying what we say about many other things. *Critical assumptions* is written for students who would like to identify more clearly their own attitudes to books. In order to illustrate the range and diversity of critical responses to literature, I have brought together numerous observations (some famous, some not, but all pertinent) on four recurrent problems in the history of criticism: the genesis, form, meaning and value of what are called literary works. While going about the business I have often thought of Walter Benjamin's dream of remaining hidden behind a phalanx of quotations which, like highwaymen, would rob passing readers of their convictions. Such a book proved impossible to write. Even so modest a task as the marshalling of quotations is a critical act, and the temptation to take part in highway robberies proves irresistible; so I have not tried to conceal my own preferences among the options surveyed.

No book can be free of assumptions, least of all a book which takes them as its subject. My major assumption is this: that although the volume of commentary on literature is immense, the number of different observations which can be made about books is relatively small. Many of the likes and dislikes expressed by literary critics can be subsumed in sets of opposites, such as originality versus imitation, inspiration versus making, clarity versus obscurity, and so on. It is also notable that such pairs function differently in literary history from the way they function in literary theory. In literary history, the binary components are mutually contradictory and always demand a commitment to one or the other. If conscious craftsmanship happens to be in vogue, for instance, people tend to keep quiet about those involuntary experiences and fortuitous discoveries which go by the name of inspiration; but if a writer is expected to be the trumpet of a prophecy, or to display graces beyond the reach of art, we are unlikely to hear much about multiple drafts and compositional agonies. In literary theory, on the other hand, binary components are not contradictory but complementary to one another and equal in value: every theoretical position on any issue whatsoever is likely to be taken by somebody at some time and defended in ways which other people will find persuasive.

Traditionally, literary criticism has aligned itself with literary history, and the range of 'acceptable' literature has narrowed accordingly, irrespectively of whether it was the old generation or the new one which shaped the standards of excellence. This difficulty would be obviated if literary criticism were to be grounded in literary theory, such as I have described it. For if all theories are possible (and capable of various permutations with one another) then the whole of literature becomes available to us as a galaxy of possibilities: there can be no dead issues, obsolete forms, unfashionable authors, or unreadable books. I find this a richer prospect than the alternative, which is to encourage inexperienced readers to despise all writing which is not in accordance with certain types of theories which happen to be fashionable at the time. The following pages accordingly document some of the possibilities which constitute our range of choice.

Christchurch, New Zealand   K. K. RUTHVEN

I

Books as heterocosms

The term heterocosm

Imaginative works make public a private view of reality, and do it so compellingly that we want to share it. A book, we say, constitutes a world of its own. Such a world may appear disturbingly unfamiliar at first; but gradually, as it comes to dominate our imagination, we begin to understand its peoples and customs, and may end up feeling relatively at home there. Later, on returning to the world we left behind, we may find ourselves noticing things we never noticed before, and will value the book for sharpening our awareness. Conversely, the imaginative world we have just explored may strike us as being altogether too bizarre to be of interest to anybody except connoisseurs of alternative realities. Whatever our reaction, we shall have made the common assumption that a book is some sort of container for a special kind of reality, which may or may not resemble that 'real' reality we experience outside books.

Current attitudes are anticipated already by Richard Hurd, who warns us in the tenth of his *Letters on chivalry and romance* (1762) that 'the poet has a world of his own, where experience has less to do than consistent imagination'. This is the conclusion generally reached by all those who look upon writers as creators who somehow make poems in the way that God made the universe. The Muse who inspired Cowley's *Pindaric odes* (1668) is praised for having, like God, a 'thousand worlds' at her disposal:

> Thou speak'st, great Queen, in the same style as He,
> And a new world leaps forth when thou say'st, 'Let it be'.[1]

If God is the Maker, then the poet becomes (said Shaftesbury) 'a second maker, a just Prometheus, under Jove' who 'like that sovereign artist or universal plastic Nature forms a whole, coherent and proportioned in itself'.[2] And what the second maker makes is a second world, a heterocosm distinct from the macrocosm of the universe and the microcosm of man. We have inherited the Greek term 'heterocosm' ('other world') from the eighteenth-century German philosopher Baumgarten, who introduced it in his *Reflections on poetry* (1735).[3] Whenever we read, we encounter literary examples of what another German philosopher, Leibniz, called 'possible worlds',[4] each coherent and proportioned in itself. What should we call them?

If 'heterocosm' is accurate but awkward in English, none of the alternatives is entirely satisfactory. The term most commonly encountered is 'world', enclosed in inverted commas (or pronounced with an odd inflection) to indicate that we are not confusing the 'world' of Charles Dickens (nineteenth-century England) with the '"world"' of Dickens' novels. Despite its ambiguity the 'world' metaphor is attractive because so easily extendable, enabling us to talk about the moral climate of Frank Sargeson's stories or the topography of Ionescoland.[5] 'Secondary worlds' is another possibility. This is the term used by Tolkien,[6] who dissociates a primary world in which we eat and sleep and work from those secondary worlds produced by 'sub-creators' who have mastered the 'elvish craft' of fantasy; and Tolkien's term is adopted by W. H. Auden in a series of lectures published as *Secondary worlds* (London, 1969). 'Secondary worlds' seems to recollect the ancient definition of art as 'second nature': Cicero, for instance, explains how we may use our hands to 'bring into being within the realm of Nature a second nature for ourselves' (*De natura deorum*, II 60). Venerable as this usage may be, 'secondary' unfortunately implies second-best, a pejorative connotation avoided altogether by Middleton Murry's beautiful if somewhat cumbersome 'countries of the mind'.[7] Other possibilities include 'mundo' (Wallace Stevens), 'private countries' (Lawrence Durrell) and 'anti-worlds' (Andrei Voznesensky).[8] We use them when we want to describe places like the Forest of Arden or Prospero's island, Yeats's Byzantium or Lawrence's Etruria, places which often bear plausibly geographical names but have no geographical location.

The usefulness of talking about books in this way is challenged by P. N. Furbank who disapproves of what he calls 'thinking-in-"worlds"'.[9] He points out that the unity we find in a book is the result of authorial decisions, and is therefore different in kind from that unity we claim for the world about us, which constitutes a whole merely by happening to be all there. Differences between the selectiveness of heterocosms and the totality of the world make any comparison invidious: 'I feel distrustful of so many worlds being discovered or created', he complains, 'and suspect that entities are being multiplied needlessly' (p. 122). Yet anybody who follows Milton's advice and reads promiscuously will readily confess that a primary attraction of reading is the plurality and variety of literary worlds. Even if we were able to envisage (as E. M. Forster once invited us to do) all the great novelists sitting together in the British Museum writing their novels con-currently,[10] we could hardly imagine them contributing to one another's novels. As Dorothy Walsh once observed, Dostoevsky's Underground Man could never turn up for tea at a Trollope parsonage:[11] for heterocosms are very much divided and distinguished worlds, to their credit and our delight. Nevertheless, Furbank's strictures are valuable in that they discourage glib talk about literary 'worlds'. Insisting, as he does, that the form of a book is radically different from the form of the world, and that the excellence of a book is dependent on the amount of reality it can ingest, Furbank clearly locates the points at which opinions divide. I propose, therefore, in probing more deeply into the nature of heterocosms, to pose his conclusions as questions, and to ask, in the first place, how we are able to say that a literary work has unity and form.

The sense of form

'Form' is fundamental to most definitions of art. A spatial concept, it can be applied literally to spatial media like painting or sculpture, where form is manifestly a visual or tactile experience. In a temporal medium like literature, on the other hand, 'form' can never be more than a metaphor, and this has led people to suppose that 'form' is a concept best approached through the psychology of perception: there is no objective 'form' in a literary work, but merely a subjective 'sense of form' or Formgefühl, as Wölfflin called it.[12] In that case, plays and novels have form because of our readiness to confer form upon them. We appear to be inveterately form-finding creatures like Tennyson, who (Carlyle told Emerson) was always 'carrying a bit of Chaos about with him' and 'manufacturing [it] into Cosmos'.[13] If this seems a perfectly natural thing to do, it is worth bearing in mind that the construction of highly organised heterocosms may be peculiar to certain cultures and even to certain social classes within those

cultures. We are told, for example, that such practices are inimical
to Islamic thought, which sees the world as being already complete
and therefore incapable of being 'supplemented' by art.[14] We are
also warned that 'form' is ideologically suspect, and that one of
the aims of Marxists is 'to liberate criticism from the magic spell
of that liberal dogma which sees art as organising the "chaos"
of reality, as imposing form on the formless, order on the
amorphous'.[15] For all that, it would be difficult to imagine a
'heterochaos': where, outside *Finnegans wake*, would one search
for a 'chaosmos'?[16] Moreover, we continue to create order even
when evidence of disorder appears to be overwhelming. Henry
Adams made this point strikingly when he remarked that the
kinetic theory of gas proved that 'Chaos was the law of nature'
whereas 'Order was the dream of man'.[17] And as a dream, the
dream of order cannot be destroyed by chaotic reality.

Comparable investigations of the problem in aesthetics result
in George Boas's claim that 'the formless is usually that form for
which we have no name'. 'Even a blot of ink', adds Boas, 'has
the form of a blot'.[18] So strong is our impulse to order that we
may even delude ourselves into believing that we are uncovering
some kind of hidden form or 'cryptomorph' in the books we
study. The outcome is often an aesthetic version of what theologians call the Argument from Design, in so far as Boas's faith in
the ultimate form of formlessness sounds not unlike that theory
of the universe set out so memorably in Pope's *Essay on man* (1
283ff):

> All nature is but art, unknown to thee
> All chance – direction, which thou canst not see
> All discord – harmony, not understood...

and so forth. Wherever we see chaos, we are guaranteed to find
cosmos, provided we take the trouble to look properly; in
Dryden's words:

> No atoms casually together hurled
> Could e'er produce so beautiful a world.[19]

Art is often suspected of harbouring hidden order.[20] Even the
most intractable of books may yield conclusions which parallel
those recorded in William Paley's *Natural theology* (1802), whose
title-page promises 'evidences of the existence and attributes of the
deity collected from the appearances of nature'. Where design
does not exist we feel obliged to invent it, and set about the task

as diligently as those early Christians who imposed a symbolic order on that heterogeneous collection of writings known to us as The Holy Bible. In the process, we may hope to emulate not William Paley but Luke Howard, who devised in 1803 a system for classifying cloud-formations still in use today, a system which gives us the illusion that the nebulous may yet contain discoverable forms, and not be forever at the mercy of form-finders and their impositions.

Not only critics but writers too are said to be characterised by a 'blessed rage for order', to quote a much-quoted phrase from Wallace Stevens' poem 'The Idea of order at Key West'. For scientific validation of this rage for order we turn to Gestalt psychology, which developed in the early years of this century under the influence of Max Wertheimer. Gestalt psychologists claim that we have an innate preference for perceiving wholes as distinct from separate parts, and that our ability to apprehend individual parts is determined by whatever whole we see such parts as belonging to. Hence the law governing the so-called *phi phenomenon*, which is this: 'There are wholes, the behaviour of which is not determined by that of their individual elements, but where the part-processes are themselves determined by the intrinsic nature of the whole.'[21] Much of the evidence comes, of course, from experiments in visual perception; but theorists of literary form are likely to be particularly interested in the Gestalt principle of closure, as illustrated in the way we invariably 'see' a circle when confronted by a line which curves well beyond semi-circularity without actually achieving circularity. The fact that we all develop Gestalt vision as children indicates that we need some sort of mechanism for imposing order on disorder to avoid being overwhelmed by the chaos of experience. The blessed rage for order looks like an aesthetic vision of our indomitable urge to make sense of things by interposing *Gestalten* between ourselves and the outside world. But it may not be as simple as that. When Hermann Rorschach invented his famous ink-blots, he had some difficulty in finding a sequence of blots sufficiently suggestive for his purposes: some ink-blots, unco-operative patients testified, look remarkably like ink-blots.[22] Now this problem ought never to have arisen, for Rorschach's patients should have been able to interpret any blot whatsoever in terms of a suggested Gestalt, in the way that Botticelli did when he told Leonardo da Vinci that if you throw a sponge-full of paint at a wall the resultant blot will take the form of a landscape.[23] Yet one's sympathies go out to those unimaginative people who failed their Rorschach test by insisting that blots are blots. What a relief it would be if critics of arcane masterpieces like Pound's *The cantos* were to display similar candour, instead of feeling obliged to write well-intentioned apologias which point to the existence of hitherto unsuspected clusters of images or thematic threads, in the expectation that revelations of such hidden order will improve *The cantos'* stature as poetry.

So universal is the assumption that art is linked indissolubly to order that theories of artistic disorder are relatively hard to come by. Controversy centres usually on whether 'form' is a quality inherent in literary works, or whether it is something projected on them by critics: are we talking about structures we perceive, or constructs we apperceive? Neither formulation questions the importance of order in what goes on when we read a poem or novel. Indeed there is little in the history of European literature to make us doubt the inevitability of art's alliance with order. Even the neoclassical cult of negligence, with its enthusiasm for the unbuttoned and the windblown, is only an elegant pretence at disorder (with order in vigilant attendance, like the clergy at a one-day Feast of Fools). One thinks of the 'sweet neglect' praised in Jonson's exquisite lyric, or of Herrick's 'Delight in disorder':

> A sweet disorder in the dress
> Kindles, in clothes, a wantonness.[24]

It is easy to establish the consummate artistry of such artlessness. Pindaric odes are organised in such a way as to look disorganised, and we are not expected to regard eulogies of *beau désordre* as anything more serious than a calculated flirtation with chaos.

All this is far removed from the 'disorder' theories which currently command attention. One of these is documented at length by Morse Peckham in his book *Man's rage for chaos* (Philadelphia, 1965). Peckham believes it is not the function of the arts to bring us into perfect focus by offering intimations of a sublimely articulated orderliness, but rather to *dis*orientate us. We arrive with preconceptions which works of art destroy. What looks to be ordered and beautiful is really a configuration of subversive elements which will detonate the moment we make contact with it. Art upsets us for our own good by destroying the complacency which accompanies ideas of order and control; its true value is therefore propaedeutic, for it prepares us for life. 'The very drive to order which qualifies man to deal successfully with his environment', writes Peckham, 'disqualifies him when it is to his interest to correct his orientation' (p. xi). Upset by some new book, we have ample leisure in which to learn to cope with the new demands it makes on us; and the lesson will have been well learned when new demands are made on us in the course of our lives, for by then we shall have rehearsed the ritual of coping-by-adjustment. Peckham seems to assume, however, that all good art is radically disturbing. But this is a difficult thesis to defend in the case of writers outside the Romantic tradition – Joseph Addison, for instance, or Samuel Johnson – who wrote with a view to consolidating public opinion and preserving the status quo. Besides, as Peckham admits, there is no psychological verification for the theory of disorder he proposes. Jonathan Culler is therefore on much safer ground when, in claiming that the novels of Flaubert seek to disorder our expectations of coherence, he confines his attention to structures of meaning in the texts themselves.[25]

The other disturbing theory which challenges traditional assumptions about the ordered nature of aesthetic experiences has come from what is known in electrical engineering as Information Theory. In Information Theory, a series of signals constitutes a message, and the information-content of such a message is measured by the degree of unpredictability of successive items. Should the signals occur in a purely random order, each will be unpredictable from what has gone before; in which case, each signal is said to give maximum information and to have maximum entropy. A telephone number has a higher Information-content than a *Hamlet* soliloquy, where predictability makes for a high degree of redundancy. And so it has come about that in the last twenty-five years or so aestheticians have had to confront what Rudolf Arnheim calls an appalling paradox: 'that complete disorder or chaos provides a maximum of information, whereas a completely organised pattern yields no information at all'.[26] By the same token, however, it may be an extremely fertile paradox in the imagination of anybody equipped to explore it, for the most striking feature of Information is its uninformativeness by ordinary standards. One way of reading Thomas Pynchon's novel *The crying of lot 49* (Philadelphia, 1966) is to treat it as a comedy of Information. Its heroine, Oedipa Maas, spends much of her time in trying to unriddle a mystery which may not even exist, and the book stops abruptly just as some sort of clarification is about to be offered. Oedipa tries to make sense of a welter of random objects and incidents, but the more she encounters, the more she discovers to be encountered, and the less she finds out. In the ordinary sense of the word, she is deprived of information, and the novel is a compendium of redundancies; but as Information, none of these things is redundant, because Oedipa is caught up in the dimension of maximum entropy. What looks like disorder in the novel is rather what Arnheim would call a 'clash of unco-ordinated orders'.[27] *The crying of lot 49*, like that other masterpiece of disorder, *Tristram Shandy*,[28] opens up a new universe of discourse.

More often, however, it is the sillier side of randomness which is brought to our attention. George Macbeth's *Collected poems* (London, 1971) contains poems whose parts are designed like playing-cards, to be shuffled and dealt and then read in whatever order chance decrees. Works made up of loose-leaved pages refuse to commit themselves to the stability of a 'correct' order. The value of such random or 'aleatory' creations resides in their resistance to hierarchical ordering. As examples of Information they are very effective, for they maximise their entropy by evading predictability. Most of us, however, prefer information to Information, and derive satisfaction from the redundancies of more orthodox books.

Relationships to reality

Because we always compare what we read with what we know, we can hardly avoid comparing heterocosms with the world we live in. Our confused expectations of books and their authors are outlined neatly at the beginning of one of Wallace Stevens' poems, where an imaginative man confronts his public:

> They said, 'You have a blue guitar,
> You do not play things as they are.'
>
> The man replied, 'Things as they are
> Are changed upon the blue guitar.'[29]

And so they are; and the people in Stevens' poem concede as much when they go on to ask, rather unreasonably, for 'A tune beyond us, yet ourselves' – for a literature which manages somehow to be 'like' life and at the same time to transcend it, a 'mundo' not entirely detached from our ordinary universe.

We soon recognise the existence of varying degrees of proximity between heterocosms and the world. At one end of the scale we find purely imaginary places like Angria and Gondal, which the Brontë children dreamed up for their own amusement. At an opposite extreme we encounter Defoe's London or Joyce's Dublin, places described so vividly that one can trace events in the novel on a street-map, or make an Odyssey around Dublin on Bloomsday. So scrupulously specific was Joyce in evoking the Dublin of 1904 that he was careful to lodge Bloom and Molly at a house shown to be vacant in *Thom's Dublin directory* for that year.[30] The allurements of specificity are strong enough to encourage certain writers to take extraordinary care in delineating the topography of imaginary places, so much so as to render them mappable: places like Hardy's Wessex, for instance, or Faulkner's Yoknapatawpha County. Trollope's decision to make a map of his imaginary Barsetshire while writing *Framley Parsonage* (1861) would have met with the approval of Robert Louis Stevenson, who believed that factual errors in *The antiquary* (1816) and *Rob Roy* (1818) could have been avoided if Scott had taken the trouble to make maps and almanacs while writing them.[31] So powerful is our desire to make the imagined look real that fiction often attracts cartographers, as J. B. Post reveals in his intriguing *Atlas of fantasy* (Baltimore, 1973). For always there is the possibility that the imagined, however fantastic, will turn out to be rooted in reality after all, like Homer's *Odyssey*, which is now read as an account of a sea-voyage anybody can repeat, despite the fact that as long ago as the third century BC Eratosthenes declared it a waste of time to go looking for the things Odysseus saw.[32]

A heterocosm is the way it is as a result of an authorial decision to imitate life or transform it. The more familiar and popular aim is *mimesis*, or the representation of reality, which derives from Aristotle's *Poetics* and is disparaged in that ignoble analogy, *ars simia naturae*, art as the ape of nature.[33] Mirrors provide the basic conceptual model for mimetic approaches, enabling Hamlet to remind the players that the purpose of play-acting is 'to hold, as 'twere, the mirror up to nature', or Stendhal to conceive of the novel as a mirror in the roadway.[34] The mirror-model, which permits us to say that art 'reflects' life, is rejected by people sensitive to the fact that reality cannot be represented in art without some distortion. When the conceptual model shifts from mirror to glass, art no longer reflects life but refracts it, offering us a 'deflection, not a reflection, of experience' (Erlich).[35] For all their differences, however, reflectivists share with refractivists the same basic assumptions: firstly, that a real world already exists, containing real roads along which Stendhal can set up his mirror, and real toads which Marianne Moore can place in her imaginary gardens;[36] and secondly, that this real world is already formed before we begin to perceive it, and so well formed as to constitute an exemplary model for mimetic art.

This is why those who reject realistic *mimesis* direct attention away from the correspondence of art to reality, and focus instead on the imagination of the artist. 'A man's work must be the reflex of a living image in his own mind', writes Holman Hunt, 'and not the icy double of the facts themselves'; Baudelaire confesses in his *Éloge du maquillage* that he has no desire to assign to art 'the sterile function of imitating nature'.[37] Whistler should not be praised for his mimetic fidelity to Thames fogs, thought Wilde, but for having the imagination to 'invent' Thames fogs by creating an artistic awareness of them, thus proving the axiom that life imitates art far more than art imitates life ('The decay of lying').

Whenever writers are convinced that their true business is not so much to transcribe reality as to transcend it, *mimesis* is abandoned in favour of some form of meliorism. The idealised landscapes and figures depicted in Sidney's *Arcadia* (1590) or Marlowe's *Hero and Leander* (1598) are melioristic in this sense, and testify to a belief that art should not reflect but perfect life. Although obliged to begin with nature, the poet (Sidney explains in his *Defence of poesy*, 1595) will refuse to be 'enclosed within the narrow warrant of her gifts', preferring instead to range 'within the zodiac of his own wit'.[38] Confronted with a brazen world of reality, Sidneian writers manufacture a golden world of the imagination by salvaging the scattered and fragmented excellences of nature and recombining them into ideal wholes, thus creating a literature in which the Golden Age is restored, Paradise regained. 'The great design of the arts', wrote John Dennis in 1704, 'is to restore the decays that happened to human nature by the Fall.'[39] Support for such a poetics of perfectibility can always be solicited from Aristotle, who once declared that art must be superior to nature because it perfects it (*Politics*, 1255b); as Oscar Wilde would say, 'Nature has good intentions, of course, but...she cannot carry them out' ('The decay of lying'). Hence the importance recognised by Baudelaire of a decreative principle in the imagination which 'decomposes all creation, and with the materials...creates a new world'.[40]

Baudelaire's own poetry illustrates very well that what is reconstituted after dismantlement need not be idealistic in Sidney's sense. Melioristic writers often feel that the ordinary world is not particularly interesting the way it is, and refuse to accept the view that the world is all that is the case. It is true that Wordsworth claimed to have had his imagination strengthened by 'natural objects', but William Blake found that 'natural objects always... weaken, deaden and obliterate imagination'. 'Imagination is my world', he proclaimed in his *Descriptive catalogue* (1809): 'this world of dross is beneath my notice.'[41]

Literary autarchies

Any writer who rejects both the realism of *is* and the idealism of *ought* is in a strong position to sever contact with reality and produce one of those seemingly self-contained heterocosms in which, as Hurd noted, experience has less to do than consistent imagination. They are said to be autonomous because subject only to laws of their own making, and autotelic in so far as they appear to exist for no other purpose than to be what they are. 'There neither exists nor *can* exist', writes Edgar Allan Poe, 'any work more thoroughly dignified, more supremely noble than this very poem, this poem *per se*, this poem which is a poem and nothing more, this poem written solely for the poem's sake.'[42] Such works are called autarchies, and are best explained by a master of autarchic fictions, Vladimir Nabokov: '"reality" is neither the subject nor the object of true art which creates its own special reality having nothing to do with the average "reality" perceived by the communal eye'.[43] When literature achieves this degree of refinement, one can appreciate the momentous implications of heterocosmic theory. Some of these will have to be investigated more closely in subsequent chapters, but for the moment let us simply note the major points.[44]

    1. If a heterocosm need not necessarily correspond to the world we live in, it cannot be expected to observe whatever truth-standards happen to apply there. Whatever truth resides in a heterocosm is more likely to be truth-of-coherence than truth-of-correspondence.

    2. Writers who believe their most important task is to establish internal coherence in their works are likely to believe in addition that their aesthetic responsibility towards such works must take priority over any moral considerations for the people who read

them. They may well feel, as Wilde did, that there can be no such thing as an immoral book, because books are neither moral nor immoral, but merely well-written or not.

  - 3. The resultant literature will call for a new kind of reader who is 'disinterested' in what he reads, able and willing to suspend his disbelief while taking pleasure in the beauteous forms of things. In short, heterocosmic theory profoundly alters the experience of reading by redefining the truth-claims and responsibilities of the writer.

The purely aesthetic pleasure afforded by heterocosms was first defined in 1790 by Immanuel Kant as 'disinterested satisfaction', which Wellek glosses as signifying 'lack of interference from desire, the directness of our access to the work of art, undisturbed, uninterfered with (*inter-esse*) by immediate utilitarian ends'.[45] Originally, 'disinterestedness' was imported into aesthetics from theology, where 'the disinterested love of God' – loving the Good because it is good – was held by Shaftesbury to be superior to serving God 'for interest merely'.[46] In its new aesthetic context, 'disinterested' was applied to a category of statements which invite mere contemplation and are therefore quite different from moral statements, which call for commitment and action. Although it proved helpful in defences of literature against charges of immorality (for how can anybody be corrupted by a book which invites contemplation and discourages action?) the theory of disinterested satisfaction fosters the limiting supposition that literature can never be anything other than beautifully useless. This too, however, is a consequence of heterocosmic thinking, for the art-for-art's-sake element in English Aestheticism and the *poésie pure* of French Symbolism are nineteenth-century culminations of heterocosmic ideals. The dilemma is clear. On the one hand we are reluctant to shackle the arts with categories and expectations imported from extrinsic disciplines: we believe that to assert the autonomy of literature is to defend its integrity and prevent it from being treated as a defective system of philosophy, an ineffectual mode of moral exhortation, or a substitute for religion. On the other hand, in protecting literature against the wrong kind of probing, we run the risk inevitably of insulating it from life. For the theory of autonomy surrounds literature like the Great Wall of China, effectively keeping out huns and philistines, but unfortunately imprisoning those on the inside. This danger is not always admitted. A. C. Bradley, for instance, describes poetry as 'a world by itself, independent, complete, autonomous; and to possess it fully you must enter that world, conform to its laws, and ignore for the time the beliefs, aims, and particular conditions which belong to you in the...world of reality'.[47] And if one refuses? An answer of sorts is provided by Virginia Woolf, who contrasts her experience in reading Sterne and Jane Austen with what she feels when reading the novels of Galsworthy, Wells and Bennett. She finds *Tristram Shandy* (1760–67) and *Pride and prejudice* (1813) so self-contained as to leave one with 'no desire to do anything, except indeed to read the book again', whereas the other novelists she mentions engender only a restless urge to do something else – 'to join a society, or, more desperately, to write a cheque'.[48] There is no question of having to make a conscious decision not to bring the wrong expectations to books: some works are so good, she believes, that we have no alternative but to submit to their domination. Like Bradley, however, she thinks that such books are not about anything but themselves, and are good books for precisely this reason. Yet I doubt whether anybody ever read *To the lighthouse* (1927) or *The waves* (1931) merely in order to read them again, or whether anybody ever considered that E. M. Forster's *A passage to India* (1924) is flawed because it arouses non-aesthetic feelings about the ineptitudes of British rule in India. Autarchic theory, like most literary theories, is a doctrine of special instances, in this case of a mode of writing epitomised in Arthur Symons' poem about Jane Avril dancing alone in the twilight in front of a mirror, smiling to herself enigmatically, totally absorbed in an autistic act whose significance we can only guess.[49] Symons' dancer is an apt emblem for the autarchic ideal: diplomatic relations between art and reality are broken off, and the whole world exists only to end up in a book.[50]

Word-worlds

Because a writer's transactions with reality are verbal, he must bridge the traditional gap between words (*verba*) and things (*res*).[51] On the one hand, he may think of language as a kind of lens, and seek out 'transparent' words which designate things-in-the-world as unobtrusively as possible; on the other hand, he may think of language as a kind of body, and pay attention primarily to the shapes, sounds and textures of the words he uses. 'The multitudinous seas incarnadine' (*Macbeth*, II ii 61) is an example of language-as-body, in that the communicative purposes of language-as-lens could be achieved equally well by some such phrase as 'turn the many seas red'. In the case of language-as-body, words are not considered to be images of things, but things in themselves. 'I would endeavour to destroy the old antithesis of *words* and *things*', said Coleridge, 'elevating, as it were, words into things, and living things too.'[52] Whenever this is deemed possible, poems cease to be thought of as mere windows on reality, and become (in Wallace Stevens' phrase) 'part of the res itself and not about it'.[53]

Some such distinction between language-as-lens and language-as-body is often at the root of arbitrary attempts to differentiate prose from poetry. Coleridge, for instance, thought that 'the words in prose ought to express the intended meaning, and no more; if they attract attention to themselves it is, in general, a fault'. He therefore admired Southey's ability to write prose so well as to conceal the verbality of his medium. 'But in verse', Coleridge went on to say, 'you must do more; there the words, the *media*, must be beautiful, and ought to attract your notice.'[54] Prose writers such as John Lyly, whose *Euphues* (1578) is written in the same ornamental style as the poetry of Sidney and Spenser, are frequently disparaged on these grounds. For 'the object of the novelist', according to Ford Madox Ford, 'is to keep the reader entirely oblivious of the fact that...he is reading a book'.[55] And of course no reader of *Euphues* is ever likely to forget he is reading a book.

Whatever the generic differences between poetry and prose may be, they cannot be framed in terms of a distinction between language-as-lens and language-as-body, because both alternatives are available to poets and prose writers alike. In the case of language-as-lens, reality is assumed to be far more important than words, which (in philosophical tradition) are usually accused of hindering us from seeing things as they really are. 'We need only draw the curtain of words', thought Berkeley, 'to behold the fairest tree of knowledge.'[56] From this point of view, verbal style is a disposable garment, what Johnson called 'the dress of thought',[57] something that can be peeled off without damage to the subject-matter. This is how it was possible for Dryden, when he came to rewrite *Troilus and Cressida*, to see himself as doing the play a favour by salvaging it from 'that heap of rubbish'[58] – Shakespeare's language – under which it lay buried. As De Quincey points out,[59] it was Wordsworth who was instrumental in substituting for the 'dress of thought' the idea of language as the 'incarnation' of thought. 'If words be not...an incarnation of the thought but only a clothing for it, then surely they will prove an ill gift', wrote Wordsworth, whose own experience as a writer convinced him that a poet 'rather makes/Than finds what he beholds'.[60]

The ability to create such word-worlds is often described as 'Orphic', after the legendary poet Orpheus, who is credited by Ovid with the power of being able to summon things into his presence merely by naming them.[61] Orphic poets do not use words to describe something which exists already, but to create something which has never existed before. Their poetry is not expected to be about reality, nor to offer us vicarious experience of it through the medium of words. On the contrary, an Orphic poem is meant to *be* reality: it confronts us with its sheer presence, having nothing to mediate but itself, and promising nothing more than the immediate experience of reading it.

Such developments are likely to occur when writers share Yeats's belief that 'words alone are certain good'.[62] To cultivate the Orphic mode involves abandoning the idea that books are valuable for what they tell us about life. Several critics have advised against the building of such word-worlds,[63] but none more cogently than Irving Massey in *The uncreating word* (Bloomington, 1970). 'The creation of an imaginary world which has substantial reality is a normal and legitimate activity of poetry', Massey concedes, 'but the reality of the world so created cannot rest in the words; it must be an experienced phenomenon' (pp. 128f). He disapproves of the way in which Gerard Manley Hopkins severed clusters of words from the stem of experience, and concentrated too narrowly on the naked thew and sinew of language. 'If we have lost our reality', he contends, 'words will not bring it back to us' (p. 103). His book leaves one with a sense that the Orphic endeavour is magnificently perverse, and that the strain of purism which refines heterocosms into autarchies is ultimately the ruination of literature.

2

Organic and inorganic form

The forms which result from the composition of chaos into cosmos are often spoken of as belonging to one of two different types: 'organic' form, on analogy with biological organisms, and 'inorganic' form, on analogy with geometrical design. The reason for this is that organicist critics from Coleridge onwards have generally agreed that the two kinds of form are in fact antithetical to one another. A writer's choice (so the argument goes) is between organic forms which are as vibrant and flexible as life itself, and inorganic forms which are inert, coldly calculated, mathematical and dead. Romantic orthodoxy in these matters, however, has never prevented authors from avoiding the appearance of disorder by tacitly making cold calculations, and neatly packaging otherwise slovenly organic experiences into metrically correct stanzas, five-act plays, three-volume novels, and so on. Historical research into the idea of organicism[1] has made it much easier for us than it was for the Romantics to be sceptical of an aesthetic which falsely polarises the geometrical and the organic, and ends up discrediting an alternative (and indeed older) aesthetic at which we must now look more closely.

Form as proportion

Much of what goes by the name of inorganic form might equally well be styled Pythagorean, in so far as all theories which emphasise the value of such things as proportion and symmetry derive ultimately from the Pythagorean doctrine that number is the key to creation. From Plato's *Timaeus* we have inherited the Pythagorean conception of the universe as the work of a geometrician, a pagan conception easily assimilated by Christians who were led to believe that their own God had created 'all things in number and measure and weight' (Wisdom of Solomon, 11: 21). It is certainly a divine mathematician who is celebrated in

Boethius' prayer to God the Creator, who governs this world (in Chaucer's translation) 'by perdurable reason', binding its elements 'by numbers proportionable' (*Of the consolation of philosophy*, III 9). Similarly, the human *artifex* could be thought of as succeeding by his mastery of those numbers which are called metres in poetry and notes in music; and so there emerged a quantitative aesthetic in which art is equated with beauty, and beauty with mathematical proportion. Socrates, for instance, remarks in Plato's *Philebus* (64e) that measure (*metron*) and proportion (*symmetron*) are universal constituents of beauty. It is no accident, therefore, that some of the most ancient of our aesthetic terms are quantitative metaphors.[2]

In its simplest manifestations, proportionate form pleases by achieving such balances of opposites as the Miltonic diptych 'L'Allegro' and 'Il Penseroso'. We take pleasure in recognising an achieved equipoise, as when Spenser sets the House of Holiness against the House of Pride in Book I of *The faerie queene* (1590), with Seven Corporal Works of Mercy set against Seven Deadly Sins. Equally simple is 'recessed' symmetry, which occurs when one episode is framed between two others, as in the *Aeneid*, where the middle of the poem is framed by the twin tragedies of Dido (I–IV) and Turnus (IX–XII).[3] A more complicated version of proportionate form gives us the clockwork plot of *Tom Jones* (1749), where for every action there is a counteraction, awareness of which may elude the reader but not the re-reader of Fielding's novel. So entrenched is our Romantic bias against inorganic structures, however, that much of the research devoted to revealing their intricacy has met with ridicule – not so much because the evidence sometimes looks rigged, as because the whole enterprise is likely to seem quite preposterous. Yet it is much less preposterous if we think of a poem or novel not as something which 'grows' (in the organicist sense) but as something 'made'. Architecturally, the ancient ideal was the Golden Section, in which the proportion of the lesser part to the greater is identical with that of the greater to the whole (numerically, a proportion of 0.618 or 1.618:1). In poetry, this can be simulated by a precise allotment of line-length to subject-matter, as Guy Le Grelle first showed in 1949 by analysing the first book of Virgil's *Georgics*.[4] A decade later, George E. Duckworth was claiming that of the 2187 verses in the *Georgics*, 835 are devoted to matters of national or philosophical interest, whereas the remaining 1352 are devoted to farming. Proportionately, $835:1352 = 1352:2187 = 0.618$. And so Duckworth went on to publish his book, on *Structural patterns and proportions in Vergil's 'Aeneid'* (Ann Arbor, 1962), pointing to the existence of over a thousand Golden Section ratios in the poem and using these as evidence for his compositional hypothesis that Virgil 'wrote the short passages with mathematical symmetry and combined them into increasingly larger units' (p. 73). It all suggests that when Virgil announced his intention to honour Caesar by writing the *Aeneid* – 'Caesar shall be in the centre, and shall occupy the shrine' (*Georgics*, III 16) – his architectural metaphor of a *templum* was not merely decorative: the *Aeneid* was to be what Horace hoped his odes would be, 'a monument more lasting than bronze' (*Odes*, III 30). And it is in a more precise sense than perhaps Matthew Arnold intended that we can speak of the 'architectonics' of such poetry.[5]

Robert M. Jordan's *Chaucer and the shape of creation* (Cambridge, Mass., 1967) proceeds also on the assumption that architecture is a better key to the art of *The Canterbury tales* than organicist models such as trees or bodies. 'The typical Chaucerian narrative', he finds, 'is literally "built" of inert, self-contained parts, collocated in accordance with the additive, reduplicative principles which characterise the Gothic edifice' (p. xi). He takes his cue from the pedestrian Geoffrey of Vinsauf, who advises readers of his *Poetria nova* (*c.* 1200) to learn from a builder how best to dispose the parts of a poem. 'Depending on the ingenuity of the maker', writes Jordan, 'a limitless number of new divisions can be adduced or new parts added, since the work does not grow *ab ovo* but is built up of parts whose relevance to the controlling idea can be defined nominally, by rationalistic deduction' (p. 238). As a structural principle, this is very similar to the rhetorical device of *partitio*, which enables one to impose order on discourse by first dividing the subject-matter into parts, then further subdividing those parts, and continuing to subdivide the subdivisions in a manner strikingly illustrated by those diagrammatic synopses which guide us through the maze of Burton's *Anatomy of melancholy* (1621). The value of Jordan's architectural analogy is that it shows us a Chaucer who succeeds in accommodating diverse materials into an inorganic structure, rather than a Chaucer who fails to make a satisfyingly organic whole of *The Canterbury tales*. It is in this spirit that other medievalists have sought inorganic models for the art they admire, seeing in Old English poetry the panel structure of the Franks Casket or the serpentine maze of illuminated initials in the *Book of Kells*, and looking at medieval narrative structural devices on analogy with the *entrelacement* or 'interlace' of the designs on other illuminated manuscripts.[6]

Numerological form

Numerical form is often arbitrary and external, like the twelve books of a Virgilian epic, the five acts of a tragedy, the fourteen lines of a sonnet. Whenever individual details have to be made subservient to the total scheme, which is always the case in numerically based forms, admiration is reserved for the writer who can move with apparent freedom within self-imposed limits: somehow the sonneteer must create the illusion that he needs exactly fourteen lines in which to say what he has to say, neither more nor less. Numerology – the mystical science of numbers – is an altogether more complicated affair than this, for it involves conferring special significances upon certain numbers and permutations of numbers, and then organising poems and subsections of poems in such a way as to emphasise by repetition a thematically significant number. In *Paradise lost*, for instance, the seven days of Creation are said to be recessed between the thirteen which encompass the Fall of the Angels and another thirteen which encompass the Fall of Man: thirteen plus seven plus thirteen equals thirty-three, which is the number of years of Christ's incarnate life.[7] Before the publication of A. Kent Hieatt's book, *Short time's endless monument* (New York, 1960), nobody had ever noticed that the gorgeous surface of Spenser's *Epithalamion* (1596) conceals a numerological pattern testifying to the poem's deep affinities with Pythagorean form. For it celebrates in twenty-four stanzas the twenty-four hours of that midsummer's day on which the wedding took place, commemorating the days of the year in 365 long lines, and using a change of refrain between the sixteenth and seventeenth stanzas to mark the sixteen hours of solstitial daylight at that particular latitude. Predictably, *The faerie queene* yields vastly more riches to this kind of probing, as Alastair Fowler argues in *Spenser and the numbers of time* (London, 1964). Book 1 was made the Legend of Holiness because in ancient number-systems 'one is no number', and the number one (the 'monad') therefore symbolises the godhead (which is why the representative of the True Church is called Una); two, on the other hand, is the dyad from which diversity originates and therefore the multiplications which make for falsehood (so Una is opposed by an embodiment of duplicity called Duessa). Within each Book, dominant astrological and mythological symbols determine the numerical shape of individual sections, the solar numbers of Book I yielding to the lunar numbers of Book II, and so on. Far from being as shapeless as it seems to be, *The faerie queene* as Fowler reads it begins to look extraordinarily schematic, perhaps over-schematic.

That Spenser conceived *The faerie queene* much as Fowler describes it there seems little doubt, although whether he ever put into the poem all of the patterns Fowler discerns in it is another matter altogether. Because all such studies assume numerical stability in the text, authorial revisions play havoc with numerological interpretations. If Milton thought it a good idea in *Comus* (1634) to have the tempter begin to speak at line 666 (which is the number of the Beast in the Revelation of St John, 13:18) it is difficult to imagine why he should have let the same speech begin at line 665 in a later edition of the masque; and if Milton intended Christ to ascend his chariot at what is numerically the middle line of the 1667 edition of *Paradise lost*, why was that placement not retained in his revised version of 1674?[8] Nobody is more acutely aware of such problems than Fowler himself, who presents in a later study, *Triumphal forms* (Cambridge, 1970), a carefully reasoned case for admitting numerological studies into a formalist theory of literature. He argues that the analogy between poetry and architecture leads to a spatial conception of form which obliges the reader to contemplate a literary work as having extension in space rather than duration in time; numerological form is there to be observed and understood. As such, it is one of the formalist devices which contribute to the manufacture of well-wrought urns: 'numerology belongs primarily to literature considered as artifact' (p. 202). Fowler's principal endeavour is to clear our minds of expectations fostered by centuries of prose ('which has taught readers to move relatively quickly along the semantic line') and to resurrect a different kind of reading-habit altogether; namely 'to think of the literary model more as an artifact, in which meditation might frequently dwell, finding ever new aspects of a world image generated, like the world itself, by mathematical patterns' (p. 202). The Renaissance reader here imagined by Fowler sounds surprisingly modernist. For in the course of departing from the organicist criteria of the Romantics, Fowler moves towards the anti-Romantic theories of twentieth-century formalists, particularly as found in Joseph Frank's controversial essay on 'spatial form' in modern literature,[9] which sets out to prove that Eliot and Joyce and Proust write in such a manner that 'the reader is intended to apprehend their work spatially, in a moment of time, rather than as a sequence' (p. 225). Modernist literature is spatial, according to Frank, because it confronts us with fragments which we ourselves must piece together if we are to make any sense of them: it departs radically from Lessing's belief that time is the essence of poetry, whereas space is the essence of the plastic arts. Now of course evidence of spatial form in pre-modernist literature is easy enough to come by if we treat the pattern-poem (verses in the shape of wings, altars, etc.) as a spatial form and trace its fortunes from the *Greek anthology* to those seventeenth-century oddities ridiculed by Thomas Hobbes.[10] The immediate problem, however, is to integrate a spatial awareness of golden sections or symbolic numbers into one's normal experience as a reader. In the first place, it may well be wrong to assume that the numerical calculations which go into the planning of a great poem are ever intended to be known by those who read and admire it (the architect's supreme achievement, after all, is to produce by calculation effects which look incalculable). But assuming the patterns are there, and there to be noticed, one still has to concede that numerological form, like other varieties of spatial form, can be appreciated only retrospectively. The forms which Fowler detects in *The faerie queene* are no more available to readers of the poem than those configurations of images 'seen' in Shakespeare's plays by Wilson Knight[11] are available to theatre audiences while a play is in performance.

Organicist alternatives

In February 1805 Coleridge entered into his notebook a formal distinction between fabrication and generation: in the case of fabrication, he observed, the form is 'ab extra, impressed', whereas in the case of generation it is 'ab intra, evolved'. A few years later, reading the twenty-second of those lectures on dramatic art which A. W. Schlegel delivered in Vienna in 1809–10, he came upon a passage which phrased the same distinction so very well that he incorporated an unacknowledged translation of it into his lecture 'Shakespeare's judgment equal to his genius' (1808), thus committing the sin his detractors call plagiarism. Speaking of how easily one can misjudge Shakespeare by 'confounding mechanical regularity with organic form', he observes:

The form is mechanic, when on any given material we impress a pre-determined form, not necessarily arising out of the properties of the material; as when to a mass of wet clay we give whatever shape we wish it to retain when hardened. The organic form, on the other hand, is innate; it shapes, as it develops, itself from within, and the fulness of its development is one and the same with the perfection of its outward form. Such as the life is, such is the form.[12]

Or in the Imagist version by Ezra Pound: 'Some poems may have form as a tree has form, some as water poured into a vase'.[13] The pejorative sense of 'mechanical' (as a foil to the adulatory sense of 'organic') is present already in Dryden's essay on 'Grounds of criticism in tragedy' (1679), in which the neo-classical dramatic unities are dismissed as 'mechanic rules'. Just how radical a transvaluation occurred with the establishment of Romantic organicism is discernible in contemporary comments on *Madame Bovary* (1856) by Louis-Edmond Duranty, who detected in Flaubert 'only the great force of an arithmetician who has calculated' everything instead of feeling it, and produced not so much a novel as 'a literary application of the mathematics of probability'.[14] Anything remotely reminiscent of quantitative aesthetics is likely to get little sympathy from organicist critics.

The subsequent history of this Romantic dissociation of organic from inorganic form establishes Coleridge as by far the most influential English organicist. Like all successful theories, organicism is formulated in such a way as to look like a self-evident truth, and it is not surprisingly one of the most deeply entrenched of our Romantic prejudices. The critic who enabled us to see this most clearly is M. H. Abrams, who published in 1949 a short view of the thesis explored so brilliantly in *The mirror and the lamp* (New York, 1953). Here Abrams shows what happened when Coleridge changed the conceptual model of literature from mechanics to biology, from an eighteenth-century machine to a nineteenth-century tree. He notes how much of Coleridge's criticism is couched in terms which are literal for a plant but metaphorical for a work of art: 'if Plato's dialectic is a wilderness of mirrors, Coleridge's is a jungle of vegetation'.[15] It is ironic, therefore, that organic form should share the same *locus classicus* with Pythagorean form. For it is Plato who, in the very same dialogue in which God is described as a divine mathematician, asks us to think of the universe as a mathematically proportioned body; God fashioned the world, says Socrates, 'as a single, visible, living creature' (*Timaeus*, 30d). Applied to the arts, this organicist analogy makes an early appearance in Plato's *Phaedrus* (264e), where Socrates is reported as saying that 'every discourse ought to be a living creature, having a body of its own, and a head and feet; there should be a middle, beginning and end adapted to one another and to the whole'. Here we find the lineaments of what is the most familiar statement of ancient organicism: the definition of tragedy in chapter seven of Aristotle's *Poetics*. For when Aristotle confronts the awkward problem of defining the correct proportions of a tragedy, he thinks in organicist terms, and writes: 'in just the same way as living creatures and organisms compounded of many parts must be a reasonable size, so that they can be easily taken in by the eye, so too plots must be of a reasonable length, so that they may be easily held in the memory'. Perversely, however, we may refuse to be beguiled by the analogy, and emphasise its limitations by asking Wimsatt's awkward questions: 'What are the beginning, middle and end of a squirrel or a tree?. . . What corresponds to the stomach in a tragedy'?[16]

In fact, the more closely we inspect the analogy, the more problematical it becomes, especially if we try to imagine literary equivalents to the defining attributes of organic forms in the natural world. For if it is true that the origin of a biological whole precedes the definition of its parts, this is by no means the case with such things as poems, individual parts of which may lie around in a finished state for years waiting for a whole to be put into. If trees and shells reveal on inspection the various stages of their development, literary works certainly do not exhibit the drafts they have gone through in becoming what they are, although a few (like Butler's *Erewhon*, 1872) display oddities which seem to betray some authorial oversight in not bringing earlier conceptions into line with later developments. Organic forms are said to be characterised by their assimilative powers: the plant assimilates water, soil and sunshine in order to produce leaves – but what would be the correspondingly alimentary processes in a book or writer? Again, although biological determinism impels a plant to produce only that kind of flower which is latent in its seed, writers are free to abandon first thoughts as well as first drafts. Although the constituent parts of living organisms are said to be mutually interdependent we all know that plays can survive performances which omit numerous lines and whole scenes, that the 'same' novel may exist in two or more different versions, and so on. All in all, 'organic' appears to be little more than an honorific term in literary discussions.

Yet there is no denying its attractiveness in comparison with the rival Pythagorean systems, some of which look forbiddingly complicated. Perhaps this is why Romantic theorists have preferred to equip themselves with a biology instead of a physics when treating every heterocosm as a living universe and aesthetic monad. For if the universe itself may be said to consist of units ('monads', Leibniz called them) which manage to remain complete in themselves while forming part of the universe, there is no reason why heterocosms and their constituents should not be subject to the same law. Leibniz never applied his monadology to aesthetics, but it is not hard to frame a poetic monadology of one's own, as Coleridge did when he called the ideal poem 'an organised whole', and then went on to define a whole as something 'composed, *ab intra*, of different parts, so far independent that each is reciprocally means and end'.[17] The final stage in an organicist aesthetic is to rule that no part of a literary work may be judged without reference to the whole. Holism ('whole-ism') protects the autonomy of heterocosms by ensuring that no part of an aesthetic work is available for separate inspection because it has meaning only in relation to a whole which in turn depends upon that part.

Inner form and expressive form

Organicism involves letting the thing take its natural shape, whatever that might be; and to counter the objection that organic form is merely a polite name for formlessness, organicists have found it necessary to invent criteria unknown in the annals of inorganic form. One of these is the Romantic concept of immanent form, what Shaftesbury calls 'inward form' and Goethe *innere Form*.[18] This is a phenomenon as occult as numerological form, but far less accessible, since it has to be intuited *ab intra*, and cannot be observed *ab extra*. We can read a book on number symbolism before grappling with a numerological poem, and get some idea of what to expect, but we have no such external guides to inner form. Every example of inner form is unique and (by definition) inaccessible outside the work itself. Certainly, some of the most attractive descriptions of inner form are quite unsatisfactory as explanations. Pound, for example, invites us to think of the myriad details in *The cantos* as iron-filings arranged in fields of force by the conceptualising magnet of the poet's mind.[19] And when Lawrence was trying to persuade Garnett to understand that *The rainbow* (1915) departs intentionally from stock novelistic conventions, he compared the 'rhythmic form' of the characters in his novel to what happens when 'one draws a fiddle-bow across a fine tray delicately sanded: the sand takes lines unknown'.[20] Perhaps so: but how could readers of *The cantos* or *The rainbow* be expected to know this?

Much less mystifying is the theory of 'expressive' or 'imitative' form. This appears to be a development of the rhetorical principle of 'decorum', which entails matching style to subject-matter in such a way that, if the hero of one's play happens to be a nobleman, decorum is observed if his speech is elevated in diction, and in no way contaminated by those pedantries or rusticities which would be appropriate in the speech of scholars and shepherds respectively. In this context, 'decorous' speech is appropriate speech, and 'imitative' form is appropriate form, the form thought suitable for that particular subject-matter. Abundant illustrations of the art of making form 'express' content have been found in the poems of Homer, especially his description of the endless labours of Sisyphus to roll a stone uphill (*Odyssey*, XI 593ff). Dionysius of Halicarnassus noted admiringly how Homer 'depicts this imitatively with the help of the actual arrangement of the words'.[21] Monosyllable by monosyllable, the stone is heaved uphill, then down it rolls again polysyllabically. 'Does not the word-arrangement roll downhill with the weight of the rock?' asks Dionysius, some two thousand years before verse-which-enacts-its-meaning became a cliché of Leavisite criticism.[22] The English parallel to Homer on Sisyphus is Donne on Truth:

> On a huge hill,
> Cragged, and steep, Truth stands, and he that will
> Reach her, about must, and about must go;
> And what the hill's suddenness resists, win so.[23]

In producing verses arduous to read, with the intent of making us experience vicariously the arduousness of the task described, Donne produces here an 'auditory correlative' to his subject-matter which fulfils the requirement epitomised in Pope's dictum: 'The sound must seem an echo to the sense'.[24]

Not everybody is impressed, however, by such technical virtuosity. Johnson mocks his own fictitious poetaster, Dick Minim, for admiring such 'representative' metre. Well aware of Homer's lines on Sisyphus – and of Pope's skilful imitation of them in *An essay on criticism* (1711) – Johnson remained convinced that 'sound can resemble nothing but sound',[25] and was alert to the danger of bathos in expressive rhythms. Minim praises the line,

'Where one part cracked, the whole does fly', because it is *'cracked* in the middle to express a crack, and then shivers into monosyllables'.[26] Uneasily, one is reminded that a good deal of the attention paid in practical criticism to functional rhythms and mimetic syntax is vulnerable to such ridicule. For the expressiveness admired by Dionysius is disparaged by Yvor Winters as 'the fallacy of imitative form'.[27] A prime offender in Winters' eyes is Walt Whitman, whose *Leaves of grass* (1855) is a vast and sprawling poem about the vast and sprawling continent of America, and thus falsely sanctions modernist experiments like *The waste land* and *The cantos*, which deal with fragmented societies in fragmented forms. Winters objects to Eliot and Pound for much the same reasons as Minturno objected in 1564 to people who defend the episodic nature of romance narratives on the grounds that an 'errant' form somehow befits the deeds of errant knights – although a couple of centuries later, Hurd had no embarrassment in resorting to that argument when defending the episodic nature of *The faerie queene*.[28]

Our reaction to expressive form seems to depend on expectations we bring to the context in which it occurs. For instance, it seems bizarre that Richardson's freshly raped Clarissa should articulate her disordered emotions in a poem typographically tumbled;[29] and yet, to take another example, it seems particularly apt that Sterne should have designed the form of *Tristram Shandy* as a gigantic *aposiopesis*, which is the term rhetoricians use to describe those occasions when a speaker suppresses what he is about to say.[30] Always, however, the creator of expressive forms risks the kind of objections Coleridge made to the Nurse's speeches in *Romeo and Juliet*, when he complained that 'it is not possible to imitate truly a dull and garrulous discourser, without repeating the effects of dullness and garrulity'.[31] This problem arises acutely in parts of Beckett's plays which, in evoking a sense of boredom and futility, may strike us as being boring and futile. Does one respond fully to *Waiting for Godot* by experiencing boredom at the futility of it all? And if so, would *The dunciad* (1728) be a more expressive poem about dullness if Pope had made it dull? Surely not, because Pope had less faith in expressive form as a literary device than in the kind of tact amusingly displayed by Fielding at one point in *Amelia* (1751): 'But as the tea-table conversation, though extremely delightful to those who are engaged in it, may probably appear somewhat dull to the reader, we will here put an end to the chapter' (Bk 9, ch. 3).

Form as process

It is commonly agreed that form can be a property only of a finished product, and never of a process yet to be completed: we watch out for terminatory devices like epilogues and envois, or await the final instalment of the novel before talking about its form. Yet any thoughtful organicist must admit that this concept of product is quite alien to biological forms, which never achieve a state of fixity but exist as continuously changing processes. In the last century or so, works of art have increasingly tended to remain unfinalised and open-ended. An 'open form' (in Robert Martin Adams' definition) is one 'which includes a major unresolved conflict with the intent of displaying its unresolvedness'. Adams is not convinced of the value of 'open' form. 'A sort of closed effect is always available', he believes, 'to any artist who chooses to make use of it. No experience is, of its own nature, unstructurable'.[32] Why then should writers have thought otherwise? Why did Conrad, for example, consider the 'full close', the 'nail hit on the head', among the most falsifying of novelistic conventions?[33]

Walter Pater's conclusion to The renaissance (1873) gives us our bearings: 'not the fruit of experience, but experience itself, is the end.' What Pater adumbrates here is a theory of art which accommodates itself to the Heracleitan doctrine that all is flux by insisting that what we call 'being' is merely a succession of states of consciousness: there are no fixities, no fruits of experience, no finalities. If you believe that all is flux and that art should imitate life, then you are unlikely to have much faith in the possibility of closed forms in the arts, because you will regard such forms as falsifications of reality. On the contrary, you will tend to value what D. H. Lawrence called in 1920 'the poetry of the immediate present', preferring with the hero of Sons and lovers (1913) 'the shimmering protoplasm in the leaves' to the actual 'stiffness of the shape' because 'only this shimmeriness is the real living. The shape is a dead crust.'[34] And if, like Lawrence, you are a novelist, you will tend to regard your characters in the same way, warning critics not to look for 'the old, stable ego'[35] because you have dissolved it in a shimmer of relationships. Such an aesthetic involves a radical re-thinking of the nature of literary form. Traditionally, literature has been admired on account of its aspirations to permanence; writers were supposed to select details from the temporal flux and preserve them for ever in memorable

words, as the lovers on Keats's Grecian urn are preserved, caught
the moment before they kiss and so held in an eternity of
anticipation, expressing a love which the ravages of time can never
violate: 'For ever wilt thou love, and she be fair'. Keats's urn
represents a kind of art which aims at withstanding the flux by
eternising the moment and in this way creating a monument more
enduring than bronze. In a 'flux' aesthetic, on the other hand, the
process is more important than the product. Consequently, the
eternising attitude is looked upon as a falsification of reality ('there
are no gems of the living plasm', Lawrence insists) and as evidence
of our contemptible attachment to 'that finality which we find
so satisfying because we are so frightened'.[36]

We are all familiar with the bolder attempts to make flux into
art. In the visual arts they range from the Impressionism of Renoir,
which dissolves fixed forms in a shimmer of light, to more recent
Action paintings by Jackson Pollock, which aim at representing
a doing rather than a deed; the possibility of depicting a 'stream
of consciousness' has been explored by Joyce and Woolf and their
imitators, who want novels to be as subtle and unpredictable
as consciousness itself; and in criticism we have witnessed an in-
creasing interest in genetic studies of the sort Jon Stallworthy
has made of Yeats's poems by arranging the manuscript drafts of
famous pieces in chronological order, drawing attention to false
starts and cul-de-sacs, and reconstructing the creative process so
very well that we are disappointed when it suddenly stops and we
find ourselves confronted with a mere product.[37] Pound's The
cantos are the supreme example of process-form in this century.
Pound began publishing them in 1917, never substantially revised
any but the first three, and was still publishing new ones just before
he died. Over the years it became increasingly obvious that The
cantos were conterminous with the evolving consciousness of their
creator, rather in the way that Tristram Shandy was conterminous
with the mind of Laurence Sterne. For Sterne was the inventor
of a new kind of form which broke with the classical assumption
that a writer should know his end in his beginning. Instead of
aiming at closure, Sterne developed instead a completely open
form ('the continuing story') which is more concerned to record
a present than to perfect a past. He published Tristram Shandy in
instalments, dying before it was completed; but its incompleteness
scarcely matters because finality is impossible in open-ended
fictions. This is one of the reasons why The cantos could never
'end' (in the sense that Paradise lost ends) but merely stop: they

stopped when Pound died, and their formlessness then became their form.

It is characteristic of form-as-process not to know where it is going until it sees where it has been. By behaving in this way it renders obsolete a number of formal criteria which once seemed universal, but which are now seen to be relevant only to form-as-product. Most strikingly, it engenders a revaluation of so-called fragments. One manifestation of a radical shift in aesthetic values between the seventeenth and nineteenth centuries is the fact that whereas Milton preserved only one juvenile fragment, something like a third of Shelley's collected poems are described as fragments or cancelled passages.[38] Unfinished 'poetry' rates as highly as finished 'poems'. A contemporary of Pope's would not have sympathised with Paul Valéry's remark that 'a work is never *complete*...but *abandoned*', nor with the suggestion that if 'Le cimetière marin' had not been abandoned and published, Valéry would have continued to work on it for as long as he lived.[39]

When processes arouse more interest than products, the unfinished (or *non finito*) has pride of place and fosters a criticism which treats fragments as wholes. *The Canterbury tales* and *The faerie queene* are regarded by critics as being somehow 'complete' in their unfinished state, as are a number of other works, from 'Kubla Khan' to Kafka's *The castle* (1926). For somebody else to 'complete' them seems inconceivable, for everybody knows that *Hero and Leander* became a very different poem indeed when George Chapman took over from Christopher Marlowe. Although Jane Austen attracts more than her share of finishers, nobody takes the results as anything other than examples of the art of pastiche.[40] For as Beerbohm remarked, we are charmed by unfinished art; and if his proposal for 'a museum of incomplete masterpieces' is ever taken seriously, the Corns and Sparke *Bibliography of unfinished books* will give us some idea of what literary examples it ought to include.[41]

Another casualty of the shift from products to processes is the criterion of consistency. It seemed axiomatic to Horace that a poem should be 'consistent within itself', like Virgil's *Aeneid*, in which 'the middle is not inconsistent with the beginning, nor the end with the middle' (*Ars poetica*, 153). In this tradition, inconsistency is a fault because it violates the Aristotelian principle of non-contradiction, which states that something cannot both be and not be at the same time. A miserly character should therefore never be shown behaving in an unmiserly manner, for that would be an inconsistency: inconsistencies make for unconvincing books, and unconvincing books are bad books. A rival tradition, however, stemming from Heracleitus,[42] encourages the opposite view that life itself is characterised by opposing tensions, in which case one can give only qualified approval to consistency in the depiction of human affairs. 'Inconsistencies cannot both be right', said Johnson's Imlac; 'but, imputed to man, they may both be true'.[43] If so, writers who aim at being mimetically faithful to life's inconsistencies are likely to share André Gide's resentment at critics who expect fictional characters to behave consistently and therefore predictably: what is admired as consistency of character, he writes, 'is on the contrary the very thing which makes us recognise that they are artificially composed'.[44] It is for this reason that process-writers claim inconsistency as their right, even when writing in the first person singular. 'Do I contradict myself?' Whitman asks:

> Very well then I contradict myself,
> (I am large, I contain multitudes).[45]

Outside the Horatian tradition, consistency is likely to be dismissed as 'the hobgoblin of little minds' (Emerson) or 'the last refuge of the unimaginative' (Wilde).[46]

'Economy' is another formal value questioned by process-writers. The earlier tradition that an indispensable function should be assignable to every component in a work of literature is supported by Aristotle's insistence on the importance in tragedy of a carefully interlocking plot. 'Various incidents must be so arranged that if any one of them is differently placed or taken away the effect of wholeness will be seriously disrupted', he writes (*Poetics*, ch. 8). 'For if the presence or absence of something makes no apparent difference, it is no real part of the whole.' Applying the principle of economy as a criterion of style, Donne found much to admire in the Psalms, which are written in 'such a form as is both curious and requires diligence in the making, and then when it is made, can have nothing, no syllable taken from it, nor added to it'; and in the best work of Milton and Shakespeare, Coleridge thought 'it would be scarcely more difficult to push a stone out from the pyramids with the bare hand than to alter a word, or the position of a word...without making the author say something else, or something worse, than he does say'.[47] According to this view, life may be slovenly, but art is not, which is why

Virginia Woolf determined 'to eliminate all waste, deadness, superfluity' from her work, all those undesirable things which clutter up realistic novels whose authors have succumbed to the 'appalling narrative business' of 'getting from lunch to dinner'.[48] Similarly, Henry James had grave reservations about 'loose baggy monsters' like Thackeray's *The Newcomes* (1853–55) and 'fluid puddings' like the novels of Tolstoy and Dostoevsky,[49] all of which attempt an indiscriminate inclusiveness instead of focusing upon selected luminous moments.

Clearly opposed to the exclusive purism of Woolf or James are those who believe that books can be damaged by writers excessively sensitive to possible superfluities. Even Forster, whose own novels are shaped and patterned to an extraordinary degree, felt that James was wrong in sacrificing superfluities to patterns, because he ended up with a set of characters 'gutted of the common stuff that fills characters in other books, and ourselves'.[50] *Dreck* ('rubbish') is a recent and useful term for the non-functional fill which writers can shovel into their novels so as to avoid the kind of objection Forster raises. 'We like books that have a lot of *dreck* in them', somebody remarks in Donald Barthelme's novel, *Snow White* (1967); 'matter which presents itself as not wholly relevant (or indeed, at all relevant) but which, carefully attended to, can supply a kind of "sense" of what is going on.'[51] Here we have a theory of form which admits the likelihood of there being a high degree of redundancy in any series of speech-acts, and a large number of non-functional parts in any literary work. 'If a poem is to be like a living organism', writes Catherine Lord, 'then padding is inevitable, for we can say that the very nature of the organism leads us to expect accidents.'[52] This is not to deny the efficiency of imaginative works as communication systems, but merely to question the value of literary interpretations which take it upon themselves to justify the presence of every detail included by the author.

The point can be made most forcibly in connection with oral narratives, which are not at all functional in the Jamesian kind of way. To the eye of the beholder they are repetitive in structure and indiscriminately padded; but to the ear of the listener such 'faults' are functional in a different kind of way, at once clarificatory and emphatic; for the repetitions and padding put a brake on the narrative pace so as to accommodate it to the listener's rate of absorption.[53] Oral literature (if one can speak of such a contradiction in terms) was never meant to be functional in the manner prescribed by Aristotle, and neither, one suspects, was a good deal of much later literature. When functionalist criteria dominate, so-called 'digressiveness' is disapproved of. This involves condemning as excess verbiage what readers familiar with another aesthetic may value as evidence of inventive fertility or rhetorical *copia* ('fullness'). Neither Scott nor Trollope approved of the Man of the Hill episode in *Tom Jones*, because digressions (said Trollope) 'distract the attention of the reader, and always do so disagreeably'.[54] A common way of answering this charge is to show that all such digressions are related thematically to the novels in which they occur, even if not in quite so obvious a manner as Trollope expected. To do this, however, is to concede tacitly that digressiveness is bad, and that Fielding is a good novelist because he does not really digress, but only appears to. ('Of course, you must appear to digress', said Ford Madox Ford. 'But really not one single thread must ever escape your purpose.')[55] A better kind of answer would proceed along the lines of Coleridge's observation that in *Tristram Shandy* 'the digressive spirit is not wantonness, but the *very form* of Sterne's genius'.[56] In process-forms, everything is part of the organism, which is another way of saying that all parts contribute equally to the total experience of reading.

3

Criteria of complexity and simplicity

Are books better for being simple or complicated in style? Here I propose to examine some of the reasons which have led people at different times to exalt simplicity or complexity as a stylistic ideal, and to contest or to applaud Matthew Arnold's dictum that a 'perfectly simple, limpid style' is 'the supreme style of all'.[1] Let us begin by surveying what is to be said in favour of making things complicated.

The rationale of obscurity

A traditional defence of obscurity is the metaphysical premise that reality is ultimately unknowable, a mystery permanently veiled from rational scrutiny. Biblical tradition as well as pagan Stoicism lend support to this claim. In such conditions, a mimetic literature will justify its existence by trying to be as enigmatic as the universe itself and exploring what Chaucer calls 'the covered qualitee/Of thynges',[2] a quality whose nature may be evoked in ambiguous and riddling utterances. Most influential in the development of a 'covered' quality in secular literature has been the Hebrew tradition that the Bible is darkly sublime and hints at truths which must be kept from profane eyes. Milton's Penseroso devotes his attention to books in which 'more is meant than meets the ear'; and Henry Vaughan splendidly evokes the allurements of this kind of obscurity when he speaks of 'a deep, but dazzling darkness', a quality unique to a God who (in Milton's phrase) is 'dark with excessive bright'.[3] Paradoxes like this acknowledge the existence of a form of obscurity which is worth cultivating as the prelude to spiritual illumination.

The effect is to dignify obscurity by aligning it with sublimity, and to set up exploitable connotations among the metaphoric senses of darkness and cloudiness, as Spenser does when describing *The faerie queene* (1590) as 'a dark conceit' (i.e. an 'enigmatic conception'), a poem 'cloudily enwrapped in allegorical devices'. By a fertile accident in the evolution of modern English, a pseudo-etymological link was forged between 'mystic' (Middle English *mysty*, from Latin *mysticus*) and 'misty' (Old English *mistig*), providing confirmation from the world of words that sublime mysteries are immanent in the nebulous.[4] What looks like impenetrable mist to the profane may be a genuine mystery in the eyes of initiates, as Spenser's friend Gabriel Harvey implies when he says that 'mysteries are mists to us silly fools'; and if you have faith in the existence of what Purchas calls 'misty mysteries', you will appreciate the value of writing vaguely when fathoming the mysteries of existence.[5] Enlightened people, however, are not enamoured of the dark, because it obfuscates clear and distinct ideas. Consequently, whenever an Enlightenment occurs, the old terms are revalued, and what used to be admired as evocative obscurism comes to be condemned as obscurantism.

At present the most respectable defence of obscurity is still the one Eliot made in 1921 when defending the difficulty of modern poetry in his essay on 'The metaphysical poets'. Working on the mimetic assumption that literature is likely to be as complicated as modern civilisation if it is to be true to that civilisation, Eliot may not have been aware that his point had been anticipated by Oscar Wilde, who told readers of *Woman's world* in May 1889 that 'the marked tendency of modern poetry to become obscure' (and he was thinking of Browning in particular) is to be explained partly by 'the complexity of the new problems' in modern society.[6] Thirty years or so later, these problems had reached such proportions that Eliot could say

that poets in our civilisation, as it exists at present, must be *difficult*. Our civilisation comprehends great variety and complexity, and this variety and complexity, playing upon a refined sensibility, must produce various and complex results. The poet must become more and more comprehensive, more allusive, more indirect, in order to force, to dislocate if necessary, language into his meaning.[7]

Notice that the suspect word 'obscure' has been replaced by the rationally more respectable term 'difficult', which is not quite the same thing. *The waste land* has ceased to be a difficult poem (now we have traced its allusions) but remains an obscure one: it compels attention through being enigmatic, not by reflecting twentieth-century civilisation, which is merely complicated.

Renaissance humanists were convinced that the requisite obscurity of great literature could be nurtured by learnedness, and in redefining poetry as the scholar's art they treated the writer as essentially a learned man, a *doctus poeta* whose erudition guarantees an authentic obscurity. Far from being a dreary encumbrance, erudition is seen as a hall-mark of excellence. 'It is not sufficient for poets to be superficial humanists', wrote Gabriel Harvey; 'they must be exquisite artists and curious, universal scholars.'[8] The point of departure for such inferences was ultimately a passage in Horace's *Odes* (1 1 29) where the crown of ivy is described as 'the rewards of a poet's brows' (*doctarum...praemia frontium*). What Horace means here is that a poet inspired by his Muse may be said to be taught by her and manifest his learnedness in his technical skills as a writer. Later humanists assumed that a poet 'taught' or 'learned' in this special way might be 'taught' or 'learned' in the more ordinary, pedagogic sense; and it was in this way that Horace's skilled poet became the erudite *doctus poeta* encountered in Renaissance literature.[9] 'Nothing of the more solid erudition is out of place in the temple of the Muses', wrote the Italian critic Scaliger; and among contemporary Renaissance theoreticians, only Ludovico Castelvetro appeared to challenge this view.[10] Long after Francis Bacon had decided to take all knowledge for his province, Dryden could insist in 1674 that 'a man should be learned in several sciences, and should have a reasonable, philosophical, and in some measure a mathematical head, to be a complete and excellent poet'.[11] And in 1797, when Coleridge surveyed the prospect of writing an epic poem, he thought an epic aspirant would have to be 'a tolerable mathematician...[and] thoroughly know mechanics, hydrostatics, optics, and astronomy, botany, metallurgy, fossilism, chemistry, geology, anatomy, medicine – then the *mind of man* – then the *minds of men* – in all travels, voyages and histories'.[12]

But by Coleridge's time, of course, erudition had ceased to be the royal road to literary excellence: as 'original genius' became the new prerequisite, the *doctus poeta* was obliged to lie low, his highest aspirations mocked by Robert Burns in 1785:

> Gie me ae spark o' Nature's fire,
> That's a' the learning I desire.[13]

Since Burns's time revivals of obscurity have been relatively private affairs restricted to odd writers or groups of writers, and in no way motivated by any widespread belief in the unfathomable nature of reality or the necessary alliance of literature with erudition. Expediency, however (especially political expediency), has been a durable incentive to obscurity. A case in point is William Langland's refusal to decode the allegory in his prologue to *Piers Plowman*: 'What this dream means guess for yourselves, you who are carefree, for I dare not' (ll. 208f). Carefree interpreters read Langland's story of how the rats planned to bell the cat as an allegory of the commoners' attempts to curb royal power. Clearly, a coded message is preferable to no message at all; and indeed a determination to glance obliquely at matters that cannot be spoken about openly may very well stimulate an ingenuity which enriches the text.

The rhetoric of obscurity

In *The chequer'd shade* (London, 1958) John Press anatomises the main literary devices by which obscurity is created. Dominant in most readers' experience, I would imagine, is 'lexiphanic' obscurity, which arises from the systematic use of a recondite vocabulary, and which is well represented in Lycophron's 'Alexandra' (third century BC) or that poem by T. S. Eliot which begins with the word 'polyphiloprogenitive'.[14] Lexiphanic obscurity is likely to occur whenever a premium is set on verbal craftsmanship and the writer comes to look upon himself as a 'word-man' (Wyndham Lewis' term), a man with a word-hoard. It is usually defended by the claim that only verbal precision can do justice to the nuances of experience; for if, as Coleridge claimed, language has a tendency to 'desynonymise' itself, then every word necessarily develops a unique meaning, and writers must ransack dictionaries in search of the *mot juste*.[15] But there are grounds for suspecting that some writers have a taste for obscure words as such, and use them deliberately to baffle us. The effect can be intentionally comic, of course:

> How dulce to vive occult to mortal eyes,
> Dorm on the herb with none to supervise,
> Carp the suave berries from the crescent vine,
> And bibe the flow from longicaudate kine.[16]

In poems by obscurist writers, even the similes (which normally function as explanatory devices) are likely to be opaque, as in Allen Tate's Horatian epode to Webster's unfortunate Duchess of Malfi:

> You have no more chance than an infusorian
> Lodged in a hollow molar of an eohippus.[17]

Whatever the intention here, poetry has become not so much the scholar's art as the lexicographer's, and the more rare a word is, the greater the chance it has of being picked out of the word-hoard. Although it has long been known that obscurity may be accidental – 'In striving to be concise', Horace complained, 'I become obscure' (*Ars poetica*, 25f) – much of the syntactical difficulty encountered in poems by Hopkins or Dylan Thomas is obviously deliberate. For a major structural device of obscurist literature is syntactical ambiguity, where the exact relationship of one dependent clause to another is uncertain, the aim being to simulate by means of syntactical obliquities something of the indecisiveness and openness of complex emotional states. And to complicate things further, obscurists may keep us guessing by organising their work in terms of some more or less private system of symbols (as Blake or Yeats did) or by introducing masks or *personae* (in the manner of Browning or Eliot) which place on us the additional burden of trying to decide which parts of his book are ironical and which are not. This raises the question of why writers should cultivate obscurity, and why readers should be willing to put up with the results.

'*The fascination of what's difficult*'

Poetry is more tolerant of obscurist habits than prose, perhaps because it traditionally imposes the discipline of metrics on communication. Expertise with the forms of poetry may easily become an end in itself, as it seems to have been for Andrew Lang or Austin Dobson, who regarded metrical and stanzaic forms like the sestina or villanelle as technical challenges rather than as aids to expression. Anathema to admirers of first fine careless raptures, formal restrictions are a godsend to those who want art freed from self-indulgence:

> Blessed are all metrical rules that forbid automatic responses,
> > force us to choose second thoughts, free from the fetters of self.[18]

Complex metrical forms constitute a challenge by confronting writers with what Renaissance critics knew as a *difficulté à vaincre*: a successful writer is therefore one who overcomes technical obstacles placed in his way and triumphantly displays a *difficulté vaincue* (even Wordsworth testifies to the pleasure of being 'bound/Within the Sonnet's scanty plot of ground').[19] Every art has its notorious *difficultés* which have been overcome so often by so many masters that it takes a recently developed art like that of the cinema to show us the problem afresh. The fact that early movies were silent, for instance, compelled producers to invent an authentically cinematic art of communicating by sequences of moving images; and the frantic acrobatics of early movie comedy capitalise splendidly on that technical defect in frame-sequence which gives an inhuman speed and jerkiness to human actions.[20]

In medieval Provençal poetry a whole nexus of obscurity developed in the style of *trobar clus* perfected by Arnaut Daniel, a style demanding adroitness in the handling of unusual words, difficult rhyme-sounds and complicated stanza-patterns. The ability to say things clearly counted for much less than the ability to say anything at all, given the seemingly intractable materials to be worked with. Raimbaut d'Aurenga describes his own poetry as the art of 'intertwining, thoughtfully thoughtful, words that are rare, dark and coloured'.[21] It would appear that a poem in the *trobar clus* style was intended to be admired primarily as a virtuoso display of craftsmanly intricacy: in appealing to the problem-solving part of our minds it was truly a *devinalh* or riddle.

Deliberately complicated works are not designed to be read, but only to be re-read, as André Gide confesses in *Le journal des faux-monnayeurs* (1926).[22] 'Read it four times', was Faulkner's advice to people who find his work puzzling even after a third reading.[23] If you protest further, you are likely to be reminded that the best books do not surrender their secrets easily, and that the harder you have to work on a book, the more you will value it in the end. 'What is attended with difficulty in the seeking', remarked St Augustine of the Canticles, 'gives greater pleasure in the finding'; and late in the nineteenth century, Mark Pattison was offering as 'the last reward of consummated scholarship' an appreciation of Milton.[24]

Poetry becomes riddling when familiar things are made strange by means of periphrasis, kennings, circumlocutions and similar devices which contribute to what Victor Shklovsky terms *ostranenie* ('making it strange').[25] This may involve looking at things with what Lewis Carroll called 'a sort of mental squint', so that mutton-pies metamorphose into 'dreams of fleecy flocks/Pent in a wheaten cell', and a blonde combing her hair is transformed flamboyantly into something rich and strange:

> Within an open curled sea of gold
> A bark of ivory, one day, I saw.[26]

Lord Herbert of Cherbury, who Englished these lines after Marino, wrote an elegy on the death of Prince Henry which (according to Ben Jonson) provoked Donne into writing another one 'to match Sir Edward Herbert in obscureness'.[27] Any anthology of seventeenth-century Metaphysical poetry shows what can happen when ingenuity is brought to the task of making things complicated. Neoclassicists like Jonson thought that Donne would perish for not being understood,[28] but any obscurist will tell you that Donne's poetry retains its fascination by inviting and resisting intellectual solutions. For Donne's verses, said King James, 'were like the peace of God: they passed all understanding'.[29] Consequently, if Jasper Mayne is to be believed, a contemporary could get a reputation as a wit by showing he understood Donne's *Anniversaries* (1611–12).[30] Unintelligibility eternises writing by whetting and perpetuating curiosity, and it is a strategy well known to those who fear that to be intelligible is to be found out.[31]

To write notes on one's own poems, as Thomas Gray and T. S. Eliot have done, is to confirm the status of literature as puzzle by supplying some of the answers. Gray introduced notes in some embarrassment. 'They are signs of weakness and obscurity', he wrote to Walpole on 11 July 1757. 'If a thing cannot be understood without them, it had better be not understood at all.' Others are quite brazen about the business, like Browning, who said that a competent reader of his poem 'Aristophanes' apology' (1875) should have 'a knowledge of the Scholia, besides acquaintance with the "Comicorum Graecorum Fragmenta", Athenaeus [and] Alciphron'.[32] One solution to the problem posed by ill-prepared readers is to make the notes intermittently organic with one's poems. The notes to *The waste land* (1922) may very well be (as Eliot later declared) an example of bogus scholarship, but they are not therefore superfluous, for they contain important information which is not adducible from the bogus scholarship on display inside Eliot's poem: how many readers would have associated the Hanged Man with the Hooded Figure if Eliot had not left a note to that effect? Empson, on the other hand, admits that 'a sort of puzzle interest is part of the pleasure' to be derived from his poems in *The gathering storm* (London, 1940), and thinks it wrong of modern poets not to publish answers to their puzzles.[33] Is it because they fear to be found out? Writers who share Wallace Stevens' belief that 'poetry must resist the intelligence almost successfully'[34] ought not to feel that to explain something, however tentatively, is to explain it away; but obviously they do. Evading the issue, they sometimes make the progressivist claim that because advances in literary perception are likely to be as obscure to non-professionals as advances in such fields as biochemistry or astrophysics, it is unfair of us to expect writers to simplify matters for the benefit of an ignorant public. Poets are in this respect much worse off than mathematicians, Auden complains. 'No cashier writes articles in the *Sunday times*, complaining about the incomprehensibility of Modern Mathematics and comparing it unfavourably with the good old days when mathematicians were content to paper irregularly shaped rooms or fill bath-tubs with the waste-pipe open.'[35] What is overlooked here is the crucial part played by obscurity in sustaining what is felt to be the essential hermeticism of modern poetry at its best. For example, when Gérard de Nerval was questioned about the obscurity of his sonnets, he said they are 'hardly more obscure than Hegel's metaphysics or Swedenborg's *Memorabilia*', and that 'they would lose some of their charm if they were explained, supposing the thing were possible'.[36] This is Mallarmé's view: he believed that three-quarters of the enjoyment of a poem is lost if it is too explicit, and that far from aiming at clarity of outline and idea, poets should cultivate nuances and evocations: *suggérer, voilà le rêve*.[37] By weakening what I. A. Richards was subsequently to call the 'denotative' element in language, and cultivating the 'connotative', one might achieve that state of cloudy indeterminacy which Symbolists regard as quintessentially poetic. When Bridges objected in 1878 to the obscurity of *The wreck of the Deutschland*, Hopkins claimed to be indifferent to the kind of clarity Bridges was asking for: 'sometimes one enjoys and admires the very lines one cannot understand'.[38] If Bridges' criticism is condoned by the ancient rhetorical doctrine that ambiguity is the verbal equivalent to ethical malpractice and therefore suspect, Hopkins' answer corroborates Sir Peter Medawar's observation of 'a voluptuary element in the higher forms of incomprehension'.[39] An Enlightenment critique of *The waste land* might take its point of departure from Matthew Arnold's objection that 'one gains nothing on the darkness by being, like Shelley, as incoherent as the darkness itself'.[40] But I think we have to entertain the possibility that certain kinds of experience yield nothing to enlightened scrutiny because whatever characteristics the darkness may possess will always disappear whenever light is directed on to them. A willed obscurity may be our only opportunity to probe such areas; for if we are adept at what Michael Polanyi calls 'tacit knowing', then the more obscure verbal networks may well constitute a sensory system for detecting and recording what we can know only tacitly.[41]

Obscurity and obscurantism

Advocates of obscurity are generally content with minority audiences for their work. While there is general agreement that literature is a communication system, the now common assumption that everybody has a right to tune in to it is comparatively recent and consequently misleading. It is no accident that among the oldest surviving forms of literature are cryptic utterances of an oracular and riddling nature, the purpose of which is to transmit classified information from master to novice and to nobody else. The verbal form which encodes an oracle or riddle functions as a scrambling-device to confuse inquisitive outsiders: all we can be sure of is that something is being said. This is the impression one gets in books on alchemy, like those versified tracts collected in *Theatrum chemicum Britannicum* (London, 1652) by Elias Ashmole, who invokes scriptural precedent when sorting people neatly into insiders and outsiders. 'Unto you it is given to know the mysteries of the kingdom of God', he says, 'but to others in parables, that seeing they might not see, and hearing they might not understand' (sig. A2).

To assist us in unlearning our Enlightenment suspicion of jealously guarded enigmas we are fortunate in having Edgar Wind's book on *Pagan mysteries in the Renaissance* (London, 1958), which opens with a description of how Florentine Neoplatonists of the fifteenth century came to be preoccupied with the recovery and furtive transmission of what was allegedly the secret wisdom of the ancients. The cultic origin of these activities was the ancient festival of Eleusis, at which initiates were 'purged of the fear of death and admitted to the company of the blessed, to which they were bound by a vow of silence' (p. 1). Here we encounter two elements which figure prominently in most defences of obscurity: the sense of a privileged experience, and an obligation not to broadcast it. In the Renaissance, terms and images associated with cultic rites were adopted and used figuratively in the intellectual disciplines of philosophical debate and meditation. Marsilio Ficino and Pico della Mirandola read Plato in the way that Porphyry and Plotinus had read him centuries earlier, as 'the heir and oracle of

an ancient wisdom for which a ritual disguise had been invented
by the founders of the mysteries' (p. 7); and they did so despite
the fact that Plato's few references to ritual philosophy are patently
ironical. The upshot was to encourage vernacular writers to make
their own work philosophically as profound in a devious kind of
way as they were convinced ancient writers had done. Particularly
noteworthy is the assumption that obscurity is always intentional.
'Renaissance discussions of esoteric language', D. P. Walker reports, 'usually suppose that the hidden meaning could have been
expressed quite clearly and adequately, and that the writer
concealed it.'[42]

Obscurism is essentially elitist and therefore runs counter to the
egalitarian ideals expressed in all attempts to make education
compulsory and literacy universal. Mallarmé thought it deplorable
that good poetry should become available to the public in cheap
editions: 'art for everybody' is an artistic heresy, he believed,
caviare to the general.[43] At a molecular level, the anti-democratic
spirit of obscurism is manifest everywhere in Johnson's *Dictionary
of the English language* (1755), and typically in the famous definition of 'network': 'Anything reticulated or decussated, at
equal distances, with interstices between the intersections'.
Dictionaries are monuments to the democracy of letters, for
they make all words equal by including and defining every
one of them, dissolving all hierarchies except the alphabetical.
The only form of protest open to a conscientious lexicographer
with elitist inclinations, therefore, is to amuse fellow-elitists
by ensuring that anybody who is stupid enough to have to
look up the word 'network' will be sorry he ever opened the
book. Such attitudes begin to be conspicuous among English
writers in the sixteenth century, especially among those who
frequent court circles and preserve an aristocratic distaste for
'the stigma of print',[44] content to have their poems circulate
in manuscript form and be preserved only in the commonplace
books of friends. The convention of manuscript transmission,
like that of the expensive limited edition, effectively restricts
the circulation of literature and preserves its value as a non-
communication system. *Odi profanum vulgus* ('I hate the profane
crowd') is the phrase with which Horace begins his third book
of *Odes*, and it aptly characterises the obscurist. Milton was
content to expect a 'fit audience...though few' for *Paradise
lost* (VII 31); and Stendhal dedicated *La Chartreuse de Parme* (1839)
to 'the happy few'. Few understand 'young Auden's coded

chatter', Dylan Thomas complained in 1934. 'But then' (he added mischievously) 'it is the few that matter'.[45]

Social in origin, *odi profanum* contempt develops into intellectual snobbery of the sort displayed in twentieth-century avant-garde magazines like the *Little review*, which flaunted the motto 'No compromise with the public taste'. Unwanted readers are successfully fenced out of such enterprises. 'The writer expresses', proclaimed *transition*, 'he does not communicate. The plain reader be damned'.[46] Gradually, however, the elect begin to discern profane symptoms in one another, and further fences go up as writers celebrated for obscurity show themselves less than tolerant of obscurity in others. The published correspondence between Pound and Joyce reveals Pound's growing uneasiness with Joyce's work, as well as Joyce's apparent indifference to Pound's: Pound even went so far as to ask Joyce (10 June 1918) to insert a few sign-posts into the Sirens episode of *Ulysses* to make it more intelligible, although his own *The cantos* are far from adequately sign-posted. All that the word 'publication' means in such contexts is 'putting into print', not 'making public'. For obscurism is the final act of self-preservation in a hostile world. Entrance to George Chapman's *Andromeda liberata* (1614) warns off would-be trespassers with the words

> Away, ungodly vulgars, far away
> Fly, ye profane, that dare not view the day.

Chapman, who is the author of some of the most enigmatic poems in the language, nowhere sees it as his business to preach to the unconverted, but stands his ground with Boccaccio, who once epitomised a defence of obscurity by quoting the New Testament to the effect that 'one does not cast pearls before swine'.[47] The state of mind which theologians used to recognise as invincible ignorance is presumed habitual among the *profanum vulgus*. 'What is grand is necessarily obscure to weak men', wrote Blake: 'that which can be made explicit to the idiot is not worth my care'; and it was Shelley himself who pointed out that 'Epipsychidion' (1821) would remain forever incomprehensible to a certain class of readers, 'from a defect of a common organ of perception for the ideas of which it treats'.[48]

A familiar feature in defences of obscurity is the contention that literary obscurity is of two kinds, one legitimate, the other factitious. A typical discussion in Castiglione's *The courtier* (1528) dissociates the 'bad' kind (which is impenetrably obscure) from that admirably 'covered subtlety' (*acutezza recondita*) which reveals 'the wittiness and learning of him that writeth' and entices readers with 'the pleasure that consisteth in hard things'.[49] When Chapman took up the matter in his dedication to *Ovid's banquet of sense* (1595) he made that familiar distinction between subject-matter and treatment which enables one to isolate a legitimate obscurity (allegedly provoked by a complicated subject) from other kinds of obscurity which are merely stylistic and superficial. This is the basis on which Dryden discriminates between the obscurity of Donne and that of Cleveland: Donne 'gives us deep thoughts in common language, though rough cadence', whereas Cleveland 'gives us common thoughts in abstruse words'.[50] Similarly, Coleridge contrasts the poetry of the early seventeenth century, which is full of 'the most fantastic out-of-the-way thoughts, but in the most pure and genuine mother English', with that of the late eighteenth century, which communicates 'the most obvious thoughts, in language the most fantastic and arbitrary'.[51] Such an argument depends upon an undemonstrable ability to dissociate form from content, and is more often than not an excuse for condemning works one disapproves of. It turns up frequently in adverse criticism of Dylan Thomas by those who think with Julian Symons[52] that Thomas deliberately made his poems impenetrable in order to protect their paucity of thought, fearing with some justification that to be intelligible is to be found out. Yet the objection is meaningless to anybody who refuses to accept the ornamentalist view of language on which it rests, and substitutes instead an incarnational view. For to do this is to see that there can be no such thing as a detachable 'thought' (obscure or otherwise) in a poem by Thomas, but only a series of evocations generated by the interactions of the words which constitute it. What tends to be paraded as a formal distinction between thought and expression in complaints about obscurity is likely to be something else altogether, and often masks a sense of frustration or even anger at Thomas for having written poems which resist our advances. No reader is infinitely patient, and most of us expect modest returns for the attention we invest in an obscure work. When a critic complains that a notoriously difficult poem by Mallarmé 'offers no rewards remotely proportional to the effort of understanding it',[53] he records a reaction we all experience at some time or other, and his comment points in the right direction. It is more honest to admit we quickly tire of books we can get little out of, than to pretend that certain kinds of obscurity are intrinsically more justifiable and consequently more rewarding than others.

The complexity of simplicity

Customarily we equate simplicity with clarity and complexity with difficulty or obscurity – not without justification, for books with complicated structures or textures are frequently puzzling. Simplicity of outline, however, does not automatically make for clarity, as admirers of Blake's *Songs of experience* (1794) have long known. We find it deeply ironic that Joseph Conrad should have subtitled *The secret agent* (1907) 'A simple tale', because we have lost the faith – so strong in *esprits simplistes* of the eighteenth century – that there is a simple solution to everything. Our universe is no longer the one explained by Newton, who found that 'Nature is pleased with simplicity',[54] and proved his point by formulating the law of gravity, a law at once simple and parsimoniously elegant, linking the behaviour of falling apples with that of orbiting planets. But 'nature's simple plan' has become rather more complicated since then. 'The simplest form of protoplasm', Teilhard de Chardin reports, 'is already a substance of unheard-of complexity'; and new elementary particles continue to be discovered by physicists.[55] Consequently, philosophers no longer think in terms of those 'simple ideas' to which John Locke devotes a section of his *Essay concerning human understanding* (1690), each of which is said to be irreducible by virtue of containing 'nothing but one uniform appearance, or conception in the mind' (II 2). On the contrary, Bertrand Russell treats 'simples' as things which can be 'known only inferentially as the limits of analysis'.[56] Looked at in this light, simplicity is merely a cover-name for undetected complexities.

It is probably the relativity of such terms as 'complex' and 'simple' which causes confusion in literary studies. What baffles one reader may be quite straightforward to another and end up a textbook platitude to the next generation. It is hard to believe that anybody could complain about 'unintelligible wildness and incoherence' in Coleridge's 'Rime of the ancient mariner', although in fact this was the verdict of the *Monthly review* in June 1799. We grapple unavoidably with relativities, knowing that the most simple poems we can find are simple only by comparison with other poems of greater complexity.[57] How did simplicity ever come to acquire such prestige?

A dominant influence has been the moral view of simplicity as the opposite of duplicity: *simplex sigillum veri*.[58] Just as Protestant Reformers did away with vestments and ornaments in the expectation of recapturing the pristine simplicity of the original Church of Christ, so those who cultivate a plain style of writing often see themselves as working in a medium not yet rotten with gratuitous ornamentation. This is what Richard F. Jones calls 'the moral sense of simplicity':[59] a plain style for plain dealing. Seventeenth-century controversies about preaching-styles centre accordingly on whether or not pulpit oratory is equivalent to gilding the lily, for if the truth contained in the Bible is no less truthful for being homespun, is there really any need to embellish it? Support could always be mustered from the oratorical tradition that clarity is the supreme virtue in public speaking, 'the first essential of good style', as it is called by Quintilian, who neatly summarises ancient opinion on this matter in the eighth book of his *Institutio oratoria*. 'Unaffected simplicity' is Quintilian's ideal: obscurists, we are led to believe, are generally up to no good. None of this has ever been challenged more effectively than by George Orwell, who exposes the *im*moral sense of simplicity in creating Newspeak, which parodies two twentieth-century attempts at simplifying our language, C. K. Ogden's Basic English and Lancelot Hogben's Interglossa. A Newspeak expert in *Nineteen eighty-four* (1949) puts the matter succinctly when he envisages 'every year fewer and fewer words, and the range of consciousness always a little smaller'.[60] If the drive towards simplicity eliminates those verbal complexities which enable us to identify moral issues, it must inevitably annihilate the moral issues themselves and form part of the rhetoric of totalitarianism. This is rank heresy in the annals of simplicity.

'Simplicité' and 'simplesse'

When Matthew Arnold came to write his 'Last words on translating Homer' (1862) he felt it necessary to distinguish genuine *simplicité* from a counterfeit thing called *simplesse*: natural *simplicité* is what we find in Homer and Wordsworth's 'Michael', and it is markedly different from that artificial *simplesse* encountered in Tennyson's 'Dora' and the pastoral idylls of Moschus (second century BC). Arnold's distinction, like F. R. Leavis' dissociation in *New bearings in English poetry* (London, 1932) of good 'poetic' qualities from bad 'poetical' ones, promises to be extremely helpful until one discovers that there are no rules for deciding which is which. What is claimed to be a formal distinction is in practice determined by feeling, with the result that one man's *simplicité* is another man's *simplesse*. More accurately, *simplesse* is probably the name given to a *simplicité* no longer found authentic; and those who pursue the elusive ideal of simplicity must resign themselves to the probability that what they and their contemporaries admire as *simplicité* will strike their children or grandchildren as an unbelievably arch *simplesse*.

This is borne out by the changing nature of the homage paid to simplicity during the eighteenth and nineteenth centuries in roughly the era from Collins to Wordsworth, when faith in the value of natural simplicity sustained various theories about the inherent excellence of noble savages, primitive and passionate bards, and untutored working-class poets. Many of the dominant cultural assumptions inherent in this aspect of eighteenth-century taste are on view in William Collins' 'Ode to Simplicity' (1746). Simplicity here is apostrophised as a nymph who is the sister of Truth and receives her education from Nature, which gives mythical expression to the contemporary scientific opinion that the fundamental truths of nature are perfectly simple ones; and she wears an 'Attic robe' to persuade us that simplicity is a defining characteristic of Greek civilisation and a mark of its excellence. Politically, Collins' nymph prefers life in an Athenian democracy, and lights out for the territory whenever monarchy is instituted, thus confirming the republican alliance of liberty with simplicity which enables people to detect symptoms of institutionalised tyranny in the abandonment of simplicity. In more narrowly literary matters, simplicity is held to be characteristic of great poetry and the only true source of the sublime, a claim ironically undercut by the fact that this elegant eulogy of simplicity is made in the context of a complicated book of odes for which even Collins himself felt obliged to supply footnotes.

If the eighteenth-century demand for simplicity was such that supplies had to be faked, it is largely because *simplicité* cannot compete in elegance with *simplesse*. And after all, elegance was the decisive factor, not simplicity; 'simplicity passes for dulness', said David Hume, 'when it is not accompanied with great elegance and propriety.'[61] Authentic 'savage' song was hardly what the age demanded, as is evidenced by Fanny Burney's account of how polite society reacted to the performance of a visiting 'savage' who shattered salon tranquillities with his caterwaulings.[62] Cultivated ladies and gentlemen felt more at ease with the bogus primitiveness of those cleverly counterfeited 'translations' which James Macpherson claimed to have made from the Gaelic (*Fragments of ancient poetry*, 1760). Similar deceptions had to be practised in the quest for peasant-poets whose formal education could rightly be presumed minimal in the eighteenth century, and whose writings might therefore be supposed to have escaped the complex artificialities which blight the hypercivilised. Such writers were not unknown in the seventeenth century. One example is John Taylor the Water Poet, who published *Taylor's water-work* in 1612, but whose writings stand as an amusing oddity rather than the embodiment of a cultural theory.

Unlike Taylor, eighteenth-century peasant-poets were expected to be unconsciously excellent, not unconsciously funny. Thomas Gray was not alone in entertaining the possibility that rural Britain might have a crop of what Southey was soon to call 'uneducated poets' (currently wasting their sweetness on the desert air) whose natural simplicities might revitalise late Augustan poetry.[63] The logical absurdity of a 'mute, inglorious Milton' – as impossible a figure as a Leonardo who never got around to painting the Mona Lisa – was overlooked by enthusiasts. To the astonishment of Coleridge, it was Wordsworth who declared that

> many are the poets that are sown
> By Nature; men endowed with highest gifts,
> The vision and the faculty divine,
> Yet wanting the accomplishment of verse.[64]

If Nature is so prodigal in creating untutored poets, then where are they all, Coleridge wanted to know. For as Crabbe notes in *The village* (1783):

> few, amid the rural tribe, have time
> To number syllables, and play with rhyme (1 21f).

All that was proved by the publication of 'uneducated' work by condescendingly labelled Poetical Washerwomen and Poetical Shoemakers and so forth was that to be deprived of an extensive formal education is no more likely to guarantee a simple style of writing than a country upbringing will make for simplicity of subject-matter. For instead of producing untutored simplicities, peasant-poets tended to write in the stale Augustanisms of better educated contemporaries whose works they read and tried to emulate, since this seemed the gateway to recognition and publication. Even the one authentic poet of working-class origins in this period, Robert Burns, pretended to a genteel taste for 'the elegantly melting Gray'.[65] It would seem that simple styles, like simple pleasures (in Wilde's aphorism), are the last refuge of the complex.

The art of artlessness

Admirers of old-style *simplesse* were disturbed by the publication in 1798 of *Lyrical ballads*, a book which, in advocating simple poems about simple people – even simpletons – seemed to confuse simplicity with simple-mindedness (one of the parodies of *Lyrical ballads* is called *The simpliciad*, 1808). 'It was as if a nudist had appeared among advocates of simpler clothing', R. D. Havens comments.[66] Much of the time, Wordsworth's poems were insulated against corrosion from his own theories by an abiding respect for the dignity of literary language. Coleridge noticed that the vigorous speech of Wordsworth's Cumberland shepherds is more attributable to the King James Bible and *Book of common prayer* than to the Cumberland way of life. Vulgarisms doubtless came his way, but Wordsworth kept them out of his poetry, with the result that his bad poems are more silly than vulgar. Later advocates of a truly vernacular poetry have claimed that Wordsworth did not go far enough: Robert Bridges, for instance, praises Kipling for having written the kind of poems Wordsworth could only talk about, poems in a language *really* used by men.[67] Nowadays, it looks as though Wordsworth's instinct was right after all, for *Barrack-room ballads* (1892) have dated far worse than *Lyrical ballads*. For the true end of all such experiments, Ezra Pound would say, is not 'the simplicity and directness of daily speech' but 'a simplicity and directness of utterance which is...more dignified'.[68]

A perennial attraction of simple styles is their seeming artlessness. Anybody who did not know that Burns synthesised half-a-dozen Scottish folk-songs in order to create the seamless web of 'My love is like a red, red rose' would be tempted to regard that poem as a practically unmediated expression of what Burns himself calls 'the spontaneous language of my heart'.[69] Here if anywhere is a masterly demonstration of those 'calculations that look but casual' which Yeats admired so much and which confirm the truth of an old maxim of uncertain provenance, *ars celare artem*: in Dryden's gloss, 'it is the greatest perfection of art to keep itself

undiscovered'.[70] 'Oratory is like the human body', wrote Tacitus:
'it is beautiful only when the veins do not stand out and the bones
cannot be counted' (De oratore, 21). By the same token, nobody
should be so naive as to assume that bodies are devoid of veins
and bones just because neither happens to be conspicuously on
display.

It is common to discover on looking closely at the work of a
writer usually praised for his simplicity that he has calculated his
stylistic effects to an extraordinary degree. Mary Ellen Rickey's
study of George Herbert[71] – a poet who made no secret of his
determination to break with the currently fashionable complexities
of Donne and his imitators – demonstrates that if a writer chooses
to emphasise simplicity he is obliged to be much more devious
in concealing his art than would otherwise be necessary. She calls
her book Utmost art, and rightly so: it is the supreme sophistication
to manipulate calculations that look but casual and artfully
contrive the illusion of artlessness. To analyse the simplicity of
Blake's Songs of innocence (1789–90) is no act of ridiculous
pedantry, equivalent to trying to photograph the Emperor's New
Clothes. The limpidities of a simple style are as worthy of note
as the opacities of more complicated modes of writing.

Nevertheless, the risks to be taken in cultivating simplicity are
serious, if only because simplicity is a privative ideal. In eliminating
so-called superfluities and renouncing the gaudy colours of rhetoric, a writer may discover that he has sacrificed the very qualities
which make literature attractive. The problem is entertainingly
explored in Love's labour's lost, in which the courtier Biron is
persuaded to exchange his highfalutin manner of speech for
something more simple and direct. Biron vows to give up

> Taffeta phrases and silken terms precise,
> Three-piled hyperbole, spruce affection,
> Figures pedantical

and confine himself instead to 'russet yeas and honest kersey noes'
(v ii 406ff). This sharp contrast between upper-class ornateness and
lower-class plainness gives point to the Marxist claim that so-called
aesthetic values are fundamentally class-values.[72] At the same
time, we are meant to savour the irony of a situation in which
simplicity is defended so elaborately. The disingenuousness of it
all reverberates beyond the immediate context of this play. By and
large, literature is made out of taffeta phrases, and we should be
thankful, for a literature made out of yeas and noes – however
honest, however kersey – would be monumentally boring.

4

Inspiration

This and the following chapter are concerned with two interrelated sets of speculation concerning the genesis of literature. Is writing a technique or a mystique, a matter of visions or revisions? Is the writer an agent or patient? Here we begin with the view that no matter how skilled a writer may become in verbal craftsmanship, his best work will always be in some sense involuntary because it is the expression of powerful forces which are beyond his control and located either deep within his unconscious mind or else in the mind of some supernatural being.

The miracle of fluency

Many writers admit that inspiration and perspiration are equally necessary, although the ratio of one to the other varies and can never be computed exactly. Most would therefore agree with Shelley that 'the source of poetry is native and involuntary but requires severe labour in its development'.[1] That was a private remark to Thomas Medwin, and quite different in emphasis from the full-blown inspirational doctrine publicised in Shelley's *Defence of poetry* (1821) and 'Ode to the west wind' (1820), and different again from his preface to *Prometheus unbound* (1820), where the finest poetry is said to be the product of revision. Why should Shelley have made public statements which contradict one another and the evidence contained in his own notebooks? A similar problem is explored by Norman Fruman in connection with Coleridge, who liked people to believe that poems he had laboured over for days on end were spontaneous effusions of the moment, if not always in quite so spectacular a way as the genesis alleged for 'Kubla Khan' (1816): 'all the images rose up before him as *things*, with a parallel production of the correspondent expressions, without any sensation or consciousness of effort'.[2] How impressive this would be if only it were true, for Coleridge here bypasses the obstacle traditionally confronted by theoreticians of the impulse to write and admits no distinction between the subject-matter of his poem (*suggestio rerum*) and the words with which to communicate it (*suggestio verborum*).[3] Miraculously, the 'images' Coleridge received in his vision were both things and words, *res et verba*. The possibility that Coleridge made it up is less interesting than his obligation to talk about the poem in this way, as though its excellence were somehow guaranteed by the facility of its composition.

Inspirationists associate 'ease' with the effortlessness often held to be characteristic of genius. The publishers of the 1623 Folio said that Shakespeare wrote with such 'easiness, that we have scarce received from him a blot in his papers'; and Milton was equally willing to concede that Shakespeare's 'easy numbers flow . . . to the shame of slow-endeavouring art'.[4] Facility is felicitous. 'Easy' became a cliché of approval in the later seventeenth century as reaction set in against the complicated Metaphysical style of poetry. 'Wit is best conveyed to us in the most easy language', wrote Dryden, dismissing Cleveland; and Samuel Johnson went on to extol the virtues of 'easy poetry . . . in which natural thoughts are expressed without violence to the language'.[5] Inevitably, a new kind of unintelligibility appeared when writers forgot Pope's dictum that 'true ease in writing comes from art, not chance' (*An essay on criticism*, 362). As Sheridan complained of a poetaster:

> You write with ease, to show your breeding;
> But easy writing's vile hard reading.[6]

Both Sheridan's comment and Pope's reflect standard advice in the rhetorical tradition: only an ignoramus, wrote the first Samuel Butler, 'professes to write with as great a facility, as if his Muse was sliding down Parnassus'.[7]

A genuinely spontaneous author such as Thackeray, who wrote good books and bad ones equally fluently,[8] is therefore a puzzle to rhetoricians, who prefer to think of spontaneity as an illusion, one of those arts which art conceals. 'In a good written speech', the Younger Pliny told Tacitus, 'there are always innumerable "extemporary" devices to be found' (*Letters*, 1 20). These could be tabulated, learnt and used in order to create 'conversational' effects far superior to what turns up in transcripts of spontaneous conversation (which make for vile hard reading). A good example is Cowper's parody of Robert Lloyd's improvised style:

> First, for a thought – since all agree –
> A thought – I have it – let me see –
> 'Tis gone again – plague on't! I thought
> I had it – but I have it not.[9]

Similarly, the effervescent liveliness of Thomas Nashe's tumbling sentences betokens an ease that comes from art, not chance, although of course Nashe, like all master illusionists, wants us to believe that he improvises as he goes along. 'Give me the man whose extemporal vein in any humour will excel our greatest art-master's deliberate thoughts', he wrote when introducing Greene's *Menaphon* (1589).[10] Inspirationists would be inclined to take Nashe at face value, and see the prose-style (warts and all) as evidence of a spontaneous impetuosity. Verbal craftsmen, however, are more likely to accept Yeats's endorsement of the rhetorical tradition in his poem 'Adam's curse':

> I said, 'A line will take us hours maybe;
> Yet if it does not seem a moment's thought,
> Our stitching and unstitching has been naught.'[11]

Drafts of Shelley's 'To a skylark' vindicate the rhetorical tradition. The Muse, it appears, made rather a botch of the opening:

> What art thou blithe spirit
> For bird thou hardly art.

Shelley knew better, and exercised craftsmanly know-how in producing

> Hail to thee, blithe spirit!
> Bird thou never wert.

The Muse also got the order of the stanzas wrong, dictating as the second stanza lines which (Shelley discovered) belonged in the seventh.[12] The excellence of the finished poem is not dependent on the effortlessness of the first draft. What the Muse tends to give a writer, Yeats discovered, are not so much poems as bits of poems, 'metaphors for poetry'.[13]

Inspirational moments are generally unfit for publication in their raw state. In public pronouncements, however, writers have tended to play up or play down the importance of inspiration, presenting themselves as dreamers *or* makers, not dreamers *and* makers. And in this they have been abetted by readers and critics who, for obscure psychological reasons, feel either thrilled or threatened by the idea of things beyond their control, and react accordingly to testimonies of inspirational involuntariness. Falsely, we are expected to choose between an inspired Blake and a craftsmanly Valéry.

The experience of involuntariness

Inspirationists commonly feel that what they write is somehow being dictated to them, and that their main problem is to get it all down before the dictation stops. The fluency of such moments is unpredictably intermittent, and may come at any stage in the writing. Richard Aldington wrote the first part of *Death of a hero* (1929) fluently, but then 'the mysterious sense of somebody dictating vanished'; R. L. Stevenson, on the other hand, reached a certain stage in the composition of *Kidnapped* (1886) when 'the characters took the bit in their teeth... turned their backs on [him] and walked off bodily; and from that time [his] task was stenographic'.[14] Afterwards, an author may look back in amazement at what he has written, thus inviting the derision of more conscious craftsmen, who diagnose fluency as logorrhoea. Mr Barbecue-Smith in Aldous Huxley's novel *Crome yellow* (1921) is one such figure of fun who has learned the secret of automatic writing by hypnotising himself with an electric light, and can now 'turn on the Niagara of the Infinite' (ch. 6).

Reports of involuntary writing are not easily verified. In Cross's biography of George Eliot, for instance, we are told that in all the novelist 'considered her best writing, there was a "not herself" which took possession of her' and made her feel 'merely the instrument through which this spirit was acting'. The example given as evidence is the meeting between Dorothea and Rosamond in chapter eighty-one of *Middlemarch* (1871–72), in which Eliot, 'abandoning herself to the inspiration of the moment... wrote the whole scene exactly as it stands, without alteration or erasure'.[15] Scholarly study of the notebook for *Middlemarch*, however, reveals that Eliot planned the episode very carefully and was still revising it when the novel was in proof.[16] Cross's anecdote tells us less about George Eliot's way of writing novels than it does about his own commitment to the Romantic supposition that unpremeditated effects betoken genius.

Freudian psychology, with its dissociation of conscious from unconscious thought, is frequently referred to in accounts of involuntary experience. E. M. Forster speaks of the writer as someone who 'lets down as it were a bucket into his subconscious,

and draws up something which is normally beyond his reach';
naturally, 'he will wonder afterwards how he did it'.[17] In the
more technical language of Ernst Kris, it is the 'withdrawal of ego
control from many of the higher mental faculties' which creates
the illusion, when we write, of giving expression to someone else's
thoughts and feelings. For when conscious control is relaxed,
unconscious materials are released: 'an alteration of cathexis inside
the person, the bursting of the frontiers between the unconscious
and the conscious, is experienced as an intrusion with without'.[18]
What George Eliot experienced as the '"not herself"' might be
called more accurately the '"not her conscious self"', and was
presumably the source of the first drafts of what she considered
her best writing.

The doctrine of involuntariness seeks to protect the mystery of
creation against scientific investigations which, it is feared, would
try to explain it away. 'How can I know what I think till I see
what I say?' asks Auden, quoting Forster.[19] What else could
motivate the willed irrationalism of such a statement but a desire
to complicate matters for anybody ambitious of converting the
art of literary creation into a science? In surrendering their claim
to conscious control over their work, however, writers inevitably
surrender their claim to freedom of choice, because the Unconscious or Wholly Other or whatever one likes to call it is an
uncompromisingly deterministic influence. Indeed, Stanley Burnshaw would even go so far as to say that what we are in the habit
of calling 'conscious artistry' is not really that at all, but the
manifestation of 'inscrutably collaborative processes' quite beyond
the writer's control. 'A poem', he concludes, 'is something that is
done to a poet.'[20]

Authorial prerogative in the creative process is eroded also by
structuralists like Roland Barthes, who believes that writers do not
'write' but are rather 'written' by the language they use. Far from
exercising freedom in the selection and arrangement of words,
they are on the contrary bound by strict laws of language if their
writings are to communicate any meaning. To Barthes, the
statement 'I write' is a naive account of a situation depicted more
accurately by 'it is writing' or 'I am written'.[21] Such speculations
accord with the behaviourist psychology of B. F. Skinner, who
believes that freedom is a humanist illusion which prevents us from
facing the fact that everything we do is conditioned by our own
individual histories. Poets have poems, he claims, in the sense that
women have babies, for the poet is merely 'a place in which

certain genetic and environmental causes come together to have a common effect'.[22] A writer may alter a word here and a phrase there, but freedom eludes him, for even 'selection is a special kind of causality', the product of inscrutable processes. All those inspirational testimonies of authorial involuntariness, which craftsmen are inclined to dismiss as so much mumbo-jumbo, become intellectually more respectable in the light of such theories. For if everything in a poem is predetermined to this extent, involuntary experiences bring us about as close as we are ever likely to get to an awareness of those unconscious drives which shape everything we do.

Authorial passivity

In pre-behaviourist accounts of literary genesis, the ability to create alternative realities is seen as a sign of human freedom, and the plurality of heterocosms attests the boundlessness of human invention. All this is seriously imperilled by the doctrine of inspiration, particularly when it holds that the best parts of any writer's work are unlikely to be his own. Although Shelley could laud inspired poets as 'hierophants of an unapprehended inspiration',[23] everybody knows that this is only a polite way of calling them ventriloquist's dummies. For the prototype of the inspired poet is the Pythoness of the Delphic oracle, who suspended her rational faculties so that the god might speak through her. Is this the best a writer can hope for? When the Spirit moves him, should he (as Hopkins believed) respond with an 'aspiration in answer to his inspiration'?[24] Or can he get beyond subordinate passivity and strike a bargain with his Muse, as Pindar did: 'Prophesy, Muse, and I will be your interpreter' (fr. 137).

Plato's *Ion* reveals the difficulties faced by any writer who is content to be a medium for parapsychological experiences. Ion is a rhapsode, that is, somebody who makes his living by reciting and commenting upon poems. When he admits to being most successful with Homer, Socrates claims that Ion's ability is not a product of learning, but a gift, and that Ion recites Homer well only because he does so hypnotically, in a state of trance-like inspiration. As with rhapsodes, so with poets, according to Socrates: a poet has to be out of his mind before he can write well, but who ever pays any attention to a man out of his mind? Hebrew prophets, on the other hand, cannot be dismissed so easily, for they always put up a struggle before accepting their calling as the trumpet of a prophecy. Jeremiah resisted so long that it left him a broken man; and Isaiah experienced all the agonies of the delivery-room in evacuating the holy word.[25] The prophetic utterances induced by a dynamic Hebrew God are made all the more turbulent by the rugged individuality of those chosen to transmit them. Early Christians therefore had a choice of models when considering the prophetic state, and a surprising number (Tertullian and Origen among them) concluded that, in trans-actions with the divine, the Platonic patient is a much more admirable ideal than the Hebrew agent. When the Hebrew prophets were inspired to utterance, wrote Athenagoras in the second century, the divine spirit made use of them 'as a flute-player breathes into a flute'.[26] A related image – the prophet as harp or lyre – was also introduced in the second century by Justin Martyr, and proved popular among Romantic inspirationists. Shelley calls on the west wind to use him like a lyre, but the favourite Romantic model is the Aeolian harp, named after the god of winds, Aeolus.[27] An Aeolian harp is a box with strings across it and a lid designed to let in air. Suitably placed in an open window it performs melodiously when caught by intermittent breezes; made by man and played upon by the winds, it is an apt symbol of the encounter between Self and Other. Although Shelley gave the Aeolian harp pride of place in his *Defence of poetry* (1821), he was not really happy with it as a model of the mind, which he imagined to be much less passive than the model suggests. Passively, the Aeolian harp produces melodies; but if these melodies were ever to become harmonies, human intervention would be necessary, he thought, so that 'the lyre could accom-modate its chords to the motions of that which strikes them'.[28] It is as if Athenagoras' flute were expected to align itself correctly in anticipation of the time when the Holy Ghost whistles through. Clearly, when a model of the mind has to be tampered with to this extent, it is time to abandon it for something more suitable.

The incept

Ovid calls poetry 'the gift of the gods' (*Tristia*, IV 10). A 'gifted' poet is believed to be the recipient of a divine grace which enables him to write with a fluency denied less privileged mortals, who are condemned to earn their poems in the sweat of their brows. Such grace is what theologians call 'prevenient' because it is given before one has the opportunity to accept or reject it. 'Supremely blessed, the poet in his Muse', writes Pope in *An essay on man* (II 70). The gift of a poem (Mallarmé's *don du poème*)[29] is our opportunity to share the grace infused into the poet. In such a system, 'writer's block' is explained as a sudden withdrawal of grace; for the Lord giveth, and the Lord taketh away. Should one's inspiration flag in the course of writing a tragedy, this can only mean that the tragic Muse Melpomene is dissatisfied and has withdrawn her favour.

It is not unusual for the most rational of writers to admit that a seminal suggestion for a certain book came suddenly, as it were, out of the blue. At present, there is no generally accepted literary term for such experiences, although we might well adopt Beardsley's term 'incept',[30] which has the advantage of being descriptively more neutral than the usual alternatives, some of the more celebrated of which turn up in a retrospective preface written by Henry James for *The spoils of Poynton* (1897). James was aware of the instigatory value of incepts but rated craftsmanship more highly, and here he runs through a number of picturesque terms, evidently unable to decide which is the best: 'germ', 'precious particle', 'grain of gold', 'virus of suggestion'. These images all tend to suggest something very small but perfectly intact, with a potential ability to grow or spread in a suitable environment such as the writer himself can best provide. 'If one is given a hint at all designedly', James warns, 'one is sure to be given too much'. This is about as far as craftsmen are willing to go in conceding the importance of inspirational moments, for they are a proud lot, reluctant to compromise themselves in the way that inspirationists inevitably do when accepting their role of stenographers to the Muses. 'The gods in their graciousness give us an occasional first line *for nothing*', Valéry once wrote; 'but it is for us to fashion the second, which must chime with the first, and not be unworthy of its supernatural elder.'[31] So it was that Rilke set about writing the first of his *Duino elegies* in 1912 after 'hearing' a disembodied voice call out through the roaring wind and surf of the Adriatic coast: 'Who, if I cried, would hear me from among the angelic orders?'[32]

Despite their fascination for writers and biographers, incepts are of limited interest to literary critics. In the first place, there is nothing intrinsically valuable in the thing given (*la donnée*), for it can be given only to somebody who knows what to do with it. Furthermore, we know that the particle which was so very precious to the writer may be completely valueless to everybody else (except to people especially interested in literary origins) because the original incept may be abandoned as the work takes shape. Valéry doubted whether 'the idea which engenders the work is always the idea of the work engendered',[33] and cases where an incept is known to have been discarded are not hard to come by. Yeats said that his play *On Baile's Strand* 'came to [him] in a dream, but it changed much in the making'; and the poem we now know as 'Leda and the swan' started out as a political poem, but in the course of writing 'all politics went out of it'.[34]

Psychic intervention

No adequate explanation has yet been given of inspirational experiences, although everybody seems to agree that we are now on the right track in believing them to be psychological rather than psychic phenomena. Just how unorthodox this modern view of the matter is (when placed in the context of speculation from roughly Homer to Pope) may be gauged at once from the fact that the word 'inspiration' means literally a 'breathing into', and presupposes the existence of something outside the writer which bloweth where it listeth. Any writer blown upon in this way was believed to betray the fact stylistically in a so-called afflatus (from *afflare*, 'to blow upon'), that 'divine afflatus' which Cicero thought distinctive of great poets (*De natura deorum*, II 66). An afflated style is not to be confused with an *in*flated one, said Thackeray, for the afflated manner is produced whenever a writer sits 'like a Pythoness on her oracle tripod, and mighty words, words which he cannot help, come blowing, and bellowing, and whistling, and moaning through the speaking pipes of his bodily organ'.[35] The Bible is said to be inspired in this pneumatic sense, which is why the Four Evangelists are sometimes depicted at work on the gospels with pens poised and clothes fluttering in the breeze as the Divine Spirit (*spiritus*, 'breath') passes through them.[36] As St Paul said, 'all scripture is given by inspiration of God' (2 Timothy, 3:16).

The reputation of inspiration as a literary theory is often affected by contemporary attitudes towards inspiration in the theological sense. It has always been difficult to authenticate inspirational experiences and separate those sanctioned by the Bible from those vouched for by later sectarians who threaten the established Church by claiming that their activities are divinely inspired. People whose own religious convictions coincide with those deemed correct by the state are generally in a strong position to disparage inspiration as the vehicle of dissident opinion. As an Anglican convert, John Donne felt that we should no longer expect God to speak to us 'mouth to mouth, spirit to spirit, by inspiration', because God 'hath constituted an Office, and established a Church, in which we should hear him';[37] but this presupposes a conviction that God is an Anglican, and it is therefore not the best of arguments for curbing religious 'enthusiasm'.

'Enthusiasm' means literally 'the state of being possessed by a god': the Greek word was translated by the Latin *inspiratio*, which embodies a different metaphor altogether. How does one know that Enthusiastic inspiration is inferior to that of the original Evangelists? When Henry More tackled this question in *Enthusiasmus triumphatus* (1662) he found his answer in Burton's *Anatomy of melancholy* (1621). 'The spirit...that wings the Enthusiast in such a wonderful manner', More writes, 'is nothing else but that flatulency which is in the melancholy complexion, and rises out of the hypochondriacal humour upon some occasional heat.'[38] Some forty years later, Jonathan Swift was to develop the same point with savage ingenuity in the eighth section of *A tale of a tub* (1704) when caricaturing an imaginary sect of Aeolists, who 'maintain the original cause of all things to be wind' and are thoughtfully attentive to oracular belching.[39] If this seems bizarre, it is worth noting that modern psychoanalytic theory supports Swift's equation of eructation with speech. 'The acts of breathing and speaking', observes Ernest Jones, 'are both treated in the Unconscious as equivalents of the act of passing intestinal flatus.'[40] Speech is the expiration of inspiration.

The indignities engendered by too literal an understanding of what is known as *inspiratio* in the Latin tradition are avoided altogether by the Greek word ἐνθουσιασμός, which explains involuntary experiences in terms of what Dodds calls 'psychic intervention'[41] by some divine being. Even here, however, ambivalences exist, as Chapman points out in dedicating his translation of the *Odyssey* to the Earl of Somerset in 1614: for 'poetic rapture' can be either a divine *furor* or a mere *insania*, the 'one a perfection directly infused from God, the other an infection obliquely and degenerately proceeding from man'.[42] Two conflicting traditions develop accordingly and run concurrently: one finds expression in Plato's *Phaedrus* and ennobles the writer as a *vates* or prophet of sublime truths and mediator of divine visions; the other, found in Plato's *Ion*, treats inspiration as a kind of madness and is at the root of later attempts to ground artistic activities in neurosis and insanity. Hence the Earl of Roscommon's warning:

> Beware what Spirit rages in your breast;
> For ten inspired ten thousand are possessed.[43]

A psychic intervener is usually named and made responsible for one particular activity which mortals would perform rather badly if left to their own devices. In the classical tradition, the arts come under the surveillance of nine Muses, each of whom exercises a tutelary function over a specialised area, so that a historian will know to invoke Clio rather than (say) Thalia, whose special competence is displayed in comedy. So influential was this tradition that Christian admirers of pagan literature felt it expedient to invent a Christian Muse who is called Urania by Du Bartas and invoked by Milton at the beginning of Book VII of *Paradise lost*.[44]

Contact with the deity may be sexual, as it was for the Pythoness, who squatted on her tripod and was entered by the god; or for St Teresa, who was pierced ecstatically by the dart of a seraphim. A more common way of getting the god inside one for enthusiastic purposes is to eat something known to be associated with him. Because laurel leaves are the emblem of Phoebus Apollo the god of poetry, the priestess at Delphi (where his shrine is located) chewed laurel leaves, no doubt experiencing mild inebriation as a result of the small amount of cyanide contained in them. Poets were sometimes called δαφνηφάγοι, writes a French commentator on Alciati's *Emblematum liber* (1531), because of their habit of munching laurel leaves for inspiration.[45] Primitive peoples who eat peyote or hallucinogenic mushrooms do so because they believe their gods to be immanent in them; and for what is basically the same reason, poets in search of inspiration pretend to drink from the Castalian spring, the well of Aganippe, the pure waters of the Hippocrene or similar streams associated with the Muses and Apollo. Excellent results are obtainable from fermented liquors derived from the grape, which is sacred to Dionysus or Bacchus:

> For Bacchus' fruit is friend to Phoebus wise.
> And when with wine the brain begins to sweat,
> The numbers flow as fast as spring doth rise.[46]

So there developed the convention familiar in Renaissance Ana-

creontic and medieval Goliardic poetry that the best inspiration
comes out of a bottle, the kind of bottle eulogised by Rabelais as
'mon vraie et seule Helicon...ma fontaine Caballine...mon
unique Enthusiasme'.[47] More temperate souls transformed such
bacchanalian excesses into the sober conceit of imbibing inspiration
at a sacred fount, and it was in this bowdlerised form that
enthusiastic drinking could become a decorous ornament of polite
literature.

Blake disliked the Greeks for making the Muses the daughters
of Memory (Mnemosyne) instead of Imagination.[48] Yet the
genealogy of the Muses is probably more sound than Blake
suspected. In a civilisation which lacks written documents, history
is in the mouths of people with reliable memories: the court poet
in Beowulf (ll. 867ff) is one such memory-man who 'remembered
many old traditions' (ealdgesegena/worn gemunde). Homer likewise
thinks of his Muse as somebody who knows everything; and
because he relies on her for matters of fact rather than for stylistic
embellishment, he invokes her in Book II of the Iliad before listing
the names of the captains and chieftains who sailed to Troy.
Memory is enormously important to the rhapsode, but appreciably
less so to the writer, who keeps no audience fidgeting impatiently
while he thumbs through his notebooks for some point of
information. What the Muses were held to guarantee was a fluent
mastery of the factual, plus an extraordinary vividness in
recapturing a scene no living person was old enough to have
witnessed. Odysseus admires Demodocus for singing about the
Trojan War so well that you would think he had got it from an
eye-witness (Odyssey, VIII 487ff). Only a Muse or Apollo himself,
Odysseus is convinced, could create that kind of effect – the same
effect, presumably, which Defoe creates in his Journal of the plague
year (1722) or Stephen Crane in The red badge of courage (1895),
two works of fiction which masquerade successfully as eye-witness
accounts. With the shift from an oral to a literary situation,
invocations were retained in a fossilised form as a conventional
ornament, although the Muses now tended to be called upon for
technical assistance in the handling of some unusually intricate
set-piece. When Milton invokes his Muse it is not for mere points
of information (readily available in written sources like the Bible
and commentaries upon it) but for ease in writing, since it is the
Muse alone who

> dictates to [him] slumbering, or inspires
> Easy [his] unpremeditated verse (Paradise lost, IX 24).

What is known to Biblical scholars as 'plenary inspiration'[49] is that rare phenomenon experienced by Moses, who went up Mount Sinai and had the Decalogue dictated to him there and then by God. This is stenographic inspiration in the most literal sense, with the writer functioning as an amanuensis in the presence of his God, granted a personal audience of a kind no classical poet ever expected to secure. Much more common than plenary inspiration is the so-called 'mantic' or prophetic mode which is symbolised by the Greek myth of the Muses, and in Biblical tradition by the idea that holy scripture is the outcome of promptings from the Holy Ghost rather than of interviews with God himself. The actual division of labour is spelled out in the preface to the 1611 translation of the Bible, where Miles Smith says that the real author of the Bible is God, the inditer is the Holy Spirit, and prophets are the penmen. Among secular writers who have laid claim to mantic inspiration is Harriet Beecher Stowe, who finally said of her best-selling novel, *Uncle Tom's cabin* (1852): 'God wrote it. I merely did his dictation.'[50] The confidence gained from being able to write with divine authority is often neutralised by a tendency observable in the poetry of George Wither, who undoubtedly became a more slovenly writer in the 1620s when he convinced himself that he was in possession of divinely prophetic gifts.[51] The greatest and most eccentric of our inspirationists is William Blake, who said that his poem *Milton* (1800–04) was dictated to him in batches of twenty or thirty lines at a time, 'without premeditation, and even against [his] will'.[52] Concerning the origin of such poems, he claimed that 'the authors are in Eternity', and that he himself was merely their 'secretary'.[53] He began *Jerusalem* in 1804 after

> God commanded [his] hand to write
> In the studious hours of deep midnight.[54]

Yeats, who studied and edited Blake, aspired to similar compositional privileges. He managed to overcome the handicap of his agnosticism by substituting occultism for Christianity, and finally succeeded in getting *A vision* (1925) dictated to him through the medium of his wife by a supernatural being called Michael Robartes.

Understandably, there is a close connection between inspirationism and the occult, for spiritualists often claim to experience psychic intervention from deceased authors. In a recent case, and in a matter of months, a medium took down over 100000 words of fiction 'dictated' to her by Conan Doyle, H. G. Wells, Edgar Wallace, Somerset Maugham, G. B. Shaw and Ian Fleming. 'However you look at it,' Peter Fleming concludes, 'a lot of *energy* was at work here.'[55]

Unconscious projections

Outside the mysterious world of the seance, however, inspiration is commonly explained in terms of dispatches from the unconscious to the conscious mind. The process by which external inspiration was internalised begins with late eighteenth-century speculations about the nature of original genius, and culminates in Freudian psychology in the early years of this century. The Muses, which had survived as a pleasant fiction in Renaissance literature, became an embarrassment in the Enlightenment. 'Lord Shaftesbury observes that nothing is more cold than the invocation of a muse by a modern', writes Fielding in *Tom Jones* (1749); 'he might have added that nothing can be more absurd' (VIII 1). Muses were outmoded, an unwanted legacy from crudely superstitious times, good only for burlesque or travesty: 'Hail Muse! *et caetera*' is Byron's mock-heroic opening to Canto 3 of *Don Juan* (1821). After all, people who deplore Enthusiasm in religion can hardly be expected to tolerate such nonsense in literature; but at the same time, poets of the Romantic generation wanted to believe in the existence of some sort of inspiration, although not so primitive a form as psychic intervention.

One solution was to demythologise the 'god within'. In the *Odyssey*, for instance, when Phemius talks about the source of his own poetic powers, he says 'it was a god who implanted all sorts of lays in [his] mind' (XXII 347f); and Ovid similarly explains that 'there is a god within us, at [whose] instigation we are fired' (*Fasti*, VI 5). Demythologised, the 'god within' ceases to be a temporary visitor bearing gifts for his fortunate host, and takes up residence instead as a latent imaginative potential in the writer. For however problematic the concept of 'genius' might be, it was easier to accept in the late eighteenth century than Greek mythology was; and it seems inevitable that when Edward Young considered genius in his *Conjectures on original composition* (1759) he should have spoken of it as 'the god within'.[56] The Romantics, however, often equivocate on this matter, and even Wordsworth was never quite sure how to explain his own inspirational experiences. When he speaks of 'visitings of imaginative power' (*Prelude*, XII 203) –

for which one can only wait expectantly in a state of wise passiveness – he seems to have in mind some form of psychic intervention rather different from the experience recorded in *The waggoner* (1819) of inner promptings by 'a shy spirit in [his] heart/That comes and goes' (IV 208ff). Perhaps it was neither one nor the other, but 'an ennobling interchange/Of action from within and from without' (*Prelude*, XII 375f).[57]

Herbert Read once conjectured that Shelley intuited the origin of poetry in the Unconscious, citing as evidence a passage in the *Defence of poetry* (1821) where Shelley speaks of an 'imperial faculty, whose throne is contained within the invisible nature of man'.[58] Without the benefit of Freudian or Jungian hindsight, however, it would be difficult to see in Shelley's remark much more than a reformulation of earlier views of genius as the 'god within'. For Shelley's image lacks the specificity of Freud's model of the human mind, in which consciousness is symbolised as a clean well-lighted place built over a murky basement where the Unconscious resides. In terms of this model (as already noted), moments of inspiration occur when matter is released sporadically from the Unconscious, which accounts for the involuntariness of such experiences as well as the element of surprise at what they contain. Experiences explained in unenlightened times as dictation from external and supernatural powers are now interpreted as 'projections' from the Unconscious into consciousness. Literary critics are more attracted by the mechanism of Freudian projection than by Freud's explanation of why such projections occur. For seeing that the Freudian Unconscious is a hoard of repressions, any work of literature inspired by unconscious projections is likely to record little more than the spontaneous overflow of powerful neuroses. Literary critics would like to dissociate the mechanism of projection from what is projected, but this is not advocated by those best equipped to test the Freudian hypothesis. The director of an interdisciplinary investigation into the creative process, Albert Rothenberg, certainly makes no such distinction when reporting on work-in-progress: 'psychodynamically', he explains, 'the inception of a poetic process and the inspirations that occur at the beginning or along the way are metaphorical embodiments of the poet's unconscious or pre-conscious emotional conflicts'.[59] How remote this is from traditional reports of sudden glory in those moments when the poem or novel starts to write itself, and everything comes so quickly that one has barely time to get it all down.

Where psychoanalytical explanations appear to go astray is in the assumption that the only purpose of an inspirational moment is to supply subject-matter otherwise inaccessible to the writer, and that this subject-matter is bound to be neurotic in nature because it is neurotic in origin. But we know very well that 'content' is not necessarily the only product of an involuntary experience, for poets in particular often find that inspirational promptings take the form of wordless rhythms. '*Le cimetière marin* began in me by a rhythm', writes Valéry. 'I had as yet no idea with which to fill out this form. Gradually a few hovering words settled in it, little by little determining the subject'; and corroboration of the theory is to be found in an essay on 'The music of poetry' (1942) by T. S. Eliot, who testifies that a 'rhythm may bring to birth the idea and the image'.[60] Actual examples of rhythmic genesis are on view among Shelley's manuscripts, where the poem which eventually is to begin with the words 'Oh, world! oh life! oh, time!' first pulses rhythmically to a mindless sequence of *na-nas*, and a few tentative *hum-hums* finally evolve into 'The beauty hangs about thee'.[61] In a line by Tennyson – 'The mellow lin-lan-lone of evening bells' – we have perhaps an example of a rhythm which develops into a unit of sound without ever reaching the final stage and acquiring a meaning: for what exactly *is* a 'lin-lan-lone'?[62] If rhythmic genesis is a type of inspirational experience, it cannot be accounted for satifactorily by those content-oriented explanations currently in favour.

5

Making

The maker likes to think of himself as a man alone. Unlike dreamers, who merely edit divine dictation, makers see themselves as wordsmiths like the poet of the Old English *Widsith*, who 'unlocked his word-hoard' (*wordhord unleac*) in order to begin a composition. To wordsmiths, writing is a matter of building the lofty rhyme, not of uttering native woodnotes wild. So they will make a point of telling you, as the Roman poet Persius does in a prologue to his *Satires* imitated by Sidney in the 1580s, that they themselves have never had the benefit of drinking from springs sacred to the Muses, nor of any other form of supernatural assistance.[1] 'I do not write with a goose-quill, winged with two feathers', says Webster in his preface to *The white devil* (1612); and indeed he did not, for source-studies enable us to appreciate Webster's synoptic skills in making coherent plays out of ideas and images drawn from a wide variety of other people's books. Extremists want us to believe that every literary effect is the perfectly controlled result of meticulously accurate planning. The parodic ideal of sheer craftsmanship, therefore, is Edgar Allan Poe's account in 'The philosophy of composition' (1846) of how he set about writing his poem 'The raven'. It would have to be no more than a hundred lines long, Poe decreed, because long poems are not really poems; it would need to have a raven in it, because ravens are traditionally birds of ill-omen; it would have to have a refrain with the word 'nevermore', and so on. Taking account of these and other 'preconsiderations', he then set to and wrote it. It comes as no surprise to learn that 'The raven' was not produced in quite this way, and that Poe concocted the story of its genesis as a joke, although with the qualification that the poem might well have been put together in precisely the way described without adversely affecting the finished product. For the method revealed in 'The philosophy of composition' is not nearly so remote from Poe's actual practice as it seemed to be to Baudelaire, who believed that Poe ('one of the best inspired men I know') affected calculation in the way that other writers affect negligence.[2] Here again, as in the case of Coleridge's claims to spontaneity, it is less profitable to wonder whether Poe is telling the truth, than to ask why he should go to the trouble of encouraging us to think of him as the dispassionate manufacturer of something which, after all, is no less mawkish than many another minor poem of that period written (as they say) with feeling. In its historical context, Poe's account of 'The raven' is anti-Romantic in its rejection not only of inspirationism but also of the expressivist view that genuine poetry is a spontaneous overflow of powerful feelings. It makes us entertain the possibility (commonplace in later formalist criticism) that the emotions evoked by a poem may be altogether different from those experienced by the poet in writing it. It was this aspect of 'The philosophy of composition' which led Valéry to ignore the element of spoof in it and praise Poe as the creator of an 'extremely original poetic theory' as well as a 'splendid piece called "The raven"'. As a result of Poe's discovery, said Valéry, the poet 'is no longer the disheveled madman who writes a whole poem in the course of one feverish night', but rather a cool scientist, almost an algebraist, in the service of a subtle dreamer'.[3] Thanks to Poe, poetry could now become truly experimental, perhaps in ways analogous to those envisaged for the novel by Émile Zola in Le roman expérimental (1880): 'the tower of ivory', Eliot notes laconically, 'has been fitted up as a laboratory'.[4] Eliot himself was to benefit from Poe's manner of treating the creative act as primarily a technical problem. It happens to be Eliot who once spoke of poets as 'concentrating upon a task which is a task in the same sense as the making of an efficient engine or the turning of a jug or a table-leg'.[5] In spirit, however, this pronouncement comes from Poe and Valéry, who believed that poets are no more obliged to feel what their poems express than locomotive-builders are obliged to work at eighty miles per hour while constructing locomotives to travel at that speed.[6] To Eliot and Valéry, writers are primarily people who know how to do things with words.

The suggestion that writing is a craft is not at all well received by those who distinguish inspiration from making only in order to denigrate making, as Coleridge does when remarking upon an 'essential difference betwixt the shaping skill of mechanical talent, and the creative, productive life-power of inspired genius'.[7] Here, as so often in the Romantic style of criticism satirised by Poe in 'The philosophy of composition', genuine poetry is regarded as a state of mind rather than a verbal art, and technique as the concern only of writers who are so devoid of genius as to have to make do with mere talent. Goethe did not like to think of poetry as an art, and told Eckermann how much he hated that 'thoroughly contemptible word *composition*, which makes out a work of art to be no better than a piece of cake or biscuit'.[8] Pope had such culinary associations in mind when he published his mock 'recipe' for an epic poem in 1713.[9] There is a feeling that poetry is necessarily belittled if treated as a craft, because poetry is a noble thing conceived in the soul and therefore a proper occupation for gentlemen amateurs, whereas crafts are practised by socially inferior artisans and tradesmen. To call a dramatist a playwright was to stigmatise him socially, as Henry Fitzjeffrey well knew when he mocked John Webster in 1617 for being a 'playwright-cartwright'.[10] Carlyle could draw on similar responses as late as 1832 when castigating 'novelwrights'.[11] Curiously, the usual derogatory analogy is with shoemaking, perhaps because of the success of cobbler-poets like Hans Sachs. Aristocratic contempt for poetry-cobbling is clearly evident in *English bards and Scotch reviewers* (1809), where Byron mocks currently fashionable working-class poets, among them the shoemaker Robert Bloomfield, who 'St Crispin quits and cobbles for the Muse'.

> Ye tuneful cobblers! still your notes prolong,
> Compose at once a slipper and a song. (ll. 791–2).

So successful were formalist critics like Valéry and Eliot in eradicating such prejudices that nobody is scandalised nowadays by Stravinsky's remark that 'the composer should practise his trade exactly as a shoemaker does'.[12]

One of the ironies in the cold war between inspirationists and makers is that the dissociation of exalted 'poetry' from a more pedestrian activity called 'making' is a distinction without a difference, since both words mean the same thing. Sidney was intrigued by the convergence of English and Greek usage. 'The word "poet"', he writes, 'cometh of this word *poiein*, which is "to make": wherein I know not whether by luck or wisdom, we Englishmen have met with the Greeks in calling him "a maker"'.[13] Far more mysterious is why the Greeks themselves should have settled upon a word which suggests a degree of voluntary activity quite remote from the idea of psychic intervention symbolised in their mythology of Apollo and the Muses. Whatever the reason, the English have been reluctant to accept 'making' as an exact synonym for 'poetry'. As a result, 'poetry' has tended to be thought of as that sublimely mad activity Plato talks about in the *Phaedrus*, whereas 'making' has acquired something of the present connotations of 'manufacture'. The rift between the two terms widened because of the way standard English evolved from southern Middle English, in which 'making' is a less dignified term than 'poetry'. 'Making' has no such derogatory connotations, however, in northern English. William Dunbar refers to himself as 'Dunbar the Mackar' and is the author of a 'Lament for the makaris' (1508); Puttenham had no other motive than to praise Wyatt and Surrey when he called them (in 1589) 'courtly makers'.[14] It seems probable that the status of 'making' has been affected adversely by the stigma of its nomenclature, which has given people the impression that only such mechanical skills as versification constitute making. Poetry, it is felt, is something rather different and much better.

The primacy of the word

Inspirationists certainly look upon making as an inferior kind of verbal craft which can be learned in the way that one might learn plumbing. Shelley's *Defence of poetry* (1821) expresses the inspirationist attitude memorably and succinctly in describing the mind in creation as 'a fading coal, which some invisible influence, like an inconstant wind, awakens to transitory brightness'. Writing it down afterwards is a miserable makeshift, like a black-and-white photograph of a peacock, for 'when composition begins, inspiration is already on the decline, and the most glorious poetry that has ever been communicated to the world is probably a feeble shadow of the original conceptions of the poet'. Shelley said that 'compositions...are to poetry what mosaic is to painting'.[15] Verbal technique is in this context an unglamorous and irksome activity. In what is one of the earliest inspirationist statements in English, a character in *The shepherd's calendar* (1579) asserts that the Muses do not approve of 'crabbed care'. An introductory note explains that poetry is 'no art, but a divine gift and heavenly instinct not to be gotten by labour and learning, but adorned with both, and poured into the wit by a certain ἐνθουδιασμός and celestial inspiration'.[16] If crabbed care is called for at all, it should be at the end rather than at the beginning of the poetic process.

Shelley told Trelawney that his brain got so heated that it threw up images faster than he could skim them; and that the few he managed to retrieve in his 'frightful scrawl' he would leave to cool for a day before starting work on them.[17] Two things are involved here: the involuntary experience (which is allegedly the real thing), and the complementary labour of revision, which involves bringing all one's technical skills to bear upon a scrappy inspirational *donnée* and working it up so well as to enable somebody else to experience vicariously what Shelley himself experienced in the heat of the inspirational moment. Updated with the help of Freudian psychology, Shelley's scheme reappears in Robert Graves's *Poetic unreason* (1925), where *données* are equated with Freudian wish-fulfilling dreams, and the writing-process made equivalent to the dream-process which Graves calls 'secondary elaboration', a common mistranslation of Freud's *sekundäre Bearbeitung* ('secondary revision').[18] No more than Shelley could Graves condone the 'automatic' writing encouraged by Surrealists like André Breton, who hope to pump poetry straight from the Unconscious. First drafts are private, Graves insists, 'none but the poet's own business'.[19] Now it is precisely this commonly accepted explanation of the relationship between dreaming and making, incept and artifact, that the maker challenges, and he is able to do so by pointing out that there is more to writing than the expression of preconceived ideas. Supposedly 'secondary elaboration' has a mysterious habit of throwing up primary materials, and the ornamentalist view of language proves quite inadequate to makers who are accustomed not to know what they are going to say until they have said it. 'Words are the colouring of the work', Dryden once wrote (from the ornamentalist point of view), and therefore 'last to be considered'.[20] But others are tempted to treat 'thought' as the *product* of making, rather than the incentive to make (just as in the visual arts 'making' is now held to come before 'matching').[21] What the theory of making does is to reverse the ornamentalist relationship between word and idea and to give primacy to the word, thus creating a new credo: in the word is the beginning. When Degas remarked that he found difficulty in writing poems (despite the fact that he was never short of ideas), Mallarmé told him that poems are not made with ideas but with words.[22] The writer's first job, Ford Madox Ford told Pound, is to 'get a dictionary and learn the meaning of words'.[23] The bigger his word-hoard, the more efficient a writer is likely to be. In fact, he can hardly ever know too much about the history and structure of the medium he has chosen to work in. A writer 'can learn more from Jespersen's *English grammar* than from Sainte-Beuve', Eliot once wrote.[24] Modernist literature from Mallarmé onwards is lexiphanic for similar reasons. Readers of Auden's poetry get into the habit of reaching for a dictionary, for there are passages in Auden's poems which look as though their main purpose is to provide a suitable environment for exotic words. Both Hopkins and Dylan Thomas seem to have been spurred on by a fascinated doodling with words irresistible in texture, connotation or ambiguity.

Although the modernist emphasis on craftsmanship is historically an anti-Romantic phenomenon, it is of course not so much a new departure as a restoration of pre-Romantic attitudes. One of the things Julius Caesar noted about the British was the long apprenticeship served by those responsible for composing and transmitting epic verses. He was told that the education of a Druid lasted twenty years, during which time he learnt poetry which he was forbidden to commit to writing; and according to the eighth-century *Book of Ballymote*, the bards and *filid* spent somewhere between seven and twelve years learning sagas, antiquarian lore, metrics and so forth. Investigations begun half a century ago by Milman Parry into the oral-formulaic method of epic composition focus attention very properly on the craftsmanly intricacy of the Homeric poems, which were put together by somebody skilled in the fitting of conventional phrases ('formulae') into metrical patterns.[25] The outcome of such a process is likely to be what Bernard Huppé calls (in the context of Old English poetry) a 'web of words'[26] – a phrase which serves to remind us that one of the earliest and most durable metaphors for the art of verbal composition comes from the craft of weaving. As long ago as the fifth century BC Aristophanes was calling poets 'masters of speech subtly woven'; and dominant in the mind of modern structuralists like Barthes is the image of the text as something woven.[27] Weaving is a particularly apt model for the art of narrative. 'If a chap can't compose an epic poem while he's weaving tapestry', said William Morris, 'he had better shut up, he'll never do any good at all.'[28]

For work on a smaller scale, however, weaving has been considered a less suitable model for poetic making than medallions and cameos. Although Jane Austen claimed to have worked exclusively on a 'little bit (two inches wide) of ivory',[29] her example was less influential than that of Théophile Gautier in persuading Anglo-American writers in the late nineteenth and early twentieth centuries to think of poems as cameos. Gautier's professed aim in writing *Émaux et camées* (1852) was to treat 'tiny subjects in a severely formal way', as a worker in precious metals does: 'each piece would have to be as finely chased as an image for the cover of a jewel box or seal ring – something reminiscent of ancient medals'.[30] A famous poem written to this formula is Ezra Pound's *Hugh Selwyn Mauberley* (1920). It is a far cry from the harps and flutes which symbolise the inspirationist's ideal.

The prestige of revision

Revision is important to a craftsman because it enables him to call his work his own. The more he tampers with it, revising his revisions, the more remote it becomes from any inspirational *donnée*, and the more certain he feels he is exercising freedom of choice, however illusory this may be in the opinion of behaviourists. The maker's presumption is to believe in improvement by revision, and to echo Laura Riding's apology to the Muse:

> Forgive me, giver, if I destroy the gift:
> It is so nearly what would please me
> I cannot but perfect it.[31]

What the labour of revision guarantees is independence of mind and excellence of product. 'If you want to write something worth re-reading', Horace advises, 'keep your eraser busy'; and you will need a large eraser too, if you are to do as Horace suggests and wait nine years before publishing your poems.[32] For literary works are not born fully-formed, like Athene out of the head of Zeus, but start out inchoate and have to be licked into shape. A recurrent image for the labour of revision derives therefore from bestiary-lore concerning the habits of the female bear, which gives birth to cubs at a premature stage of their foetal development, and was once thought to lick them into shape. As a metaphor of the compositional process, this vulgar error was sanctioned by Suetonius, who said that Virgil produced verses in a bear-like manner, and wanted the *Aeneid* destroyed because he had not had time to perfect it.[33] An influential modern occurrence of the image is in Du Bellay's *Défence et illustration de la langue française* (1549), where it is used in a gloss on *émendation*; and it had obviously become something of a cliché by the time William Rawley used it when commenting on the fact that Bacon revised his *Novum organum* a dozen times in as many years, 'as many living creatures do lick their young ones, till they bring them to their strength of limbs'.[34]

The analogy is striking but not quite apt. A female bear knows it is time to leave off licking those shapeless lumps she has given birth to when they begin to look like bears, but writers have no such external check on their activities. How does a poem know when it is finished?[35] Is revision a never-ending process, as Valéry feared, and must the writer resign himself to the probability that a work is never finished but merely abandoned?[36] Even the act of publication is not necessarily final. 'I add, but I correct not', said Montaigne of his essays, for the good reason that growing older does not guarantee growing wiser.[37] Others, such as Yeats and Auden, make substantial stylistic and thematic changes when reissuing work already in print, and then mislead the public by back-dating the revised text.[38] In addition to betraying anxiety about past performances, such activities are anti-historical and indefensible when (as is often the case) copyright is refused to original versions subsequently revised. In spite of what authors say to the contrary, a text which is revised after publication becomes in fact another text – something to place alongside the earlier one, but in no sense a substitute for it. *The American* (1877) became a new novel by the author of *The golden bowl* (1904) after Henry James had minutely revised it for the New York edition of 1907.

Can a work be spoiled by revision? Dryden thought so. 'A work may be over-wrought, as well as under-wrought', he declared: 'too much labour often takes away the spirit by adding to the polishing, so that there remains nothing but a dull correctness'.[39] Many readers accordingly prefer the 1805 version of *The prelude* to Wordsworth's overwrought version of 1850, and the 1798 version of Coleridge's *Rime of the ancient mariner* to the Christian version of 1817; but which of the four versions Fitzgerald published of *The Rubáiyát of Omar Khayyám* is the best? The existence of optional texts tends to increase our dissatisfaction with what we have got. The 1712 version of *The rape of the lock*, for instance, is regarded as a better proportioned but less well-written poem than Pope's augmented version of 1714; and a reading of all three versions of *Lady Chatterley's lover* (1928) conjures up in most people's minds an ideal fourth version which Lawrence never got around to writing. Certainly there is no guarantee that second thoughts are always best, and studies of authorial revisions show how often a revised wording may be cancelled in favour of the original.[40] Dylan Thomas liked people to believe that he was a conscientious verbal craftsman, and left worksheets to prove it; but a close examination of those manuscripts reveals that Thomas' first thoughts were often superior to the rest.[41] Elizabeth Barrett tried to dissuade Browning from correcting his work because she felt that his efforts at improvement did more harm than good.[42] This disturbs admirers of calculated artistry, who feel more at ease with the news that the excellent touches in Dickens' well-known scenes were the result of second thoughts.[43]

The mere fact that critical scholarship pays attention to unpublished authorial revisions is an indication of the extent to which the craftsmanly approach to writing has shaped the way we now talk about books. An obvious reason why makers have had such an influence on literary studies is that whereas we have no way of locating or verifying an inspirational moment, we can approach with some confidence the material contained in an author's notebooks and worksheets. Besides, they afford us the delights of vicarious creation, an experience acknowledged for perhaps the first time by Samuel Johnson in connection with Milton's draft plans for *Paradise lost*. 'It is pleasant to see great works in their seminal state pregnant with latent possibilities of excellence', Johnson wrote; 'nor could there be any more delightful entertainment than to trace their gradual growth and expansion, and to observe how they are sometimes suddenly advanced by accidental hints, and sometimes improved by steady meditation.'[44] Here speaks a maker who knows that writing is hard work and likes to see evidence of it in others. Inspirationists react very differently indeed. 'I had thought of the "Lycidas" as a full-grown beauty – as springing up with all its parts absolute', Charles Lamb confessed. 'How it staggered me to see the fine things in their ore.'[45]

Evidence of making is so much more tangible than evidence of dreaming that pedagogues have long had a penchant for it and turned out rhetorical treatises by the gross. All those books which Charlton calls 'Helicon in tabloids' and Kenner 'subways to Parnassus' are conceived in the belief that writing is a technique and that all techniques are teachable.[46] 'We undertake to create a poet', Scaliger announces proudly in his *Poetices* (1561); and it is only when you bother to read the fine print in such policies that you come upon the words Pound discovered at the end of Duhamel and Vildrac's *Notes sur la technique poétique*: 'mais d'abord il faut être un poète'.[47]

Making something out of nothing

Theologians have taught literary critics to distinguish two different theories of creation. One is the pagan Greek tradition that everything in the world is made out of something, and that literary making is best understood as the reshaping of something already in existence. Such is the theory of universal creation set out in Plato's *Timaeus* (27ff), where the Demiurge acts in accordance with the Epicurean doctrine that 'nothing is created out of nothing' (*ex nihilo nihil fit*) and constructs a universe by rearranging chaos as cosmos. Plato's Demiurge is a maker and the universe is his artifact, but the analogy is only unilateral. For although Plato finds it helpful to compare the divine Demiurge to a craftsman, he does not think of craftsmen as possessing divinely demiurgic powers, because he prefers to think of artists as dreamers rather than makers. It is in Aristotle's *Poetics*, therefore, that we must look for something approaching the current view of poetry-as-making. Here Aristotle treats the best Greek tragedians as high-class technicians who are good at manufacturing neatly dovetailed plots populated with plausible characters. Not burdened as Plato was with a transcendental theory of reality, Aristotle feels no urge to presuppose a transcendental origin for literature. He is content to treat Greek tragedies as artifacts whose dimensions and qualities can be described and analysed: *Oedipus Rex* is simply a well-made play, a new play made out of old stories, and in no sense something made out of nothing. In an aesthetic context, therefore, demiurgic creation is likely to engender such comparisons as the one Dryden makes between the poet and the watchmaker, who is able to invent new kinds of watches, but is never allowed to forget that 'the iron or silver is not his own'.[48]

In the Christian tradition, on the other hand, the universe is created by a God who distinguishes himself from demiurgic rivals by making it out of nothing. Although there is no justification in canonical scripture for the doctrine of 'exnihilistic' Creation, the dualistic account in Genesis is usually interpreted to imply an exnihilistic act. The closest approach to a textual justification is to be found in the apocryphal Second Book of Maccabees, where a mother comforts a son who is about to be tortured to death by advising him to 'look upon the heaven and the earth, and all that is therein, and consider that God made them out of things that were not' (7:28). Educated Christians from Justin and Clement of Alexandria to Bacon and Milton found the Platonic account of Creation more plausible than the exnihilistic interpretation foisted upon Genesis,[49] and saw in the apocryphal Wisdom of Solomon proof of demiurgic activity by an 'Almighty hand, that made the world of matter without form' (11:17). Meanwhile, a textually unsupported belief in exnihilistic Creation became practically universal among Christians from the second century onwards, to be dogmatically formulated in 1215 at the Fourth Lateran Council and reaffirmed by the Vatican Council in 1870.

To transfer the idea of exnihilistic creation from theology to aesthetics is to come up with something which is much more impressive than is possible by casting writers in the role of demiurgic makers. To think of the poet as a *creator* enables one to exploit what Milton C. Nahm calls 'the Great Analogy' between God and the human artificer,[50] an analogy which seems to sanction man's ability not merely to reproduce nature but to transcend it. It is the poet-as-creator rather than the poet-as-maker who is God in a heterocosm of his own invention. 'The artist should be in his work like God in creation', Flaubert once told a correspondent, 'invisible and all-powerful; he should be felt everywhere and seen nowhere'.[51] Potentially blasphemous, the Great Analogy at first had to be handled with care, and the key texts betray a predictable caution. Some time before 1474 Marsilio Ficino wrote a book published in 1482 as *Platonic theology*, in which he claims that 'man's power is nearly similar [*ferme similis*] to the Divine Nature', because works of art rival those of nature.[52] The first explicit acknowledgement of the poet's divinity, however, occurs in the introduction which Landino wrote to his commentary on *The divine comedy* in 1481. Tactfully, Landino does not make poets coequal with God, but at the same time he places them above ordinary men. He argues that whereas God 'creates' by making something out of nothing, and man 'makes' by making something out of something else, poets 'poetise' their poems 'not entirely out of nothing [*non . . . altutto di niente*]'. Less than divine, though more than human, the poet is in possession of powers which can only be described as God-like.[53] As the creator of 'another world' (*altera natura*) he may properly be spoken of as 'another god' (*alter deus*), declares Scaliger in his *Poetices* (1561); and this is the view Puttenham takes in his *Art of English poesy* (1589) when he says that because poets write about things which have never happened, 'they be (by manner of speech) as creating gods'.[54] The idea of God-as-poet helped sanction the idea of poet-as-God. St Augustine speaks of the world as an exquisite poem (*Civitas Dei*, XI 18), prompting Abraham Cowley to imagine God going about the business of Creation in much the same way as Cowley himself might have set about writing his *Davideis* (1656):

> As first a various unformed hint we find
> Rise in some God-like poet's fertile mind,
> Till all the parts and words their places take
> And with just marches verse and music make,
> Such was God's poem, this world's new essay.[55]

Chaos was given form, Cowley believes, by 'the Eternal Mind's poetic thought', and thus was created the Book of Nature, that 'universal and public manuscript' which Sir Thomas Browne took pleasure in reading, and which gives moral guidance to anybody prepared to look around him and learn the knack of finding sermons in stones, books in the running brooks, and good in everything.[56]

Sidney was afraid the comparison between makers and their Maker might appear to be 'too saucy', and accordingly steered clear of the word 'create'. Even Dryden felt it necessary to defend Shakespeare against those who might think the author of *The tempest* had displayed an unjustifiable boldness in having 'created a person [Caliban] which was not in Nature'.[57] Throughout the Middle Ages, verbal custom excluded the Great Analogy which Landino entertained. The verb *creare* ('to create') was reserved for the work of God, and the corresponding human activities were expressed by *condere* or *effingere* ('to fashion'). Pious people were always likely to be disturbed by the secularisation of creation which Renaissance humanism brought about. It was Coleridge himself who deleted from a copy of *Biographia literaria* (1817) the famous passage in which the creative imagination is defined as 'a repetition in the finite mind of the eternal act of creation in the infinite I AM'; and it is only a generation or so since C. S. Lewis expressed his aversion to the idea that 'poetry is "creative" in the strict (theological) sense of the word, for no one really believes that the poet *facit e nihilo*'.[58] Such fears are understandable among Christians, but by no means inevitable, for the attribution to man of God-like powers of creation need not result in the apotheosis of man, but rather in a new reverence for what Sidney calls 'the heavenly Maker of that maker'.[59] The point is elaborated in the second of Thomas Traherne's *Centuries of meditation* (written 1669–74): 'God hath made you able to create worlds in your own mind, which are more precious unto Him than those which He created' (II 90). The existence of human creations within Divine Creation is therefore providential, for human makers neither rival nor blaspheme against their Maker, but graciously pay homage to him by making: 'the world within you', claims Traherne, 'is an offering returned'.

Nowadays, the most strenuous objections to the Great Analogy come from Marxist critics.[60] Because they like to think of the literary work as conditioned by the historical moment in which it is written, Marxists oppose what they call the 'mystification' of literature by the Great Analogy, which misleads us into thinking of authors as God-like creatures who miraculously transcend their own times in creating works of universal significance and everlasting value. Eager to relocate writers in history (where meanings and values are relative to particular times and places), Marxists would like us to abandon the Great Analogy altogether.

The ordeal of creation

When making is considered to be hard labour, it is tempting for those engaged in it to solicit sympathy by publicising their sufferings. Not everybody is a disciplinarian like Trollope, who set himself to write 2500 words in two-and-a-half hours every day until he reached his weekly total of 10000 words, repeating the performance week by week throughout the year, thus furnishing himself with enough material for three three-volume novels a year.[61] The distinction drawn by Hannah Arendt between enjoyably vocational 'work' and mere bread-and-butter 'labour' is not always acknowledged by makers, who sometimes forget that nobody ever compels them to write. If their agonies seem endemic to their craft, it is largely because they are victims of their own fastidiousness. The perfectionist cult of the *mot juste* in Flaubert and his imitators is a widely esteemed form of masochism. 'Whatever one wishes to say', writes Maupassant in his preface to *Pierre et Jean* (1888), 'there is one noun only by which to express it, one verb only by which to give it life, one adjective only which will describe it. One must search until one has discovered them.' Valéry detected in himself 'a kind of *Ethic of Form* that led to infinite labour', a 'perverse taste for endless revision' which left him unable to finish anything to his own satisfaction. 'I consider *work itself* as having its own value', he concluded, 'generally much superior to that which the crowd attaches only to the product.'[62] It is significant therefore that when English literature entered its aestheticist phase in the nineteenth century, a dominant symbol of the creative imagination should have been the *femme fatale*, a Medusan beauty who destroys any man associating with her, a Salomé whose dance cost John the Baptist his head. In a religion of art, the ordeal of creation ends with the martyrdom of the artist, because devotion to an aesthetic ideal calls for self-sacrifice: this is the lesson taught by such a work as Oscar Wilde's *The picture of Dorian Gray* (1891) and studied by Mario Praz in *The romantic agony* (London, 1933).

If literary excellence and personal suffering are equally the product of hard work, it is easy to mistake suffering for a sign of excellence. When Flaubert tells his correspondents that he has spent a whole night in search of one adjective and the best part of a week writing one page, we feel he is really asking them to concede that any book on which so much labour has been expended cannot possibly be a failure. Much the same conclusion is to be drawn from Conrad's recollection of those twenty months of his life which he devoted to writing *Nostromo* (1904), 'neglecting the common joys that fall to the lot of the humblest on this earth' in order to raise up a monument in which 'there was not a single brick, stone, or grain of sand of its soil I had not placed in position with my own hands'.[63] What Roland Barthes calls 'the "Flaubertization" of writing' developed in response to the problem of self-justification in the literary profession, and the subsequent replacement of genius by labour as a value (*labor omnia vincit*).[64] As an ideal, this departs radically from the tradition of *ars celare artem*. The classical attitude to craftsmanship is to acknowledge the existence of painstaking qualities without dwelling indulgently on the pains taken. Horace, building his odes brick by brick, won the admiration of Petronius for his 'studied felicity' (*curiosa felicitas*); Suetonius was clearly impressed by the slow rate at which Virgil composed his *Georgics*.[65] The evident point of such anecdotes is to solicit admiration for dedicated craftsmanship rather than pity for the expenditure of immense effort: that 'painfulness in poets' which Davenant observed is no more than a craftsmanly painstakingness.[66] 'Flaubertization', however, eliminates such reticence by substituting a work-ethic of the sort displayed in Ruskin's chapter on 'The lamp of sacrifice' in *The seven lamps of architecture* (1849), where evidence of 'apparent labour' becomes a criterion of beauty and value. In the gospel of work, leisure-pursuits like the arts are inevitably suspect because only work is truly virtuous; and in the resultant work-aesthetic, evidence of industriousness is a criterion of value.

The fallacy here is neatly exposed in Congreve's prologue to *The way of the world* (1700):

> He owns with toil he wrote the following scenes,
> But, if they're naught, ne'er spare him for his pains:
> Damn him the more; have no commiseration
> For dulness on mature deliberation.

The point is generally overlooked by modernists who mention their compositional problems as a way of signalling their emancipation from what is felt to be a naively Romantic inspirationism. Dylan Thomas used to get very annoyed at the suggestion that his poems were produced by 'automatic' writing. 'I am a painstaking, conscientious, involved and devious craftsman in words', he told Richard Jones in 1951; and to prove it, Harvard University now possesses forty-seven manuscript sheets of his poem 'Over Sir John's Hill', with some of the phrases reworked forty-one times.[67] The knowledge that we are awed by such revelations encourages writers to supply them. Irving Wallace, for instance, has published an account in *The writing of one novel* (London, 1969) of how he spent 582 days or 3101 work-hours on his best-selling novel *The prize* (New York, 1962). Wallace's testimony points to another error in allowing value-judgements to be influenced by this kind of confession: for if compositional difficulties are to be taken into account, the second- or third-rate writer constitutes a much more poignant case than the first-class writer, who at least has the consolation of an occasional masterpiece for his troubles.

Compositional ordeals are likely to seem inevitable whenever 'making' is interpreted as meaning 'exnihilistic' creation. If you always set your sights on things unattempted yet in prose or rhyme, then your chance of suffering increases every time you set pen to paper. Frank Kermode puts the matter very well when he says that for a modern writer 'the craft of poetry is no longer the imitation of what has been well made, but the return to brute elements', and that this makes the writing of poetry an increasingly 'ruinous and exhausting undertaking'.[68] Too late, the maker discovers that he has a kind of Muse after all, but that she is a Medusa who demands exorbitant prices for favours rendered, and forces him to face the dilemma which Yeats confronted time and again:

The intellect of man is forced to choose
Perfection of the life, or of the work.[69]

The poet in Hermann Hesse's short story of that name deserts both
home and fiancée in order to apprentice himself to the Master of
the Wholly Perfect Word, and by the time he has learned all there
is to be known of such matters, his family and fiancée are dead.[70]
Either you live, or you write. Would-be makers are advised to
brace themselves for the worst by studying the bloodier pages in
the book of literary martyrs, with its gruesome anecdotes about
'the pains of turning blood into ink' (T. S. Eliot) or shedding
poems in 'syllabic blood' (Dylan Thomas) or undergoing the
'imagination's haemorrhage' (George Barker).[71] Such is the price
which makers pay for their freedom from inspirational passivity,
and in moments of despair they may well echo the agonised cry
of Gottfried Benn: 'We are using our own skins for wallpaper and
we cannot win.'[72]

6

The autobiographical element

If we reject inspirationist accounts of how books come into existence, we are likely to wonder whether they are the result of 'making' or 'creating'. Are writers *bricoleurs* who make new objects out of old materials which lie to hand, or the God-like inventors of things that never were? If we treat them as makers, much of what they do may be explained by the ancient rhetorical doctrine of imitation, and will stimulate inquiries into sources and influences. But if we treat them as creators, we may find ourselves paying more attention to their lives and personalities than to the books they read, and looking to psychoanalysts for insights into the nature of creative genius. Such are the options to be explored in this and the following two chapters. Let us begin with the assumption that because nothing is more important to a writer than his own experiences, what is known neutrally as the biographical approach to books and their authors (and disparagingly as the biographical fallacy) is a justifiable concern of literary critics.

The author in the book

Biographical modes of criticism are always sustained by some expressivist theory of literature. Whenever writers themselves ask us to believe that their works constitute 'fragments of a great confession', which is how Goethe describes his own writings in the seventh book of *Dichtung und Wahrheit* (1831), readers will feel justified in piecing together the fragments in the hope of discovering the complex identity of their author. 'I have never affected anything in my poetry which I have not experienced, and which has not urged me to production', Goethe told Eckermann.[1] An expressivist is content to look into his heart and write, in a more emotional sense than Sidney perhaps intended by that phrase: Byronically, he may bear the pageant of his bleeding heart around Europe, or emulate the sensationalism of Baudelaire in displaying *un cœur mis a nu*.[2] 'Every inch of me is in what I write', Tolstoy reminded his wife; and Montaigne could preface his 1580 volume of *Essais* with the declaration, 'It is myself I portray'.[3] The aim in all such endeavours is to create the kind of book Montaigne describes as being 'consubstantial' with its author.[4] *Leaves of grass* is another such 'attempt, from first to last, to put *a person*, a human being (myself, in the latter half of the nineteenth century, in America), freely, fully and truly on record'; and to show how seriously he meant it, Whitman cautioned readers who might be brutal in their clumsiness: 'Who touches this touches a man.'[5] Taken at face value, such confessions encourage us to believe with Yeats that 'only an aching heart/Conceives a changeless work of art'.[6] And if we do, we may well get into the habit of persevering with the art in order to gain insights into the ache. This is what often happens in Freudian analyses of literature, although it is only fair to point out that Freud himself was alert to the limitations of Freudianism. He introduced his essay on Dostoevsky with the disclaimer that 'before the problem of the creative artist analysis must, alas, lay down its arms'; and Jung was even more sceptical of psychoanalytical approaches to imaginative literature, being convinced that 'the creative act, which is the absolute antithesis of mere reaction, will for ever elude the human understanding'.[7] Freudians, however, are more bold in designating the literary work as a kind of 'autopsychography'[8] and treating it as an unreliable document which, if interpreted correctly, will throw light on the author's personality. For justification, they are at liberty to cite the verses Yeats wrote in defending the practice of constantly revising his poetry:

> The friends that have it I do wrong
> When ever I remake a song,
> Should know what issue is at stake:
> It is myself that I remake.[9]

If the poet whose personality develops as he grows older feels it necessary to rewrite earlier poems before he can claim them once more his own, he must feel there is some one-to-one relationship between what he is and what he writes. To re-write earlier work in order to eliminate elements one now finds embarrassing or untrue, as Auden has done, is to falsify history in the pretence that one's personality is monolithic and immutable. It takes a Whitman to admit that fragments of the great confession may eventually contradict one another, and that contradictoriness reveals personality.

Ought we to take expressivist claims at face value? Apparently not. The same Goethe who claimed to write in a wholly confessional manner also denounced mere subjectivity as 'the general sickness of the present day'; and biographical inquiries reveal that the 'Walt Whitman' in *Leaves of grass* is not identical with either Whitman the man or Whitman the poet.[10] Innocently intending to tell us all about himself, Montaigne discovered that he was not so much depicting as creating his personality as he went along. 'I have no more made my book', he confessed, 'than my book hath made me.'[11] Ideally, the consubstantial relationship between an author and his book is best expressed in the language of Shakespeare's 'The phoenix and turtle' ('Two distincts, division none'): but in actual practice the distinction between books and writers, between public *personae* and private personalities, signals a real division which we must acknowledge when evaluating what authors have to say about their own work. It is no more possible for an expressivist to reveal an unstructured personality than it is for an inspirationist to communicate an unmediated vision.

Disagreements about the advantages of a biographical approach to imaginative literature are likely to stem from divergent views of the part which writing plays in an author's life. Expressivists are inclined to believe that the writing of books is as much an expression of personality as collecting stamps or climbing mountains, and have no qualms in using biographical facts or speculations in order to open up obscure passages in imaginative works. Nor do they see anything wrong in reversing the whole process so as to reconstruct from *The Canterbury tales* the personality of Geoffrey Chaucer; and in more bizarre moments they will even prove that the *Odyssey* must have been written by a woman, or that John Milton was an albino.[12] Formalists, on the other hand, prefer to think of literature as an autonomous phenomenon, and know enough about the fictive imagination to insist upon the essential separateness of art from life. The Dylan Thomas we imagine when reading his poems is the author of some of the most intricately original verses in the English language, and not at all like that money-cadging, adulterous alcoholic who appears in some of his published letters. Formalists see no advantage in identifying Thomas the poet with Dylan the bar-fly, or in using John M. Brinnin's harrowing account of *Dylan Thomas in America* (London, 1956) as a commentary on Thomas' last poems. Similar instances spring to mind. Thomas Hardy, for example, seems to have been far more cheerful than the pessimism of his novels would suggest, for like Samuel Beckett he found unhappiness a more fertile subject than happiness; and biographers of Richard Crashaw have difficulty in reconciling the known temperament of the man with the religious complexities of his verse.

In opposing formalist arguments, expressivists can cite the case of Ernest Hemingway, who made a point of behaving like people in his own books, so much so that the man who hunts and fishes and goes to war is not easily distinguishable from the novelist who writes about hunting and fishing and going to war. Believing that one should 'write when there is something that you know, and not before',[13] Hemingway thought it necessary to experiment with life in order to guard against the atrophy of his art. To have stayed in Oak Park, Illinois (where he was born) would have involved rewriting Sherwood Anderson's *Winesburg, Ohio* (1919). *Farewell to arms* (1929) is dependent upon Hemingway's wartime experiences on the Italian front, and there would have been no *For whom the bell tolls* (1941) if Hemingway had not been in Spain at the right historical moment. Against such a Hemingwayan view of Hemingway, however, we have the evidence adduced in Carlos Baker's biography[14] that Hemingway lied habitually about himself and the origins of his work. What we witness in the case of Hemingway is not so much an expression of the man's life in fiction as the sometimes desperate attempt to live his own novels, fictionalising the record of his own past whenever the reality seemed insufficiently impressive. Now the Hemingway who experimented with his own life in order to understand a situation which would turn up in his next book was undoubtedly going about things quite differently from the Solzhenitsyn who drew on experiences enforced by unavoidable circumstances, but the relationship between art and life looks much the same in the end. It is merely a question of priority. Strindberg is known to have set up controlled experiments in his own home in order to find out for himself what (say) extreme jealousy feels like.[15] Rilke would sometimes desert his mistress Loulou Lazart so as to give himself the literary opportunity to write passionate love-letters to her.[16] 'An artist with certain imaginative ideas in his head may then involve himself in relationships which are congenial to them', writes Auden. He was thinking of Wagner's affair with Mathilde Wesendonk, which was 'the "result" rather than the "cause" of

Tristan'.[17] And when it was necessary to terminate the affair in order to write the last act of his opera, Wagner did so. Life, too, is an art.

The irrelevance of biography

When formalist assumptions oust the expressivist, biographical readings of books are stigmatised as an irrelevance. What is condemned by C. S. Lewis as 'the personal heresy' is classified by Wellek and Warren as one of those 'extrinsic' approaches which deflect attention from books to authors.[18] Memories of nineteenth-century opposition to the academic study of English literature ('chatter about Shelley') may underlie the formalists' fear that biographical inquiries might reduce literary criticism to one of those arts William H. Gass calls 'gossipacious'.[19]

Most perniciously of all, biographism encourages people to substitute a moral evaluation of the writer for an aesthetic evaluation of his work. Sainte-Beuve, for instance, found it difficult not to let his judgement of the work be affected by what he knew of the writer as a person. *Tel arbre, tel fruit* was his motto,[20] a modification of that passage in the Gospel according to St Matthew (7: 18ff) where it is said that a corrupt tree cannot bring forth good fruit. Matthew Arnold's attitude to the writings of Byron and Shelley and their associates was similarly coloured by feelings of revulsion for their domestic arrangements ('What a set!'); Burns too, he thought, was blighted by 'Scotch drink, Scotch religion, and Scotch manners'.[21] One is reminded of that lady in Jane Austen's *Sanditon* (1817) who found her enjoyment of Burns's poetry spoiled by an awareness of 'poor Burns's known irregularities'. But as Burns would say, a man's a man for all that, and if moral immaculateness were made a condition of literary excellence, the number of masterpieces would shrink alarmingly.

A classic exposition of antibiographism is C. J. Sisson's attack on late Romantic attempts to detect emotional crises in Shakespeare on the evidence of his plays.[22] Not until the eighteenth century, when Malone attempted to settle the chronology of Shakespeare's plays, was it possible to treat them as fragments of a great confession and to speculate (as Coleridge does) about the state of mind Shakespeare must have been in when he wrote *Troilus and Cressida*. After that, it was only a matter of time before Edward Dowden provided a switchback version of the dramatist's career, with Shakespeare up on the heights at one moment and down in the depths at another.[23] Sisson, however, sees no reason why anybody should have to feel tragic in order to write a tragedy. And here the confession of a renowned melancholic bears him out: 'Strange as it may seem,' wrote William Cowper, 'the most ludicrous lines I ever wrote have been written in the saddest mood, and, but for that saddest mood, perhaps had never been written at all.'[24]

Testimonies like this jeopardise attempts to equate literary works with states of mind. Even more striking is Northrop Frye's mockery of consubstantialist readings of Blake, which assume that *Songs of experience* were written by an experienced thirty-seven-year-old, whereas *Songs of innocence* are the work of a mere boy of thirty-two.[25] Further complications arise from the fact that dates of publication are no reliable guide to dates of composition. Readers who believe that Swift's misanthropy had reached pathological proportions by the time he wrote the fourth book of *Gulliver's travels* (the one Thackeray advised us not to read) do well to remember that Swift in fact finished the fourth book before beginning to write the third.[26] It is all very well to pin one's faith on the consubstantiality of books and their authors, but in the absence of accurate information about chronology of composition, criticism based on such a premise is bound to be conjectural.

At the heart of Sisson's argument is a conviction that the biographical approach is essentially a Romantic discovery and therefore irrelevant to the criticism of non-Romantic literature. Johnson's *Lives of the poets* (1779–81) illustrates the mere curiosity value which biographical information holds for critics not yet conditioned by Romantic expressivism. 'The biographical part of literature', Johnson told Boswell, 'is what I love most', but he never thought of probing a writer's inner life for clues to his works.[27] If Johnson seems to overlook opportunities to connect tendencies in the life with tendencies in the poetry, it is because he saw writing as a craft rather than the revelation of hidden ambitions and obsessions. Reticence, however, is another force to be reckoned with in pre-Romantic criticism. Although Thomas Sprat had access to private papers when writing a life of Cowley (1668), he decided to omit letters full of 'native tenderness and innocent gaiety' because Cowley's soul there appeared 'undressed' and 'fit to be seen by one or two in a chamber, but not to go abroad in the streets'.[28] Accordingly, the very parts of Cowley's life which Romantic critics would make so much of are not even entered for the record. How ironic that Johnson himself should

have become in 1791 the subject of a biographical study by
Boswell which anticipates the Romantic taste for detailed accounts
of the man behind the masks. Asked to comment on the
manuscript of Boswell's *Journal of a tour of the Hebrides*, Johnson
said 'it might be printed, were the subject fit for printing'.[29] It
was not the propriety of Boswell's study which Johnson queried:
he simply could not believe that anybody would be interested in
such trivia.

An important objection raised by the antibiographist is that
literature is not self-expression but shaped expression, and that the
shaping process produces distortions which make it impossible for
anybody to deduce biographical evidence from literary works.
When it is possible to check the facts in allegedly autobiographical
works, errors and misrepresentations often abound. Wordsworth's
version in *The prelude* (1805) of his formative years is a less accurate
account of what actually happened than letters he and Dorothy
wrote in the years 1787–95; and Dickens scholars come up against
even more complicated problems with the pseudo-autobiogra-
phical *David Copperfield* (1849–50).[30] Pseudo-biographical statements merely complicate matters if (as is often the case) they turn
out to be based on the same imaginative works they are supposed
to explain. Some of the biographical notes on Shelley's poems
written by Mary Shelley are obstacles of this kind, as Carlos Baker
shows in the case of *Julian and Maddalo* (written 1818) which, far
from being as autobiographical as we are invited to believe, is
rather 'a semi-fictionalised treatment of the poet Tasso's impris-
onment for real or alleged madness in the year 1579'.[31]

So successful have rhetoricians been in teaching the art of
feigning feeling that we have no way of assessing the degree of
personal involvement in any statement whatsoever. The most
banal of clichés may be committed to paper with far more feeling
than a brilliantly original phrase. For instance, the autobiography
of the Elizabethan Thomas Whythorne contains a number of
verses which are so stereotyped in diction and phrasing that
nobody would ever guess they glanced originally at certain real-life
situations which Whythorne describes by way of explanation.[32]
'The supposed intensity, inwardness, immediacy of an experience',
Wellek asserts, 'can never be demonstrated as certain, and can
never be shown to be relevant to the quality of art.'[33] This
seems especially true of Renaissance literature, where personal
idiosyncrasies are often effaced in the desire to conform to a
universal type. So Walton made Donne's life conform to the

pattern of a 'salvation narrative' modelled on the life of St Augustine; and when the wounded Sidney refused water at Zutphen, he no doubt expected those about him to observe the parallel with Alexander the Great, who is said to have refused water in the Baluchistan desert.[34] What such instances compel us to recognise is that we are in no position to choose between expressivist and formalist readings of Elizabethan literature, because we have no way of knowing whether its commonplaces are intended to embellish a set-theme or articulate (however inadequately) the true voice of feeling.

The place and nature of experience

In antiquity, 'experience' posed no problems for writers who kept to an ornamentalist theory of language and saw their job as primarily suasive. Cicero notes that an ignorance of astronomy did not prevent Aratus from writing a brilliant poem on the heavens, and that Nicander of Colophon, who 'could hardly have been more remote from the countryside, wrote successfully on agricultural matters by virtue of a poet's abilities, not a farmer's' (De oratore, I 69). First-hand knowledge seems to have counted for less than the ability to make excellent use of second-hand information. Yet the confusion of books with authors occurred even in antiquity, notably in the allegation that Aeschylus introduced drunken characters into his satyr-plays because he was drunk at the time of writing them.[35] It was perhaps to counter such objections that Aristotle argued that opinions expressed by the dramatis personae are not necessarily those of the dramatist himself, whose art is to observe 'decorum' in composing plausible speeches for the characters he has created (Poetics, ch. 25). A foolish character says foolish things in order to convince audiences of his folly, and not because the dramatist himself is a fool. Put like that, the argument is elementary. But the point is less obvious if we substitute 'libertine' or 'atheist' for 'fool', and think of expressivist responses to dramatic decorum in such cases. Blake and Shelley, for example, were sure that the author of Paradise lost was of the devil's party without knowing it, for how could Milton have given Satan such sweetly plausible speeches if he had not secretly sympathised with the devil?[36]

Modernists in search of alternatives to Romantic expressivism, therefore, had to re-learn certain commonplaces of the rhetorical tradition. The results still shock readers who assume that self-expression is the only worthy motive for writing, and who would think it perverse of Valéry to claim that 'a poet's function...is not to experience the poetic state' but rather 'to create it in others' – or to define a poem as 'a kind of machine for producing the poetic state of mind by means of words'.[37] Following Valéry, and separating the experiences of a writer from those embodied in his work, we can use Susanne K. Langer's distinction between 'actual' experiences (which happen in life) and 'virtual' experiences made available by those affective machines we call books. 'Actual experience just "happens"', writes Dorothy Walsh, whereas 'virtual experience is "made"'.[38] It is therefore possible to redefine the expressive function of literature in a way not envisaged by expressivists. Literature need not be thought of as 'expressing' a writer's personal experience, but as being 'expressive of' those virtual experiences which make art what it is.

The concept of virtual experience helps us to understand why the author of A Shropshire lad (1896) should want to say he had never spent much time in Shropshire, and why he turned down a request for biographical information on the grounds that to include such material in a literary article would be 'low, unworthy, and American'.[39] Eliot would have us believe that he himself was a creator of virtual experiences and never got involved in Prufrock in the way that Dickens confessed to be involved in The old curiosity shop (1841) when writing the death scene of Little Nell ('If you knew what I have been suffering in the death of that child!').[40] Dickens here makes no pretence at supplying virtual experience or of constructing an affective machine for jerking tears out of sensibilious readers. Instead, he conceives of writing as a kind of emotional contagion, as the handing on of actual experience to readers who would feel cheated if they found out that their author did not himself feel the things he writes about so feelingly. 'If you want me to weep [si vis me flere], you must first weep yourself.' The formula (an oddly sentimental intrusion into classical rhetoric, and rejected by Cicero and Seneca) is from Horace, and is resorted to frequently by expressivist critics.[41] Verlaine told Yeats that Tennyson ruined In memoriam (1850) by reminiscing instead of being heartbroken; and Johnson surprisingly dismissed Milton's Lycidas (1638) with the verdict that 'where there is leisure for fiction there is little grief'.[42] To accept such judgements, however, is to believe that the prime function of writing is to convey deeply felt emotions, and that a manifest concern with the literary work as a verbal artifact smacks of 'insincerity'.

The criterion of sincerity

Formalists declare the question of sincerity out of order in literary discussions. 'The goodness or badness of poetry has nothing to do with sincerity', according to Wellek, because 'the worst love poetry of adolescents is the most sincere'.[43] Grief is another emotional area in which sincerity may be a liability, as is shown by the platitudinous doggerel on display in the *in memoriam* columns of newspapers. Wordsworth, however, treated infelicities of style as marks of sincerity in writers of epitaphs, believing that they would betray a self-regarding insincerity if they went to the trouble of articulating their grief in a more polished manner.[44] Where there is leisure for grief, in other words, there is little room for fiction.

At first glance, the formalist rejection of 'sincerity' seems a timely reminder that critics should concern themselves with literary texts rather than authorial motives. Yet the formalism which superseded expressivism has in turn been challenged more recently by a neo-expressivism sanctioned by Allen Ginsberg's *Howl* (1956) and more especially by Robert Lowell's *Life studies* (1959), the latter a literary event of such magnitude (according to Donald Davie) that 'the question of sincerity can never again be out of order'.[45] But exactly what kind of sincerity are we being asked to condone? Should we distinguish (as Lionel Trilling does) an old-style 'sincerity', which involves communicating non-deceptively with others, from a new-style *sincérité*, which sanctions 'the unmediated exhibition of the self, presumably with the intention of being true to it'?[46]

Although the word 'sincerity' occurs in sixteenth-century texts, it tends to be used there in the Latin sense of *sincerus* ('clean, pure'). An emblem book of 1586 explains that the swan is sacred to Apollo, the god of poetry, because its

> colour white Sincereness doth declare:
> So poets must be clean, and pure, and must of crime beware.[47]

It is in this sense that Robert Herrick, half a century later, could praise the 'sincerity' of Julia's legs.[48] Instances of modern usage in literary contexts are not recorded before 1828, when Carlyle declared that 'the excellence of Burns is...his *sincerity*, his indisputable air of truth'; but by 1865 G. H. Lewes had made sincerity one of the three fundamental principles of literature.[49] Of course the idea of sincerity may well antedate the first appearance of the term in print, but when Henri Peyre published a comprehensive study of *Literature and sincerity* (New Haven, 1963) he was hard pressed to find any evidence even for the idea of literary sincerity before Rousseau. Earlier than that, 'sincerity' is a word more often applied to authors than to their works. 'He that courts his mistress with Roman imagery deserves to lose her', Johnson said of Hammond, 'for she may with good reason suspect his sincerity.'[50] But when John Ruskin remarks that 'the greatest art represents everything with absolute sincerity, as far as it is able', he is evidently thinking of sincerity as a quality of artifacts rather than of artificers.[51] The need to distinguish between these two kinds of sincerity is prompted by *A sentimental journey* (1768), which records with admirable fidelity the experiences and behaviour of an insincere man. Clearly, a writer can be sincere about insincerity by delineating it faithfully. Despite its subject-matter, *A sentimental journey* is 'sincere' in Ruskin's sense, or in the sense intended by Edouard Roditi when he describes Oscar Wilde as being 'most sincere, as an artist, when depicting insincere characters'.[52]

The attractions of anonymity

Judging from the way many writers react to biographical readings of their work, few of them regard their books as nothing but fragments of a great confession, and the majority object to having their private lives investigated.

> For now the poet cannot die,
> > Nor leave his music as of old,
> > But round him ere he scarce be cold
> Begins the scandal and the cry.[53]

Such was Tennyson's reaction to the publication of Keats's love-letters in 1848. George Eliot thought biographers 'a disease of English literature';[54] and like-minded writers (Arnold, T. S. Eliot and Auden among them) have tried to protect themselves posthumously by proscribing official biographies. T. S. Eliot complained that he had become more or less resigned to having his biography reconstructed on the evidence of passages he had copied out of other people's books,[55] and to screen himself from biographical inquisitiveness he framed an extremely influential theory of impersonality which we must look at shortly.

E. M. Forster argued in 1925 that every writer has two personalities, one of them superficial and in possession of a name and social identity, the other an unconscious, nameless and amorphous creature having no identity of its own. It is Forster's contention that 'creation comes from the depths', not from that surface personality which is merely a signature or a name. 'While the author wrote he forgot his name', says Forster, and 'while we read him we forget both his name and our own'. So he concludes that since 'all literature tends towards a condition of anonymity', any signature on it can only be a distraction.[56] As if to test the truth of this claim, I. A. Richards was shortly to circulate unsigned poems for comment among Cambridge undergraduates, and analyse the alarming results of this experiment in *Practical criticism* (London, 1929). Is the greatest literature always 'Seraphically free/From taint of personality', as Quiller-Couch believed?[57]

Anonymity evades the iniquities of a *tel arbre, tel fruit* kind of criticism which measures works by reputation rather than quality. 'If I were responsible for the administration of the museums', Valéry wrote in 1935, 'I should have all the painters' names removed' so that the eye might judge for itself.[58] A couple of years later he went on to suggest that a serious history of literature could be written 'without so much as mentioning the name of any writer'.[59] Behind such proposals lies Heinrich Wölfflin's call for an art-history without names (1899), which in turn rests on Auguste Comte's conception of history without names (1877).[60] A move in this direction is Ernst Robert Curtius' investigation of some of the major commonplaces in European literature. Although his masterly study of *European literature and the Latin Middle Ages* (London, 1953) names names in tracing the history of various commonplaces or *topoi*, Curtius engenders a strong feeling that these commonplaces are far more durable and important than many of the writers who transmit them, and his book accordingly illuminates the collective rather than individual characteristics of European authors.

Forster's emphasis on anonymity reminds us also that the concept of authorship is itself a relatively recent phenomenon, and that biographical critics would work at considerable disadvantage if they were to concentrate their attention on English literature written before the late fourteenth century. Of all the Old English poems which have come down to us, only four carry signatures and they are all the work of Cynewulf, who wove his own name into those texts by means of runic letters. Only in a couple of instances (the hymn which Bede attributes to Caedmon, and

Bede's own death-song) is the authorship of Old English poems established externally; and J. A. Burrow remarks that an early English poet's motive in mentioning his own name is in any case less likely to be proprietorial than 'petitionary', in that he wants readers to pray for *his* soul rather than for somebody else's.[61] Nobody knows why Old and Middle English literature should have been largely anonymous when the authors of medieval Provençal poetry are mostly named and over a hundred of them are the subject of contemporary biographies. Many attributable poems from Chaucer to Wyatt and beyond, however, might just as well be anonymous, so stylised and commonplace are the materials from which they are made. Somehow, scholars manage to talk intelligently about them without having to take into consideration the personalities of those who produced them. Yet for all that, many readers like to feel the presence of a known poet behind a poem, and therefore find anonymous poems much less appealing than those with known authors.[62]

Empathy and impersonality

The theory of impersonality and its associated doctrine of *personae* or masks cuts right into the heart of the biographical approach. Although it is not at all what one associates with highly subjective poets like the Romantics, it was nevertheless a Romantic poet, John Keats, who first defined impersonalism in the course of dissociating his own experience as a writer from that of the 'Wordsworthian or egotistical sublime'.[63] He seems to have experienced what later generations called 'empathy', a term which came into English about 1912 as a translation of the German *Einfühlung* as used in Wilhelm Worringer's classic contribution to the theory of non-representational art, *Abstraktion und Einfühlung* (München, 1908). Empathy, in Theodor Lipps's definition of 1903, is the ability to 'feel something, namely oneself, into the aesthetic object' – a definition not markedly different from what A. W. Schlegel had in mind in 1791 when he imagined being able to 'enter into the structure of a foreign being, to know it as it is, to listen to how it became'.[64] Compulsive empathy is exhausting, as Katherine Mansfield found while standing for hours on the Auckland wharf being a ship 'waiting to be berthed...a seagull hovering at the stern and a hotel porter whistling through his teeth'.[65] In the case of Keats, it meant watching a sparrow so intently as to peck about on the gravel with it, or lying awake at night 'listening to the rain with a sense of being drowned and rotted like a grain of wheat'.[66] More frighteningly, the process would go into reverse, and alien personalities would seem to annihilate his own in a crowded room.[67] Empathy can therefore be a perilous experience, resulting in *déréglements* like those Rimbaud records (' *I* is someone else'),[68] but it is a risk willingly taken by defectors from the egotistical sublime. Virginia Woolf felt that '"I" is only a convenient term for somebody who has no real being'; Norman Mailer, like Henry Adams, occasionally writes of himself in the third person.[69] There is a parable by Jorge Luis Borges which is about the subtle difference between himself and that world-famous author who shares his birth-certificate: 'I live, let myself go on living, so that Borges may contrive his literature, and this literature justifies me.'[70] Which Borges does the biographical critic have access to?

In the intervals between pecking with the sparrows and rotting with the wheat Keats was reading and re-reading Shakespeare, and discovering that Shakespeare (unlike Wordsworth) did not have a personality to express, but rather a variety of personalities in the form of *dramatis personae*. It was an experience which forced him to recognise that a great writer may entertain ideas he does not necessarily believe in (as Wordsworth himself demonstrated in writing the 'Immortality' ode, adapting the Platonic doctrine of remembrance or *anamnesis* without implicating himself in the heresy that newborn souls can in fact recollect the eternity they have so recently vacated).[71] Because Shakespeare understood too many philosophies of life to formulate a coherent philosophy of life, Keats concluded that a great poet is a man without an identity, a man who is 'continually informing and filling some other body'.[72] What Keats detected in Shakespeare, Wilde was later to find exemplified in Swinburne, 'the first lyric poet who has tried to make an absolute surrender of his own personality, and he has succeeded'.[73] For lacking an identity of his own, the Keatsian poet cultivates 'negative capability', which is the ability to remain 'in uncertainties, mysteries, doubts, without any irritable reaching after fact and reason'.[74] By refusing to define and then fortify a personality of his own, Keats hoped to remain sufficiently open to experience to approach the imaginative range of Shakespeare. 'The only means of strengthening one's intellect', he wrote, 'is to make up one's mind about nothing – to let the mind be a thoroughfare for all thoughts.'[75] Anybody who succeeds in such an ambition will seriously mislead critics who approach his work biographically.

Another awkward fact which a biographist has to face up to sooner or later is that self-revelation is a pleasure only to those who first master the art of self-concealment, as Sir Thomas Browne did when writing *Religio medici* (1643). 'Men wear masks not merely to conceal their true characters from the world', Morse Peckham observes, 'but...to conceal their true characters from themselves.'[76] This is why even that most patently confessional of forms, the autobiography, has its reticences and distortions, sometimes so extensive that the final product is more a work of fiction than anything else, which appears to be the case in Hale White's *The autobiography of Mark Rutherford* (1881).[77] Role-playing is so much more diverting than the quest for identity that the humanistic ideal of *nosce teipsum* ('know thyself') becomes in practice the business of identifying the image of yourself you wish to project. Instead of confronting their readers directly, most writers would rather ape Eliot's Prufrock in preparing a face to meet the faces that they meet.

Since Keats's time, the doctrine of impersonality has been an article of faith among those programmatically anti-Romantic writers we call modernists. A key text is *Madame Bovary* (1856), in which Flaubert hoped there would not be 'a single reflection of the author'.[78] It was to be an exercise in empathy or imaginative projection, with the male author suspending his maleness to become a female personality for the duration of the book, much as Tolstoy tried to do in the sixth book of *War and peace* (1865–72) when imagining Natasha's feelings before going to her first ball. As a novel seemingly without an authorial presence, *Madame Bovary* was a staggering achievement in the eyes of those who understood it – 'it was life itself making an appearance', commented Maupassant.[79] Such too was Joyce's ambition in writing *A portrait of the artist as a young man* (1916), whose hero preaches an impersonalist doctrine of the artist as God, 'within or behind or beyond or above his handiwork, invisible, refined out of existence, indifferent, paring his fingernails'.[80] No survey of these matters can overlook the distinction Eliot drew in 1919 between 'the man who suffers and the mind which creates'. A generation of critics made common coin of phrases Eliot minted from this dissociation: 'the poet has, not a "personality" to express, but a particular medium'; 'emotions which he has never experienced will serve his turn as well as those familiar to him'; 'poetry is not the expression of personality, but an escape from personality.'[81] Much of this was retracted in 1940 when Eliot published his lecture on Yeats, but the drift away from impersonalism was discernible already in the 1930 essay on Dante, with its concession to personal suffering in the poetic process. Since then, impersonalism has come under attack from critics who argue that no writer can ever avoid being personal, because however careful he is not to intrude, anything he writes will sound unmistakably his.[82] If he is honest with himself, he will have to echo Flaubert's 'Madame Bovary, c'est moi'. For example, *The ring and the book* (1868–69) is quintessentially Browning's in spite of his disclaimer: 'I disappeared: the book grew all in all' (1 687). As Eliot's own mentor, Remy de Gourmont, once remarked: 'to be impersonal is to be personal in a special kind of way'.[83] And if so, then the most an impersonalist can claim is that he is not an exhibitionist.

A further objection raised against impersonalism is that those who preach it (especially Joyce and Eliot) do so because they are sensitive to the highly personal nature of what they write, and invoke *personae* as a diversionary tactic to protect their privacy. ('If you can read this you've come too close' was Dorothy Parker's epitaph for herself.)[84] Even their *personae* are a give-away. 'The moment a poet starts putting on his masks', says Leon Edel, 'he puts his heart on his sleeve, he invades his own privacy, he parades it before everyone.'[85] Such revisionist readings of the great impersonalists come in the wake of Leslie Fiedler's claim that by the 1950s 'the dogma of antibiographism' had outgrown its usefulness as a corrective to Romantic excesses.[86]

By far the most damaging accusation brought against impersonalism is the claim that it corrodes literature by dehumanising. Just as it is humanly impossible for a writer to stay out of his own work, so it is humanly impossible for readers to eradicate all curiosity about the writer himself: it is not the well-wrought urn which attracts us, Walter J. Ong would say, but the jinnee inside.[87] 'For poetry to be great', writes Donald Davie, 'it must reek of the human, as Wordsworth's poetry does.'[88] Modernist literature from T. E. Hulme to Alain Robbe-Grillet provides ample evidence of experiments in the art of dehumanisation.[89] Lawrence's attempt to create in *The rainbow* (1915) a sense of the inhuman otherness of people is a well-known dehumanising ploy. He told Garnett that he found the 'non-human in humanity... more interesting... than the old-fashioned human element', and was fascinated by 'the inhuman will'.[90] Consequently, the dehumanising trend has provoked a great deal of anxiety about the desirability of authorial detachment.

It is curious that in the years when antibiographism was becoming a critical orthodoxy, far more biographical information went on deposit than Romantic critics ever managed to amass. The discrepancy between high-brow formalist contempt for biographical information and the actual accumulation of it in vast quantities can only mean that impersonalism has influenced critical theory much more than it has influenced critical practice. Significantly, it is a formalist, Victor Erlich, who warns us not to disregard important 'extrinsic' evidence 'for the sake of methodological purity'.[91] No reader of Richard Ellmann's work on Joyce (or of Leon Edel's on Henry James) will want to call biographical inquiries irrelevant to the critical enterprise.

Style and personality

We think it a truism to say that a writer's individuality will determine not only the content but also the style of his work, and that differences in style between one writer and another are the result of differences in personality. Proof, however, is hard to come by, for we have yet to discover the mechanism by which dispositions in the writer become characteristics of his style. Theoretically, the style is the man. 'For man is but his mind', wrote Puttenham in 1589, 'and as his mind is tempered and qualified, so are his speeches and language at large.'[92] Are we justified, therefore, in seeking structures of thought in figures of speech, and neurotic obsessions in recurrent imagery?

Ancient rhetoricians were aware of the psychological dimensions of rhetoric and recognised that emotional disturbances could be simulated by deviations from normal usage. When Wilson Knight analyses a passage from *Cymbeline* and remarks how it manifests the 'cramped, interjectory style variously used by Shakespeare for expression of nervous disorder', he is developing an observation Demetrius made long ago on the emotional effects created by the omission of conjunctions (asyndeton).[93] Where modern analysts and ancient rhetoricians are likely to part company, however, is on the use of such figures. Ancient rhetoricians treat the figures as illusionist. The writer or speaker is advised to use such and such a figure because it is known to induce a certain effect in the audience; he is not advised to use it in order to express his own state of mind.[94] Rhetorical analysis of the classical kind aims accordingly at illuminating the writer's art rather than his psyche. For example, in reading or hearing Hamlet's soliloquy, 'To be, or not to be', we are to notice how Shakespeare reaffirms our impression of the hero's indecision by composing the speech in antitheses, because antithesis is an appropriate figure for the presentation of a divided mind. More recent stylistic analyses differ in orientation by trying to make contact with the author himself through the rhetorical pattern of his work. Instead of admiring (say) Hopkins' use of elliptical language to create the illusion of a mind under duress, we expect to find in the very structure of those 'terrible' sonnets evidence of the mental duress Hopkins himself experienced. The style is not the medium but the man.

In the 1920s Leo Spitzer set about tracing the 'philological circle' binding style to psychology. 'The linguistic surface is a biologically necessary effect of the poet's soul', Wellek paraphrases; 'the observation of a stylistic trait allows the critic to infer the biography of a soul.'[95] Spitzer aimed at closing the gap between formalist descriptions of literary texts and expressivist speculations about the people who write them. Stylistic mannerisms were to be treated as a kind of psychic outcrop. The critical task was to deduce from a text its 'spiritual etymon' or 'radix in the soul' of the writer, and in this way to delineate his 'psychogram'.[96] Examples put forward by Spitzer in support of his theory are disappointingly banal (Charles-Louis Philippe's addiction to the phrase *à cause de*, for example, is shown to signal a prevalent fatalism). More boldly, Spitzer is tempted to look for collective psychograms in entire languages, and see in the *fait-accompli* construction in Spanish 'a linguistic reflection of Spanish Utopianism, of the Spanish *plus ultra* will'.[97] Others have followed these leads. Can it be accidental that the absolute construction 'nothing but' figures prominently in so reductive a work as Hobbes's *Leviathan*?[98] Or that the rhetorical figure of litotes (understatement) should characterise the poetry of Germanic peoples who rate deeds more highly than words?[99] Spitzer himself later expressed doubts about his method, and it is certainly unfortunate that he had no means of telling the difference between a rhetorical trick and a psychological tic. Think, for instance, of all those reduplicatory patterns in the poems of T. S. Eliot:

> to prepare a face to meet the faces that you meet
> the voices dying with a dying fall
> assured of certain certainties
> I no longer strive to strive towards such things

end of the endless/Journey to no end
the roses/Had the look of flowers that are looked at
distracted from distraction by distraction.[100]

Here we seem to catch Eliot standing at one remove from experience, aware of his awareness. Can we infer a 'psychogram' from such reduplicatory patterns? Or was Eliot merely taken with the pattern as a pattern (in the same way as Andrew Marvell was partial to 'reflexive' images of rivers drowning themselves, or mowers mown down by their own scythes, and so on)? A choice seems called for, but the evidence is inconclusive, for a 'psycho-rhetoric' of literature has yet to be written.

Spitzer assumes that the personality 'behind' a text is a stable one, and that no matter what the occasion, a stylistic trait will always refer back to the same psychological disposition. Here his method is open to the objection raised by structuralist critics like Tzvetan Todorov, who thinks that 'the idea of an author as a homogeneous source of his texts, as an invariant behind the variables, a stable and primary essence looking out upon fugitive and derived appearances belongs to a philosophy which is no longer that of our own time.'[101] French 'criticism of conscious-ness' (*critique de la conscience*) of the kind conducted by Georges Poulet and J. Hillis Miller accordingly looks for the author *in* the work instead of looking behind it for that spectrally 'stable ego' which Lawrence believed obsolete when writing *The rainbow* (1915).[102] 'For these critics', writes Sarah N. Lawall, 'the "author" is not just the man who wrote the book but the implied being who gradually assumes form as the work is created. The text itself depicts this "author", just as a photograph would depict the historical author.' Consequently, 'the "author" is incarnate in the book because he does not exist outside it'.[103] Methodologically, this is no doubt a convenient stand to take, as it rules out 'extrinsic' evidence assembled by biographers, and frees the critic to deconstruct the text in front of him. Nevertheless, the historical author is often a residual presence in literary works, well-known for his deeds and opinions, and we cannot make him disappear by declaring our knowledge of him inadmissable evidence. If the links between style and personality merit investigation, it is surely the historical author we must concern ourselves with.

7

Imitation and originality

That writers must be original is so ubiquitous an assumption in our time as to appear a self-evident truth. A couple of hundred years ago the situation was very different, although a few writers here and there were beginning to confer on originality something of the prestige it enjoys nowadays. For the majority, however, no defence of originality was a match for the cultural pessimism epitomised in Ecclesiastes' verdict that 'there is nothing new under the sun' (1:9). In such a situation, the best one can hope for is a recovery of forgotten knowledge, since there is nothing fresh to be discovered:

> out of olde bokes, in good feyth,
> Cometh al this newe science that men lere.[1]

Adam was thought to have known everything by virtue of divine grace and to have forfeited that knowledge at the Fall, although in Calvinist theology he was believed to have retained the intelligence which enables his descendants to embark upon the arduous task of trying to re-learn what our first father once knew effortlessly by grace.[2] Knowledge is here conceived of as something to be *re*covered rather than *dis*covered, for knowledge is only recollection, as Plato's *Phaedo* (72–3) and *Meno* (81–2) teach. What Francis Bacon boldly called in 1605 *The advancement of learning* might more properly be designated *A restitution of decayed intelligence*, which is the title of Richard Verstegen's book of the same year.

It follows that one can hardly expect writers to have anything new to say in a world devoid of novelty, although they themselves do not always take kindly to the idea. One of the most ancient and recurrent complaints of writers is memorably expressed in a misquotation from Terence's *The eunuch* (161 BC): 'There's nothing said nowadays that hasn't been said before' (l. 41). Three centuries earlier still, the Greek lyric poet Bacchylides was already voicing the familiar complaint that 'it is not easy to find words which have never been pronounced' (fr. 5); and Walter Jackson Bate, in his book on *The burden of the past and the English poet* (Cambridge, Mass., 1970), quotes similar sentiments expressed by Khakheperresenb, an Egyptian poet who lived some four thousand years ago. If you feel that everything has been said before, what can you do about it? A common response is to indulge in melancholy resignation, as Eliot does in 'East Coker', and carry on with the irksome task (in 'conditions/That seem unpropitious') of rehearsing themes already rehearsed 'by men whom one cannot hope/To emulate'.[3] Such anxieties are avoided nowadays only by a Beckett or a Borges, who has the brilliance to take as his theme the 'ultimacy' of his place in literary history.[4] Yet there was once a time, not so very long ago, when it seemed the sensible thing to accept the impossibility of saying anything original, and to devote one's energies instead to saying what has been said before, but in a manner much superior to that of one's predecessors. This is what the theory of imitation is all about.

Imitation, emulating and overgoing

The earliest surviving literary theory of imitation is in the *Poetics* of Aristotle, who applies the term *mimesis* to the dramatist's transactions with reality. *Mimesis* here means imitation in the sense of a 'representation of reality'; but some three centuries later, and for inexplicable reasons, *mimesis* had come to mean 'the imitation of authors'. Two-thirds of the now lost work *On mimesis* by Dionysius of Halicarnassus were devoted to authors suitable for imitation and the best ways of imitating them; and in the Latin rhetorical tradition, Dionysian *imitatio* supplanted Aristotelian *mimesis* as a literary method. Some agreed with Cicero that one's style should be moulded on that of a single author, whereas others favoured Quintilian's view that a synthesis of many styles would be preferable.[5] Nobody doubted that the best way of mastering the medium was to compose detailed imitations of other people's styles. Playing the sedulous ape to acknowledged masters was still recommended practice for Robert Louis Stevenson and Ezra Pound,[6] who recognised that this is the only way to get first-hand experience of the verbal dexterity which makes for literary expertise. Abuses of the method reveal most clearly what is involved. A canon is drawn up of the 'best' writers whose works are then treated as normative. In prose it is typified by

'Ciceromania', which Erasmus mocks in his dialogue *Ciceronianus* (1528). Ciceromaniacs assume that Cicero's prose style is at once so timeless and perfect that disciples must restrict themselves to words and expressions used by the master; and it was for the benefit of such aficionados that Marius Nizolius compiled his *Thesaurus Ciceronianus* in 1535, those 'Nizolian paperbooks' ridiculed by Sir Philip Sidney.[7] The parallel phenomenon in poetry is 'Maronolatry' or adulation of Virgil (Publius Vergilius Maro), which led Scaliger to declare that since 'nothing was omitted by the celestial poet, nothing is to be added (unless by ignorant fools) and nothing to be changed (unless by impudent rascals)'.[8] This is the kind of thing which has given *imitatio* a bad name.

Since Roman times, however, imitators have been expected not so much to imitate as emulate. A respectable imitator, Petrarch told Boccaccio, will see to it that 'what he writes resembles the original without reproducing it. The resemblance should not be that of a portrait to the sitter...but...of a son to his father'.[9] Where *imitatio* might appear slavish, *aemulatio* is challenging, for it encourages the intrepid beginner to surpass the authors he studies. 'It is shameful to be content merely to reach the level of your model', warned Quintilian (*Institutio oratoria*, x 2). As a result, literary history is turned into a series of contests at which acknowledged masters are taken on by all-comers. Gabriel Harvey saw that *The faerie queene* was Spenser's attempt to 'overgo Ariosto' in some sort of literary contest not unlike what Pound had in mind when he described Jules Laforgue (whose poems helped shape 'The love song of J. Alfred Prufrock') as 'an angel with whom our modern poetic Jacob must struggle'.[10] Milton engaged in conscious and serious rivalry with ancient and modern poets in practically everything he wrote, knowing that the process is never ending. 'Future generations', wrote Pliny, 'will challenge us to battle as we ourselves have challenged our predecessors'; and an emulator who happens to be a novelist is always likely to see himself as boxing an elimination-contest Hemingway-like with Turgenev before the title-bout with Tolstoy.[11] Anthologies are littered with inconspicuous examples of the overgoing principle. Keats, for instance, wrote melodiously of 'the murmurous haunt of flies on summer's eves' before Tennyson celebrated

> The moan of doves in immemorial elms,
> And murmuring of innumerable bees.[12]

Undoubtedly, some overgoings are overdoings, but the principle is not invalidated by abuses. 'I cannot think that real poets have any competition', Blake wrote in his copy of Wordsworth's poems, and of course he is right.[13] For whereas poetasters never get beyond pastiche, the successful overgoer ends up with something altogether his own: 'The love song of J. Alfred Prufrock' may have begun as an attempt to out-Laforgue Laforgue, but it grew into the first mature poem by T. S. Eliot. Such are the benefits to be gained from wrestling with angels.

It is characteristic of imitators and emulators alike to place a high value on tradition. The institution of exemplary canons determines the function of writing to be what Pound calls in *Hugh Selwyn Mauberley* (1920) the 'conservation of the better tradition'. Continuities are thought preferable to schisms, and tradition is looked upon in the very literal sense of the ancient Greek torch-race as a handing-on of the lamp (*traditio lampadis*):

> His only pride to tend the flame
>> That Homer and that Virgil won,
> Retain the rite, preserve the act
> And pass the worship on intact.[14]

Over the centuries, tradition acquired such honorific sanctions that even radicals who are all in favour of schismatic originality are often tempted to appropriate it and defend what Harold Rosenberg paradoxically calls *The tradition of the new* (New York, 1959).

To accept a tradition is to defer to authorities who dictate it, with the result that traditionalists may find the absence of authority a disquieting experience. Medieval poets often conceal the originality of their material because they were expected to purvey the kind of statements which can be authenticated historically. They will quote their 'auctoritees' at the very moment of departing from them, or invent imaginary authors like 'Dictys' or 'Dares', whose non-existent writings authorised the twelfth-century Benoît de Sainte Maure's additions to ancient legends concerning Troy, notably his invention of the story of Troilus and Briseida in his *Roman de Troie*, which is the ultimate source of Chaucer's *Troilus and Criseyde*.[15] The intention, C. S. Lewis deduces, was 'to hand on the "historial" matter worthily; not worthily of your own genius or of the poetic art but of the matter itself'.[16] Untraceable books, 'old' plays, 'anonymous' authors are all versions of the same authenticatory device which survives in the novelistic pretence of passing off an original work in the form

of an edition of someone else's letters or journal. Originality needs
to be handled apologetically in such an ethos, as Dryden shows
when praising Anne Killigrew. Artlessly original, she nevertheless
writes so well that you would think her work derivative:

> Such noble vigour did her verse adorn,
> That it seemed borrowed, where 'twas only born.[17]

Even allowing for the force of the witticism, Dryden's comment
was not nearly so Wildean a remark at the time as it appears to
be now.

Allusiveness and eclectic plagiarism

Imitatio results in a literature manufactured with the aid of an
assiduous eclecticism easily mistaken for plagiarism, and marketed
on the assumption that people will prefer allusiveness to novelty
any day. Emulators, it was generally agreed, are busy bees who
ransack the profusion of flowers in the Muses' garden and
transform the stolen pollen into honey. 'As...a bee gathers wax
and honey out of many flowers', writes Robert Burton of *The
anatomy of melancholy* (1621), 'I have laboriously collected this
cento out of divers writers.'[18] No author should be so completely
original as to manufacture things out of his own guts, for that is
what spiders do, as we are informed in a section of Swift's *Battle
of the books* (1704) which Matthew Arnold helped popularise in
Culture and anarchy (1869): spiders are nasty little Moderns who
spin poison out of their own entrails, and vastly inferior to those
admirably Ancient bees who search hither and yon before
producing honey and wax, 'thus furnishing mankind with the two
noblest of things, which are sweetness and light'.[19]

Pollen-gatherers operate with a clear conscience as long as they
maintain an ornamentalist attitude towards style, and treat subject-
matter as something which belongs to no-one in particular. Before
Robert Greene rewrote the apocryphal story of Susanna and the
Elders as *The mirror of modesty* (1584) he first excused himself 'with
the answer that Varro made when he offered Ennius' works to the
emperor: "I give", quoth he, "another man's picture, but freshly
flourished with mine own colours".'[20] At such times it is difficult
to assert proprietorial rights over one's work, for its subject-matter
is no more than what Horace calls 'public property' (*Ars poetica*,
131). Plagiarism is a difficult concept to formulate. 'The history
of Troy was no more the invention of Homer than of Virgil',

Dryden declared in 1697, for Homer supplied only the telling, not the tale.[21] A discerning Elizabethan reader, William Webbe, recognised that 'Homer made matter which was common to all, proper to himself'; but as late as the 1890s, Rudyard Kipling expressed what had long been the majority opinion in such matters:

> When 'Omer smote 'is bloomin' lyre
> He'd 'eard men sing by land an' sea;
> An' what he thought 'e might require
> 'E went an' took – the same as me![22]

Even in the heyday of *imitatio* as a compositional method, however, misgivings were voiced about it. John Donne graphically castigates the kind of writer who

> beggarly doth chaw
> Other wits' fruits, and in his ravenous maw
> Rankly digested, doth those things out-spue,
> As his own things; and they are his own, 'tis true,
> For if one eat my meat, though it be known
> The meat was mine, th' excrement is his own.[23]

It was after reading poems by John Soowthern that George Puttenham wrote in 1589: 'This man deserves to be indicted of petty larceny for pilfering other men's devices from them and converting them to his own use.'[24] Legal action was impossible before the 1709 Statute of Anne first gave copyright protection to British authors. Shortly afterwards, John Dennis denounced plagiarists as 'spiritual outlaws' in the commonwealth of learning, and a year later James Smith had persuaded the publisher of his poems to print borrowings in a different type so as 'to avoid the imputation of a plagiary'.[25] The new scrupulousness is neatly parodied in Swift's boast about his own originality:

> To steal a hint [he] was never known,
> But what he writ was all his own.[26]

How piquant that this protestation of independence should have been cribbed – from Denham's elegy on Cowley:

> To him no author was unknown,
> Yet what he wrote was all his own.[27]

The word 'plagiarist' is first recorded in 1598, when John Hall called one of Petrarch's many imitators a 'plagiary sonnet-wright', anglicising the Latin word *plagiarus* ('man-stealer').[28] In Roman law, *plagium* was the name given to the criminal offence of stealing a slave from his master, or a freeman with intent to enslave. Martial was the first poet to apply the legal term metaphorically to literary theft, although he seems to have had in mind 'deprivation of authorship credit' rather than the sly infiltration of parts of other people's work into something ostensibly one's own.[29] Nobody before the twentieth century entertained the possibility of psychological explanations for the plagiaristic element in *imitatio*, such as are alleged in defence of Coleridge. 'The exact phrasing of another writer's passage was for Coleridge some sort of talisman that allayed his anxieties', writes Thomas McFarland, who believes that Coleridge's plagiarisms are 'not the thefts of a poverty-stricken mind, but the mosaic materials of a neurotic technique of composition'.[30] Is this the psychological basis on which *imitatio* in general rests?

If eclectic plagiarism is the dubious origin of an *imitatio* literature, allusiveness is its affective strength. Calling for a high degree of literacy among readers, allusive literature achieves its unique intensities by treating earlier texts as a patrimony and constantly evoking other literary occasions, sometimes emphatically, sometimes facetiously, but always appositely.[31] Allusiveness makes possible the art of Thomas Gray, whose poetry is an echo-chamber resonant with the voices of earlier poets; or the art of Thomas Macaulay, who (in Thackeray's tribute) 'reads twenty books to write a sentence'.[32] Webster's plays are likewise mosaics of quotations, and pose the problem of deciding how many of the borrowed bits and pieces we are meant to recognise. Ideally, one would like to use Herman Meyer's distinction between borrowings and quotations ('the borrowing is distinguished from the quotation by the fact that it has no referential character').[33] Unfortunately, we have no way of knowing whether *The white devil* and *The Duchess of Malfi* are supposed to reverberate 'intertextually' with buried quotations, or merely dazzle us with the surface glitter of fine phrases whose primary function is to illuminate one another. We are assured that while contemporary audiences were not expected to recognise the allusions, obscure passages in the plays become more intelligible if approached by way of the texts Webster plundered.[34] Does this mean that Webster (like Eliot) mingled borrowings with quotations indiscriminately, or that scholars are glad to get what help they can from Webster's sources when the meaning of a particular passage is obscure? It is only in cases where irony is unmistakable that a referential manner can be wholly free of suspicion of plagiarism, for nobody ever accuses

Jane Austen of having anything other than a parodic interest in novels alluded to in *Northanger Abbey* (1818). For the rest, allusiveness is ever likely to be a perilous enterprise, acclaimed on the one hand as the acme of sophistication, and condemned on the other as a literary malpractice.

Individual originality

Imitation of the Ancients (*imitatio veterum*) was recommended universally to young writers until the late eighteenth century, by which time the rival and still current theory of originality had been formulated. The shift from one to the other signals a revolution in our estimation of the individual component in literary creation. *Imitatio* flourishes best among people who do not mind annihilating themselves in the functions they perform, and who think of themselves as not primarily writers but (in the Marxist formulation) people who engage in writing among other activities.[35] If it never occurs to anyone to connect original works with original minds, nobody is likely to expect preferential treatment for producing them, or to have much in the way of proprietorial rights over what is produced. Major works will be left unsigned, somewhat to the embarrassment of scholars who feel obliged to invent an author for them, like 'the *Gawain* poet' or 'the Wakefield Master'. For it is tempting to conclude that the Wakefield Master was unaware of his own unique contribution in producing a text for *The Towneley plays*, and saw no reason for attaching his signature to plays on themes he had taken out of the Bible.

To inculcate an awareness of the original contribution to such enterprises, interest has to be redirected from the structure of artifacts to the psychology of artificers. The drift from one to the other signals a change from 'medieval' to 'Renaissance' attitudes towards human potentiality. When Donne published his sombre *Anatomy of the world* in 1611 he registered disquiet at the prospect of a new age in which everybody was likely to consider himself as unique as the phoenix.[36] Sure enough, within the next few decades there emerged a new cult of eccentricity, with phoenixes preening themselves in public after the manner of Sir Thomas Browne in *Religio medici* (1643). An early intimation of this growing sense of the uniqueness of individual experience appears in a letter written by Petrarch to Boccaccio in 1359: 'Each of us has naturally something individual and his own [*quiddam suum ac*

proprium] in his utterance and language as in his face and gesture'
– something which is more easily cultivated than altered.[37] Here
we have a distinctly unmedieval recognition of the importance of
individual idiosyncrasy, an awareness which was later to drive
William Blake to the point where he had to devise an original
method of book design and even an original method of relief-
etching in order to avoid compromising the uniqueness of his
offering by more orthodox methods of publication. For Blake is
'a new kind of man', Francis Finch told Gilchrist, 'wholly
original, and in all things'.[38]

When individuals are valued more highly than the representative
or typical, it is difficult to sustain a vital interest in *imitatio*
disciplines which call for self-effacement rather than self-
exploration, and discourage the writing of advertisements for
oneself. Indeed, exponents of originality are likely to find *imitatio*
perverse. For if a writer's first responsibility is towards his *quiddam
suum ac proprium*, he is obliged to produce work as unique as his
fingerprints. 'Born originals', Edward Young observed in 1759,
'how comes it to pass that we die copies?'[39] His answer (not very
original) is to lay the blame on simian art: 'That meddling ape
Imitation, as soon as we come to years of indiscretion (so let me
speak), snatches the pen, and blots out Nature's mark of separation,
cancels her kind intention, destroys all mental individuality.'[40] If
each of us is a phoenix, we can echo with conviction one of the
opening sentiments of Rousseau's *Confessions* (1781): 'I may be no
better [than other people], but at least I am different.'[41]

Imitatio promotes the idea of the uniformity of human experience, and encourages people to emphasise the historical continuity
in that seamless web called tradition. The doctrine of originality,
on the other hand, exploits the heterogeneity of people in drawing
attention to the uniqueness of individual experience, and leads to
a schismatic view of history in which sudden mutations are the
norm. Momentous changes are then seen to occur with disarming
casualness. 'In or about December, 1910, human character
changed', wrote Virginia Woolf.[42] She was probably thinking of
that chasm between herself and nineteenth-century novelists
marked by the Post-Impressionist Exhibition, which opened in
London in November 1910. She made the remark in 1924, when
modernists contemplated their descent from eminent Victorians
with the same distaste as postmodernists nowadays contemplate
their great modernist fathers and grandfathers. Some would see
this as supporting Timothy Leary's contention that 'the generation

gap is a species mutation'.[43] The point which concerns us immediately, however, is that whenever such a schism is announced, and the 'new mutants'[44] draw their cutting line, the past is invariably in jeopardy.

Forgetting the past

To advocates of originality, knowledge is no longer the recovery of the old but the discovery of the new. In this respect, the defence of literary originality is a by-product of the Battle of the Books, that *querelle des Anciens et des Modernes* which Pico della Mirandola anticipated when he told Cardinal Bembo in 1512 that 'we are greater than the Ancients'.[45] A progressive Modern like Bacon promulgated *The advancement of learning* (1605) in the conviction that men of his generation knew more than the Ancients had known; and Joseph Glanvill, attacking *The vanity of dogmatising* in 1661, could see no point in 'doting on Antiquity' to the extent of ignoring contemporary achievements and looking with 'a superstitious reverence upon the accounts of preterlapsed ages'.[46] The orthodoxy attacked by such remarks asserted that the Ancients are superior to the Moderns by virtue of living at a time when mankind had not yet degenerated to the degree reached in the sixteenth and seventeenth centuries, when there were barely four hundred years left of the six thousand allotted to the world which God had created about 4004 BC. 'The first men', wrote Vasari, introducing his *Lives of the artists* in 1550, 'were more perfect and endowed with more intelligence, seeing that they lived nearer the time of the Creation.'[47] Understandably, they had not only originated but also perfected all the arts, which makes them giants in the eyes of a Modern, who is puny by comparison because *puis né*.

Moderns refuse to acquiesce in the subsequent historical determinism which implies that post-classical history is an uninterrupted decadence, and that modern man can have no higher aspiration than the imitation of acknowledged excellence in the forlorn hope of restituting the decayed intelligence of ancient Greeks and Romans. In the Modern transvaluation, veneration of the past is redesignated disparagingly as 'past-ism' (*passatismo* or *passéisme*). The past ceases to be a patrimony, and now becomes a burden and an embarrassment, something to be avoided in case it engenders in the Modern a sense of inferiority not unlike that 'cultural cringe' observed by Arthur Phillips in Australian writers who worry about what British critics will think of their work.[48] For *imitatio*, in the opinion of the first English polemicist on behalf of originality, Edward Young, is merely 'inferiority confessed'.[49] History becomes a nightmare from which one tries in vain to awake, and the newfoundland of America attracts a Goethe or a Heine because it has the advantage of being a sub-European continent blessedly devoid of European history. An Emerson arises in 1837 to accuse American writers of having 'listened too long to the courtly muses of Europe'; and a few years later a Melville is urging the same people to abandon their 'literary flunkeyism towards England'.[50]

The Modern hates to think of himself as merely pedicuring the past, and thinks it sufficient to discredit false Moderns merely by calling them 'men content with the connotations of their masters', which was William Carlos Williams' jibe at Pound and Eliot.[51] The literary *ancien*, on the other hand, is inclined to see the whole of modern literature as a series of footnotes to Homer. 'Modern writers are the moons of literature', said Johnson; 'they shine with reflected light, with light borrowed from the Ancients.'[52] Traditionalists are willing to accept this and make their own contribution to the poetry of mirrors, as the allusive Vladimir Nabokov does in *Pale fire* (London, 1962), taking his cue from *Timon of Athens*: 'the moon's an arrant thief,/And her pale fire she snatches from the sun.' Schismatic Moderns will have none of this, preferring (in D. H. Lawrence's image) to 'start with the sun'.[53] Or (in another favourite image) they will adopt an attitude of parricidal antagonism towards the founding fathers of traditions foisted upon them. 'One cannot be forever carrying one's father's corpse', Guillaume Apollinaire complained in his book on Cubist painters, before going on to write the manifesto, *L'antitradition futuriste* (1913).[54] 'Let the dead poets make way for the rest', cries Antonin Artaud in *Le théâtre et son double* (1938).[55]

Cultural arsonists found their spokesman in the Italian inventor of Futurism, F. T. Marinetti, who launched his attack on *passsatismo* in *Le figaro* on 20 February 1909. 'We will destroy the museums, libraries, academies of every kind', he wrote. 'We want to free this land from its smelly gangrene of professors, archaeologists, ciceroni and antiquarians.'[56] Warming to the task ahead, he urged sympathisers to 'set fire to the library shelves! Turn aside the canals to flood the museums!' (how delighted he would have been at the present plight of Venice, that '*cloaca maxima* of passéism').[57] Reiterated by the Dadaists, Marinetti's *antipassatismo* reveals a yearning for a cultural clean slate or *tabula rasa*. 'We should burn all libraries and allow to remain only that which everyone knows by heart', said Hugo Ball in 1917. 'A beautiful age of legend would then begin.'[58] Or in the words of another Dadaist, Marcel Janco: 'We demanded the *tabula rasa*. We knew then that the caveman was a great artist, and that we must start afresh.'[59] Such sentiments are intended to shock those who look upon Europe as a museum rather than a studio, and believe that the past conceals important lessons for the present. 'Those who cannot remember the past are condemned to repeat it', wrote Santayana;[60] but it is equally true that those who can remember the past are condemned to watch it repeated by those who can not.

Antipassatismo called for a willed ignorance not easily achieved by people accustomed to understand the present from the vantage-point of the past. When ignorance is held to be the best safeguard against being crushed by the burden of the past, the naturally ignorant writer is much better placed than those who consciously choose the way of unknowing. Blissful ignorance is denied a John Stuart Mill (who began learning Greek at the age of three) or a Thomas Macaulay, who had sampled Homer, Virgil and Pindar by the time he was six. Abstemiousness in later years may nevertheless repair some of the damage done during a bookishly misspent youth. 'I reckon it among my principal advantages, as a composer of verses', wrote William Cowper in 1781, 'that I have not read an English poet these thirteen years, and but one these twenty years.'[61] In a similar vein, Wordsworth told Henry Crabb Robinson that he had 'never read a word of German metaphysics, thank Heaven!'[62] Perhaps what distinguishes the 1802 Preface to *Lyrical ballads* most sharply from neoclassical criticism is its sparsity of allusions to earlier critics, typically in the feigned ignorance of Wordsworth's sole reference to Aristotle. 'Aristotle, I have been told' – he has not actually read him, we are to understand – 'hath said, that poetry is the most philosophic of all writing: it is so.'[63] Here speaks a man seemingly disemburdened of the past, a man who is aware of the existence of Aristotle's works, but feels no obligation to study them carefully. Wordsworth starts with the sun, which is Wordsworth, and so can afford to ignore both the moonlight of Aristotle and the moonshine of Aristotelians. For an 'original' writer ought not to display familiarity with the *loci classici* of his subject, even if he knows them better than most of his readers do. The illusion of ignorance has to be fostered if the illusion of originality is to be maintained. How revealing, then, to have the disingenuousness of it all exposed by Keats: 'I am reading Voltaire and Gibbon, although I wrote Reynolds the other day to prove reading of no use.'[64]

Novelty and originality

When people believe that there is nothing new under the sun, and that everything has been said before, it is up to writers to reawaken interest in the great commonplaces of human experience by learning the art of telling old stories in new ways. Here the *imitatio* writer displays his 'originality', by focusing on treatment rather than subject. Horace thought it 'better to dramatise a Trojan tale than to break new ground': any fool can be original, he seems to imply, but 'it is hard to be original in treating well-worn subjects' (*Ars poetica*, 128–30). Waller paid Davenant the compliment of having met this challenge admirably in writing *Gondibert* (1651), a work in which the judicious reader

> May find old love in pure fresh language told,
> Like new-stamped coin made out of angel-gold.[65]

In miniature, François Villon's originality was to select from the medieval literature of death the gaunt topic of *ubi sunt* ('where are they?') and transform it into 'Mais où sont les neiges d'antan?', which Rossetti Englished as 'But where are the snows of yester-year?'[66] Excellence was largely a matter of improving on someone else's discovery, for 'nothing is perfect the moment it is invented', said Cicero (*Brutus*, 71).

The upshot of *imitatio* theory was to discredit what would now be called originality by redefining it as 'novelty', and then to claim that novelty is irrelevant to excellence. An eighteenth-century critic might concede that Homer's *Iliad* is a more original work than Virgil's *Aeneid*, but still be inclined to think the *Aeneid* the better poem. This judgement would accord with Kant's claim, in the *Critique of judgement* (1790), that originality can hardly be a virtue if we can admit the existence of 'original nonsense'.[67] 'Originality is not nearly so good as goodness, even when it is good', A. E. Housman told Bridges.[68] The arts, we discover, can easily be jeopardised by what Wyndham Lewis calls 'the demon of progress', which he defines as 'a pathological straining after something which boasts of a spectacular *aheadofness*'.[69] *Imitatio*, on the other hand, ensures a continuing concern with centralities which is denied progressivists who feel compelled to explore the peripheral because the centre has already been colonised by those one cannot hope to emulate. In his introduction to Baudelaire's *Les fleurs du mal* (1857), Théophile Gautier draws attention to the way in which modern writers restlessly search out increasingly fugitive experiences of a neurotic or hallucinatory character. When a standard *imitatio* topic like the way of a man with a maid has to be dispensed with because it has already been done, the frenzied novelty of Gore Vidal's *Myra Breckinridge* (1968) becomes inevitable. We have no Samuel Johnson to reassure us that writers are not obliged to transmit 'some truth unknown', because they perform a useful enough function merely by 'diversifying the surface of knowledge'.[70]

Even in classical antiquity, however, some writers appear to ignore the persuasive apologias of *imitatio* theorists and insist on the importance of originality in something like our sense of the word, never worrying about the probability that an absolutely original work would be absolutely unintelligible. The Homeric bard Phemius describes himself as being 'self-taught' and therefore indebted to nobody; and Pindar frequently claims originality for his own compositions, offering 'the flowers of songs that are new' in one ode and 'a new-winged song' in another.[71] 'Is it a crime for us to discover something new?' asked Quintilian: but his question is deceptive to modern readers unaware of the fact that the 'claim to originality' was a conventional way of beginning a classical oration.[72]

Ambivalence concerning the importance of originality is most clearly manifest in what English writers came to call 'invention'. The word derives from *invenire* ('to come upon') and was first used in the sense it had always had in classical rhetoric: 'the discovery of valid or seemingly valid arguments to render one's cause plausible'.[73] An *inventio* is not necessarily original because one can 'come upon' suitable material in other people's books; and this is the meaning of 'invention' in the first English book on rhetoric, Leonard Cox's *The art or craft of rhetoric* (1530). But when Dryden writes, in 1695, that 'without invention, a painter is but a copier, and a poet but a plagiary of others',[74] he seems to be using the word in the modern sense. After starting out as a technical term for the selection of subject-matter, 'invention' gradually became a psychological term associated with 'imagination' and therefore a distinguishing characteristic of 'creative genius'. To Alexander Gerard, who published *An essay on genius* in 1774, invention is 'the capacity of producing new beauties in works of art, and new truths in matters of science'.[75]

New beauties, new truths: newness is the hall-mark of modernity, with Pound's 'make it new' the dominant slogan, and technical progress the dominant ideal. 'It is exactly as wasteful for a poet to do what has been done already', Eliot was to write, 'as for a biologist to rediscover Mendel's discoveries.'[76] In the later eighteenth century, writers turned aside from generalities to isolate whatever is uniquely particular in the plenitude of nature, and began to treat with contempt the kind of literature to which every bosom returns an echo. To sustain the new endeavour, a brand-new form was invented in the eighteenth century, a form unknown to the Ancients and called (with disarming candour) the novel. For if, as Johnson suspected, the plenitude of Nature ensured the existence of 'a thousand recesses unexplored, a thousand flowers unplucked, a thousand fountains unexhausted',[77] then it was up to the new novelists to do the exploring, the plucking and the exhausting.

Originality as a mark of genius

'No man was ever great by imitation', said Johnson's Imlac.[78] Towards the end of the eighteenth century, a growing number of critics agreed that no matter how creative an imitation might be, it is necessarily inferior to an original work. 'Copies surpass not their originals', wrote Edward Young in 1759, 'as streams rise not higher than their spring.'[79] And in the years which followed the publication of *Rasselas* (1759), the difference between *imitatio* and originality came to be treated as more or less the difference between talent and genius.

'Originality' acquired its current prestige in the course of new psychological enquiries into the nature of genius. It was not until the eighteenth century that the word 'genius' lost its old meaning of 'an attendant spirit' and became internalised as a mental endowment, thus enabling some unusually intelligent person to be spoken of as a 'genius'.[80] At the time, Shakespeare was a major exhibit, inviting Pope's superlative compliment that 'if ever any author deserved the name of an original, it was Shakespeare'.[81] The first writer to devote a whole book to genius in the new and still current sense was William Sharpe, whose *Dissertation upon genius* was published in 1755, four years before Young's *Conjectures on original composition* (1759) and twelve years before Robert

Wood's *Essay on the original genius of Homer* (1767) and William Duff's *Essay on original genius* (1767 also). Such investigations mark a radical shift in traditional attitudes towards the relationship between art and nature, between the labour of composition and the creative impulse, between acquired learning and spontaneous expression. When Horace, for example, asked himself whether a good poem is the product of nature or of art, he decided that he could not 'see the value of application [*studium*] without a strong natural aptitude [*ingenium*], or, on the other hand, of native genius unless it is cultivated' (*Ars poetica*, 408–11). The crucial ingredient seems to be *ingenium*. Certainly, it was Horace's lines which inspired a grammarian who lived about the year 200 (Pseudo-Acro) to formulate that much quoted aphorism, *poeta nascitur non fit* ('the poet is born, not made').[82]

Now despite this concession to *ingenium*, Horace devotes much of his *Ars poetica* to *studium*, emphasising the importance of mastering metrical systems, of revising carefully what you write, and so on. Perhaps this imbalance was inevitable: either you have *ingenium* or you do not, and if not, there is nothing you can do about it. Craftsmanship, on the other hand, can be talked about profitably, which is why books on the art of poetry from Horace's time onwards focus attention on techniques one can acquire through careful *studium*. What distinguishes the attitude of a Sharpe or a Duff is their Romantic curiosity about *ingenium*. As a result, the *studiosus* writer came to be overshadowed by the natural genius, who wanted to close up those barren leaves on which the literature of the previous two thousand years had been written and behave instead like a wild untutored phoenix, a specialist in fine careless raptures, spontaneously original, and uttering his native woodnotes wild. Johnson detected symptoms of the new fashion in 1751: 'impatience of study, contempt of the great masters of ancient wisdom, and a disposition to rely wholly upon unassisted genius and natural sagacity'.[83] But in the Romantic transvaluation which was taking place, the weaknesses Johnson detected were reinterpreted as strengths. Edward Young was soon to denounce learning as mere 'borrowed knowledge', much inferior to genius, which is 'knowledge innate, and quite our own'.[84] 'An original', he adds, 'rises spontaneously from the vital root of genius; it *grows*, it is not *made*.'[85] Out went bookish *imitatio*, to be replaced by a fresh attentiveness to those minute particularities of the way things are, an attentiveness it was still too early to call by its proper name, *mimesis*.

Laudable as such attempts were to probe the enigma of *ingenium*, they have bequeathed to us the problematic assumption that writers are somehow different from everybody else. The Wordsworthian poet, for instance, is above all else an unusual man, 'of more than usual organic sensibility',[86] and without this, he is nothing. Benedetto Croce, however, thought that a more correct formulation of *poeta nascitur* would be '*homo nascitur poeta*: some men are born great poets, some small. The cult and superstition of the genius has arisen from this quantitative difference having been taken as a difference of quality.'[87] Psychiatrists, according to Anthony Storr, frequently encounter highly original people who are unable to express their originality in any medium, and so remain mutely inglorious. 'The idea that people who practise the arts do so because they are endowed with a particular skill and need to exercise it cannot be maintained,' Storr concludes.[88]

Seeing that the processes which make for what is described as originality are inexplicable, any term we choose is likely to illustrate only what Whitehead used to call the Fallacy of Misplaced Concreteness.[89] Terms like 'creative imagination' or 'genius' have no other virtue than expediency. 'Analgesic pills which dull the aches of incomprehension', Medawar would call them, and rightly so, for to think of them as self-explanatory is to align oneself with that pseudo-scholar mocked by E. M. Forster, who 'loves mentioning genius, because the sound of the word exempts him from discovering its meaning'.[90] Nor have experiments in computer creativity illuminated original genius and its products, for computers only simulate poetic processes, and cannot yet replicate them. The IBM computer which produced for Marie Boroff the arresting phrase, 'O life,/Dance like a silent tumbleweed', was aided by a programmer who fed it words culled from two anthologies of poetry, and then obliged it to regurgitate them in the rhetorical scheme 'O *a*, *b* like a *c d*'.[91] Far from doing something original, it had no choice but to race through all possible permutations, and was wholly dependent on Marie Boroff to fish out her pennyworth of bread from an intolerable deal of sack. The computer is as yet no serious rival to Young's original genius, who can go on verbalising his *quiddam suum ac proprium* in the knowledge that the processes by which he makes poems are still inscrutable.

8

Literary influences

Authorial testimony and the reader's curiosity

No writer is an island, entire of itself, but a piece of the continent, a part of the main. Whatever he reads is likely to have an effect on what he writes, if only in the negative sense of showing him what not to do. Often, his focus on things will be sharpened by what Dryden once called 'the spectacles of books'.[1] Occasionally, he may want to acknowledge his indebtedness, as Eliot did in the case of Arthur Symons's book on *The symbolist movement in literature* (London, 1899), which introduced him to Laforgue and so catalysed the process which terminated in 'The love song of J. Alfred Prufrock' (1915).[2] However one interprets the treacherous term 'influence', Laforgue's poetry undoubtedly influenced the young Eliot, most probably in the form he was later to recollect as 'a kind of inundation, of invasion of the undeveloped personality by the stronger personality of the poet'.[3] Some writers are so wary of this that they try to avoid potentially domineering authors. It was Goethe who once said of Shakespeare that 'a productive *nature* ought not to read more than one of his dramas in a year if it would not be wrecked entirely'.[4] Auden thought himself fortunate as a young poet to have come under the influence of Thomas Hardy's poetry, the technical imperfections of which left him room to manoeuvre and subsequently overgo, whereas a more accomplished master might have had a depressive effect on the younger writer's confidence.[5] On the other hand, Longinus noted that 'many authors catch fire from the inspiration of others',[6] and the poetry of Swinburne shows that the result need not be as bookish as the poetry of George Chapman. Nor need it be only a one-way process, if the writers involved are aware of each other's existence to the degree that Eliot and Pound were, or Goethe and Schiller, or Wordsworth and Coleridge. 'Great contemporaries whet and cultivate each other', Dryden observes;

'and mutual borrowing, and commerce, makes the common riches of learning, as it does of the civil government.'[7] Influence as inundation, influence as whetstone: the two metaphors mark opposite poles of response to the same phenomenon, ranging from a seemingly helpless passivity in the presence of a stronger personality, to the abrasive stimulation of good company.

Yeats wrote in his 1930 diary that poets 'do not seek truth in argument or in books but clarification of what [they] already believe'.[8] If so, what we construe as 'influence' may be no more than confirmation of quite independent speculations. A younger writer, said Eliot, is usually 'looking for masters who will elicit his consciousness of what he wants to say himself'.[9] In other words, writers choose influences in the way that they choose friends, and experience what Goethe called 'elective affinities'.[10] Poe's influence on Baudelaire was evidently of this nature, for Baudelaire said he discovered in Poe's books 'poems and stories which I'd already conceived, but only in a vague and formless manner, which Poe had planned and brought to perfection'.[11] The establishment of a precedent offers reassurance, even justification, no matter how different one's finished work may turn out to be from the precedent invoked.

Literary critics use a number of terms which (like Eliot's 'inundation') appear to be hydrological metaphors, such as 'diffusion', 'mainstream', 'current', 'source' and (of course) 'influence'. There are numerous books with titles like *The influence of Milton on English poetry* (1922) by Raymond D. Havens. Margaret Sherwood's *Undercurrents of influence in English Romantic poetry* (1934) is less well-known than H. J. C. Grierson's *Cross currents in English literature in the XVIIth century* (1929); Frederick ·E. Pierce once traced *Currents and eddies in the Romantic generation* (1918), and Harry Levin *Countercurrents in the study of English* (1966). We tend to forget that the word 'influence' was originally an astrological term denoting those astral streams which allegedly control our destiny. To Richard Ellmann, who has given an exemplary account of Yeats's literary relationships with his contemporaries, it is the hydrological sense which dominates, and not altogether satisfactorily so. 'That writers flow into each other like waves, gently rather than tidally, is one of those decorous myths we impose upon a high-handed, even brutal procedure', he declares. 'Writers move upon other writers not as genial successors but as violent expropriators.'[12] Or as Eliot once put it, 'immature poets imitate; mature poets steal'.[13]

Students of literature can hardly avoid such transactions, for books and articles concerning the influence of x on y are very common, despite frequently voiced misgivings by literary comparatists. Every reader experiences the fortuitous discovery of an 'influence'. Preoccupied with other matters, one's eye may suddenly be caught by a comment James Howell made in 1628 on a poem which somebody sent him: 'it committed holy rapes upon my soul'.[14] Did Thomas Carew read this before writing that magnificent elegy in which Donne's 'brave soul' is said to have 'committed holy rapes upon our will?'[15] Quickened by the euphoria of discovery, one reads Howell as carefully as one expects Carew did (Carew also has to be re-read); and eventually, off goes a missive to a learned journal reporting anything from a borrowing to an influence. Should the isolated gold-strike turn out to be a glory-hole, two procedures are then possible. Either one can try to judge the originality of the borrower by seeing what he has done with his borrowings; or one can see in the borrowings evidence of kleptomania, in which case influence-study becomes a sort of literary criminology. Neither approach is very much liked by writers themselves. As for critics, they feel more at ease if influence-studies can be conducted in a positive spirit in the hope of assessing the borrower's originality in 'diverging' from his source. This is how the method is usually applied to Shakespeare. Certainly one learns a good deal about the moral stature of *Romeo and Juliet* by comparing it with *The tragical history of Romeus and Juliet* (1562), which Arthur Brooke says he wrote in the hope of dissuading young people from disobeying their parents and taking up with drunks and friars.[16] But it is doubtful whether any author's originality can be measured by subtracting one poem from another.[17]

Writers who equate originality with excellence find obnoxious a method of inquiry which amasses parallels and analogues to their own work. Romantic disapprobation of such activities is explicit in the 1816 preface to 'Christabel', where Coleridge complains rather crossly about critics 'who seem to hold, that every possible thought and image is traditional', and who consequently 'derive every rill they behold flowing, from a perforation made in some other man's tank'.[18] Had Coleridge written *Beowulf*, he would not have looked kindly on scholarly suggestions that Virgil's Avernus drained into Grendel's mere.[19] Tennyson was plagued by this problem. After watching water-lilies start and slide on his pond one windy day, he wrote the line, 'But as the waterlily starts and slides', and resented being told he had borrowed it from Wordsworth ('And, like the water-lily, lives and thrives'). So he too hit out against 'editors of booklets, book-worms, index-hunters, or men of great memories and no imagination, who *impute themselves* to the poet, and so believe that *he*, too, has no imagination, but is for ever poking his nose between the pages of some old volume in order to see what he can appropriate'.[20]

What heavy weather Coleridge and Tennyson make of it all in comparison with Vladimir Nabokov, who once responded to attempts to link his work with that of a wide range of celebrities (from 'Tolstoevski' to Charlie Chaplin) by confessing to have been influenced by the *Discours sur les ombres* of Pierre Delalande (1768–1849), an author Nabokov himself invented.[21] 'Every writer *creates* his own precursors', Borges concludes after surveying various precursors of Kafka. 'The poem "Fears and scruples" by Browning foretells Kafka's work, but our reading of Kafka perceptibly sharpens and deflects our reading of the poem. Browning did not read it as we do now.'[22] What seems to happen, writes Morse Peckham, is that 'an emergent style restructures one's perceptual process so that the values of that new style are now perceived in works of the past'.[23] This is what creates the illusion of 'retroactive influence', which makes Joyce a major influence on Rabelais (confirmed in the English translation by Jacques Le Clercq),[24] and Borges himself a powerful influence on Sir Thomas Browne's *Pseudodoxia epidemica* (1646). Current discussions of this phenomenon derive from T. S. Eliot, who thought we should 'not find it preposterous that the past should be altered by the present as much as the present is directed by the past'.[25] Eliot himself exercised until quite recently a powerful influence on seventeenth-century Metaphysical poets, and a generation of readers accustomed to look for Homeric elements in Joyce's *Ulysses* (1922) must have glimpsed the occasional Dubliner in the *Odyssey*. Looked at in this way, the Chinese poets who make their debut in *Cathay* (1915) owe as much to Pound as he does to them. For Pound (said Eliot) is 'the inventor of Chinese poetry for our time',[26] the man whose retroactive influence freed Li Po from centuries of detection by sinologists.

Some shortcomings of influence-studies

Our understanding of literary 'influence' is obstructed by the grammar of our language, which puts things back to front in obliging us to speak in passive terms of the one who is the active partner in the relationship: to say that Keats influenced Wilde is not only to credit Keats with an activity of which he was innocent, but also to misrepresent Wilde by suggesting he merely submitted to something he obviously went out of his way to acquire. In matters of influence, it is the receptor who takes the initiative, not the emitter.[27] When we say that Keats had a strong influence on Wilde, what we really mean is that Wilde was an assiduous reader of Keats, an inquisitive reader in the service of an acquisitive writer.

Another setback faced by the charter of influences is that he is always in danger of misconstruing resemblance as dependence and thereby committing the *post hoc* fallacy of assuming that because *b* was written after *a* it must have been written on account of *a*: *post hoc, ergo propter hoc* (a phenomenon vividly illustrated in law-suits involving plagiarism).[28] In any case, causality eludes us in literary matters, for even if we succeed in rounding up all the putative influences on a certain book, we have no way of showing how they acquired the shape they now take: they stand around it, awkwardly, while we talk about 'creative fusions', 'sea-changes', transformations, transmutations, transmogrifications or whatever process-metaphor happens to appeal to us. The truth of the matter is that there is no road to Xanadu. The only connection between 'Kubla Khan' and various phrases from all those travel-books Coleridge undoubtedly looked into is by way of unex-aminable processes hinted at by Livingstone Lowes's imagery of a Jamesian 'deep well of the unconscious' or of Epicurean 'hooked atoms of association'.[29] Somehow, the alleged influences never quite flow into the poem.

Acquaintance with the busier purlieus of influence-scholarship can be an effective deterrent to anybody considering opening up a new suburb. 'After a while', writes Robert Martin Adams, 'the more little guesses we put forward, the less probable any of them looks.'[30] He makes the point in connection with Milton, who is accused of having perforated an incredible number of other men's tanks. Some time ago, Herbert Weisinger reckoned that scholarship devoted to *Paradise lost* had named some two thousand authors to whom Milton was in some way or other indebted, which averages out at roughly one new author for every five lines of the poem.[31] When influence-studies get to this stage, they are patently destructive of their own ambitions.

Now in cases where there is no external testimony (authorial or otherwise) to an influence, the usual procedure is to accumulate internal evidence by juxtaposing parallel texts, the idea being to show that author *b* was dependent on *a* for such and such a word, phrase, image, etc. When George C. Taylor sifted through the 'deadly parallels' listed by readers of Montaigne and Shakespeare,[32] he identified seventy-five different types of so-called evidence used in attempts to prove that Montaigne influenced Shakespeare, much of it trivial and inconsequential in view of the Renaissance fondness for commonplace books, classical dictionaries-cum-encyclopedias, simile-books, volumes of *adagia* and other shortcuts to erudition. The problem is epitomised in G. K. Hunter's analysis of Seneca's alleged influence on Elizabethan drama:

The danger of charting the changes in 'Seneca' as he passes through Dolce or Corraro or Garnier and so reaches England is that elements genuinely Senecan (i.e. characteristically if not uniquely present in Seneca's plays) may cease to be present at all, while elements generally characteristic of late medieval and Renaissance taste (sententiousness, a gloomy sense of overpowering rule by fortune or fate in human affairs, a morbid interest in the limits of human suffering), or indeed characteristic of tragedy as a genre (horror, blood, desolation) come to be labelled 'Senecan' because Seneca also displays them and is thought responsible for the tradition (late medieval tragedy) in which they appear.[33]

Not even the most obvious similarities can ever be taken as incontestable proof that one book derives from another. If Johnson's *Rasselas* and Voltaire's *Candide* had not been published within a few weeks of one another in 1759, 'it would have been in vain' (Johnson told Boswell) 'to deny that the scheme of that which came latest was taken from the other'.[34]

Inventories of books are not much help to the investigator either, since we all own books we haven't read, and may have been profoundly impressed by books we never have occasion to mention (the fact that *Gargantua et Pantagruel* is not referred to in Renaissance discussions of imaginative literature does not mean that nobody read and discussed Rabelais).[35] Conversely, a writer may be influenced in ways not detectable by a parallel-passages approach, as Yeats apparently was by Shelley. So it is sometimes objected that influence-studies have no way of locating truly formative influences, but instead have developed a technique which gives undue prominence to similarities of detail perhaps incidental or irrelevant to the total design. Paradoxically, the most concrete evidence an investigator can display may occur in parallel passages of relative triviality, while a major influence will remain forever inaccessible to such positivistic probes: somehow, the method is strongest at its weakest points.

When the authors concerned are contemporaries, chronology presents further complications. Although we are unlikely ever again to witness anything like the confusion of the early centuries of the Christian era, when pagans and Christians were so struck by similarities in one another's mythologies as to accuse one another of plagiarism,[36] comparative studies of individual authors are not immune to similar hazards. A case in point is the exact relationship between Marlovian passages in Spenser and Spenserian passages in Marlowe.[37] In *Tamburlaine the Great* (1590) there is a passage about

> an almond tree y-mounted high
> Upon the lofty and celestial mount
> Of evergreen Selinus

– which is obviously akin to those lines in *The faerie queene* (also published in 1590) about

> an almond tree y-mounted high
> On top of green Selinus all alone. (I vii 32).

Eliot assumed that Marlowe cribbed the passage from Spenser, and so it became an important piece of evidence for his contention that Marlowe's major achievement was to infuse Spenserian melody into blank verse.[38] The direction of the influence, however, cannot be determined, although biographical information makes it far more likely that Marlowe saw a manuscript of Spenser's poem in London than that Spenser, in distant Ireland, had a preview of Marlowe's first play.

Meanings attached to phrases by one writer may so easily come unstuck when handled by another that the presence of the same phrase in different writers may signify less than the charter of influences might imply by quoting them out of context. When Keats wrote to Shelley advising him to '"load every rift" of [his] subject with ore' he did so without the slightest trace of irony, ignoring the context of moral disapprobation in which the phrase occurs in Spenser's description of the Cave of Mammon:

> Embost with massy gold of glorious gift,
> And with rich metal loaded every rift.[39]

Alert to such 'disjunctions',[40] some critics find it necessary to protect the poetry of William Blake against erudite 'misreadings' by scholars such as Kathleen Raine, who treats Blake as primarily a transmitter of Neoplatonic doctrines. Alleged sources are allowed to dictate what the poems mean, and sometimes inappropriately so. Blake's Oothoon, for instance, who celebrates 'lovely copulation bliss on bliss' in *Visions of the daughters of Albion*, metamorphoses rather oddly into a Plotinian angel when approached by way of her Neoplatonic ancestry.[41] Instances like this lead one to suppose that Blake treated his sources 'negatively'[42] by using traditional materials in untraditional ways and composing poems therefore innocent of traditional meanings. Readers who oppose similar tendencies among Yeats scholars (in the books of F. A. C. Wilson, for instance) take heart from Yeats's own confession that the supernatural beings who dictated *A vision* to him said their purpose was merely to give him 'metaphors for poetry'[43] and not instalments of a mystical philosophy. In Blake as in Yeats, local contexts appear to neutralise Neoplatonic images.

For all their technical shortcomings, however, influence-studies are likely to continue for as long as we go on believing that a historical sense is important to the critical moment, and that the present is intelligible only if conceived of as the product of processes which reach back into the past. 'He to whom the present is the only thing that is present, knows nothing of the age in which he lives', said Wilde. 'To realise the nineteenth century one must realise every century that has preceded it, and that has contributed to its making.'[44] From this historical or diachronic point of view, every y derives from some antecedent x, which makes it impossible to comprehend y without first coming to grips with x. Analysts of original anxiety, who believe we make trouble for ourselves by evading the raw immediacy of the present, will recognise in literary genetics many familiar symptoms of our malaise:

> When have we not preferred some going round
> To going straight to where we are?[45]

For influence-study is the most striking example in literary criticism of rear-vision driving, in which the critic behaves like those 'learned philologists' mocked by William Cowper, who chase

> A panting syllable through time and space,
> Start it at home, and hunt it in the dark,
> To Gaul, to Greece, and into Noah's ark.[46]

Such performances can be dazzling. 'To have no direct acquaintance with the Italian epic when judging Spenser', writes George Steiner, 'to value Pope without a sure grasp of Boileau, to consider the performance of the Victorian novel and of James without a close awareness of Balzac, Stendhal, Flaubert, is to read thinly or falsely.'[47] Anybody robust enough to be merely awed and not paralysed by the one-upmanship displayed here will notice that Steiner's misgivings about the self-explanatoriness of y apparently do not extend to x, in so far as he treats Italian epics, Boileau and Balzac as more immediately accessible than Spenser, Pope and James. If pressed, however, Steiner might say that we cannot value Boileau without a sure grasp of Horace, nor Horace without a sure grasp of Aristotle. Regressive exercises like this are endless and often irrelevant, for the a from which x ultimately derives is unlikely to tell us anything helpful about y. Certainly, as Leo Spitzer notes, the word 'source' no longer seems to mean what it meant in the Reformation ('*e fontibus praedicare*, "to go back to the sources", i.e. to the Bible as God's own word, as opposed to the subsequent alterations introduced by the Church').[48] Perhaps the best answer to rear-vision drivers and originologists was formulated long ago by Horace, when he said that if you want to write about the Trojan War it is not really necessary to begin with Leda's egg (*Ars poetica*, 147). A critic must not only begin but actually stay *in medias res* if he is convinced that what books are made into is more important than what they are made out of, and that good books are those which outgrow the works they grow out of.[49]

Unconscious borrowings and commonplaces

When a writer denies ever having read the texts he is said to have been influenced by, critics seek other explanations for the columns of parallel passages now before them. Forgetfulness may be given as a reason, on the grounds that writers cannot be expected to remember everything they read:

> Oh 'darkly, deeply, beautifully blue',
> As someone somewhere sings about the sky.[50]

The 'someone' Byron fails to recall is Southey, who sings not about the sky but about a dolphin 'in blue ocean seen,/Blue, darkly, deeply, beautifully blue'.[51] When there is no such indication of a conscious lapse of memory, depth psychology is often invoked, and similarities are then 'explained' by the hypothesis that the author of y unconsciously recollected certain passages in x. Phrases or images lodged in a writer's subconscious mind are then thought of as resurfacing in a 'resurgence' which feels like a moment of inspiration.[52] Shelley's recollection of passages from *Measure for measure* in *The Cenci* (1819) are perhaps examples of resurgence in this sense. So too are a few lines in Tennyson's *The princess* (1847):

> A wind arose and rushed upon the South,
> And shook the songs, the whispers, and the shrieks
> Of the wild woods together; and a Voice
> Went with it, 'Follow, follow, thou shalt win.'[53]

This bears more than a chance resemblance to a passage in Shelley's *Prometheus unbound* (1820):

> A wind arose among the pines; it shook
> The clinging music from their boughs, and then
> Low, sweet, faint sounds, like the farewell of ghosts,
> Were heard: 'Oh, follow, follow, follow me!'[54]

When this was pointed out to him, Tennyson (fearing an implication of plagiarism) contented himself with a nothing-new-under-the-sun answer: 'It is scarcely possible for anyone to say or write anything in this late time of the world to which, in the rest of the literature of the world, a parallel could not somewhere be found.'[55] Nevertheless, both passages are so interchangeable in style that Tennyson must here bear the responsibility for being Shelleyan. The theory of unconscious resurgence, although impossible to validate, has an obviously diplomatic usefulness in such cases, for it soothes ruffled consciences by disemburdening the accused of all responsibility for similarities which might otherwise be misconstrued as plagiarism.

Yet there is no need to invoke unconscious resurgence except on behalf of writers who are sensitive to questions of originality, for in *imitatio* conditions similarities are only to be expected. Given the uniformitarian hypothesis that all people are the same, and have only a limited range of experiences available to them between birth and death, it follows that the truly significant

experiences in life will tend to be repeated over and over again
and expressed in pretty much the same ways. 'Writers of all ages
have had the same sentiments, because they have in all ages had
the same objects of speculation,' Johnson concluded.[56] When
Shakespeare wrote Jaques's speech on how 'all the world's a stage'
(*As you like it*, II vii), what was he doing? Did he hit on one of
the great commonplaces of European literature quite independently of anybody else? Or did he consciously select the commonplace and then create the most memorable instance of it?

The first possibility – which amounts to a collectivist theory of
literary influence – is investigated by Ernst Robert Curtius in his
study of *European literature and the Latin Middle Ages* (New York,
1953). Writers are here regarded as being not unlike rhetoricians
in their methods of assembling and presenting their materials.
Ancient rhetoricians who engaged in public disputation were
advised to collect illustrative examples of arguments so that they
would never be at a loss for something to say. What they collected
were known as commonplaces or topics, some of them
undoubtedly commonplace in the sense of being trite, but all of
them *loci communes*. The term Curtius uses for such commonplaces
is *topoi*, and his book is an immensely detailed study of such major
commonplaces of European literature as the Earthly Paradise and
the Book of Nature and many more besides. 'All the world's a
stage' is a *topos* to Curtius, who lists occurrences of *theatrum mundi*
chronologically from Plato to Shakespeare and beyond, by way
of Horace, Seneca, Petronius, St Paul, Clement of Alexandria,
Palladas, Boethius, John of Salisbury, Luther, Ronsard and the
motto on the Globe Theatre (pp. 138–44). From the contiguity
of such isolated examples Curtius creates a theory of literary
continuity which seeks to explain similarities as the result of
conscious imitation of *topoi*.

Predictably, his conclusions have been questioned. He is accused
of having too deterministic a conception of tradition to allow for
the individual talent of individual writers; of having too literary
a conception of tradition to appreciate the importance of popular
and oral contributions; and of ignoring those local contexts which
indicate qualitative differences in successive manifestations of a
certain *topos*.[57] Most damagingly of all, he is said to have mistaken
for a conscious process something which a uniformitarian critic
would recognise as an unconscious and inevitable by-product of
the homogeneity of man. Curtius' *topoi*, Alonso finds, 'are not so
much commonplaces of literature, as commonplaces of life':[58]

what they evidence is not a consciously sustained tradition, but a spontaneous 'polygenesis' which results in the creation of identical things by different people at different times. Some of the best evidence for polygenesis, therefore, is available in studies which explore similarities between cultures known to have had no direct contact with one another until fairly recent times, such as James J. Y Liu's examination of the conventions of poetic drama in *Elizabethan and Yuan* (London, 1955), or V. Krishna Chari's study of decorum as a critical concept in Indian and Western poetics.[59]

The 'Zeitgeist'

The theory of influence envisaged by those who look upon writing as a perpetual reshuffling of *topoi* is historical in dimension and collective in emphasis. For *topoi* are older than the people who use them, and more important than any single manifestation of them: they point not to individuals, but to cultures, and perhaps even to races. Collectivist theories of influence, however, need not necessarily be diachronic in form. We often hear, for example, that writers are more readily influenced by the times in which they live than by specific books or authors from the past – which is again a collectivist theory, only this time synchronic in emphasis. People who believe this tend to think that every age has its own intellectual climate, the effects of which are inescapable. Ideas and attitudes are said to be 'in the air' and consequently find their way into books, whether an author is conscious of them or not. Often a particular mode of writing will develop – what Barthes calls *écriture*[60] – which later generations will recognise as the distinctive style of that period. Earlier critics, more mystical in outlook, see in this process the activities of a 'spirit of the age' or *Zeitgeist* which is immanent in all the most characteristic phenomena of any era. The *Zeitgeist* is responsible for the fact that people who have never read *The interpretation of dreams* (1900) nevertheless know all about Freudian symbols. Writers themselves may foster the superstition. '*Odyssey* very much in the air here', Joyce wrote to his brother from Paris in 1920. 'Anatole France is writing *Le Cyclope*, G. Fauré the musician an opera *Pénélope*. Giraudoux has written *Elpénor* (Paddy Dignam). Guillaume Apollinaire *Les mamelles de Tirésias*.' And there was Joyce writing *Ulysses*: after all, *il faut être de son temps*.[61]

Evoking and assessing the intellectual atmospheres of past ages is an occupation for intellectual barometrists like Basil Willey, whose various background books to the previous three centuries began with an investigation of the ways in which seventeenth-century poetry was 'affected by the contemporary "climates of opinion"'.[62] 'Climate of opinion' has become a somewhat hackneyed phrase since Whitehead put it into general circulation in *Science and the modern world* (1925), after taking it from Joseph Glanvill's *The vanity of dogmatising* (1661). It owes its popularity to the fact that it fulfils the same grand purposes as 'spirit of the age' but sounds more respectable, if only because meteorology is intellectually more respectable than spiritualism. The transcendental theory of a 'spirit of the age' flourished in the nineteenth century, as evidenced in the publication of William Hazlitt's *The spirit of the age* (1825) and *A new spirit of the age* (1844) by R. H. Horne; but it is difficult to trace back the idea much further than Dryden, who observed in 1668 that 'the genius of every age is different'.[63] The *O.E.D.* credits Shelley with the first occurrence of the phrase 'spirit of the age' in a letter of 1820, but the basic idea is already developed in the preface to *Laon and Cythna* (1817), in which Shelley explains why he may not have succeeded in avoiding the literary styles of his contemporaries:

There must be a resemblance which does not depend upon their own will, between all the writers of any particular age. They cannot escape from subjection to a common influence which arises out of an infinite combination of circumstances belonging to the times in which they live, though each is in a degree the author of the very influence by which his being is thus pervaded.[64]

The major English exponent of *Zeitgeist*-theory is Matthew Arnold, whose dependence on it prompted Hugh Kingsmill to caricature him as Don Matthew, 'mounted on Zeit-Geist, a hobby horse'.[65] Arnold himself appears to have come upon the term in Goethe. 'Intellectual ideas, which the majority of men take from the age in which they live, are the dominion of the Time-Spirit', he writes; and because such things are 'in the air' (was Arnold the first to use this phrase?) we are consequently at their mercy.[66] But it does not take very long to realise that a belief in the *Zeitgeist* can be sustained only if one is willing to suffuse the detailed particularities of specific books in a collective haze. Yeats wanted people to think that similarities between his own cyclic theory of history (as set out in the 1925 edition of *A vision*) and the one expounded in Oswald Spengler's *The decline of the west* (translated into English in 1925) were to be explained supernaturally, as though the *Zeitgeist* had given the same inspiration to the pair of them; but in fact, the original German edition of Spengler's book was published in 1918 and provoked such interest that neither Yeats nor the spiritualistic medium he was married to could have remained wholly ignorant of Spengler's general theory.[67]

If the *Zeigeist* exists, then it does so only in the minds of writers and critics who want it to exist, and not as an irresistible and extramundane force. To the writer, it may be a convenient fiction, because it condones failure by encouraging him to believe that conditions are not very propitious for the production of master-pieces. Pound, for instance, when his early poems failed to have the impact expected of them, was able to console himself with the belief that

> The 'age demanded' chiefly a mould in plaster,
> Made with no loss of time,
> A prose kinema, not, not assuredly, alabaster
> Or the 'sculpture' of rhyme.[68]

And it is an even more convenient fiction for critics, simplifying, as it does, the chaos of history into patterns of dominant trends and characteristics. After we have played down the differences between writers in order to emphasise their similarities, it is only too easy to detect the influence of the *Zeitgeist* in their activities. Hence the cogency of George Boas's warning that 'works of art are not expressions of an age; they help make up the age. They are not what they are because of the age; the age is what it is because of them.'[69] There can be no such thing, therefore, as an Augustan 'age' (separate from the people who constitute it) which somehow 'caused' Pope and Johnson and the rest of them to write in an Augustan manner. 'When one is in search of an age', Boas concludes, 'one ends with human beings.'[70] And when one is in search of a literary influence, one ends with a book.

Creative misunderstandings

Freud was puzzled when André Breton told him that Surrealists had derived their theory of automatic writing from Freud's account of the workings of the subconscious mind.[71] As far as he was concerned, Surrealists had completely misunderstood his whole purpose, which was to describe pathological states of mind with a view to curing them, not with a view to enabling so-called creative artists to cultivate them. His private opinion was that the Surrealists were utter fools – the exception being (ironically) Salvador Dali, whose parodies of nineteenth-century academic painting were not parodies to Freud, but technical masterpieces.[72] Consequently, the Surrealists could hardly claim to have understood Freud correctly, in so far as the intentions of the emitter were in this case not consonant with those of the receptors. At the same time, the Surrealists' misunderstanding of Freud was no mere mistake, for it contributed to the formation of a new kind of art, and is therefore described more accurately as a 'creative misunderstanding'.

This is but one of many celebrated instances in which the arts have undergone an important mutation as a result of some fertile misconception. Cubism developed from a misunderstanding of Cézanne, and modern opera from the misconception that ancient Greek drama had been sung. The fertile accident is well enough established among writers to provide the nuclear model for larger misprisions. W. H. Auden, for instance, was pleased when Isherwood misread 'poets' as 'ports' in what afterwards became 'the ports have names for the sea'.[73] Such are the *trouvailles* anticipated by Noel Stock's serious artist, who,

> Composing later, pen in hand
> Imagination fancy free
> Discovers with some slight amendment
> Profundities of poesy.[74]

The term 'creative misunderstanding' is used by Valéry ('rather facetiously perhaps') in his 'Reflections on art' of 1935, although he was already toying with the idea in the 1920s. 'I'm not interested in knowing what the author says', he once wrote. 'My error is the author!'[75] Such misunderstandings are 'more fruitful than if we understood each other perfectly', he told members of the PEN Club in 1925, doubtless to the bewilderment of those who believe that the arts promote international understanding.[76] Misunderstanding Poe was as important an experience to Baudelaire and Valéry as misunderstanding Byron was to Pushkin. The value of technical error is that it releases unpredictable potential, interrupting the slow processes of evolution with a surprising mutation. The biological metaphor is not inept if we accept Bronowski's conclusion that 'the errors that destroy the individual are also the origin of the species'. Cells are obliged to make proteins over and over again from the same blueprint, but cannot do this without making mistakes from time to time; and should the mistake occur in a master molecule, 'it will in its turn cause errors in the making of other copies, and as a result the error will be cumulative'. Life evolves only because of errors in the copy; and but for these errors 'there would be no raw material of genetic mutants for natural selection to work on. There would only be one universal form of life, and however well adapted that might have been in the environment in which it was formed, it would have perished long ago in the first sharp change of climate.'[77]

Similar assumptions appear to underlie the defence of error in the arts. By far the most prolific advocate of the theory of influence as creative misunderstanding is Harold Bloom, who believes that writers misread the past so as to prevent it from becoming burdensome. Ever prone to the astral disease ('Influence is *Influenza*'), they immunise themselves with 'a saving misprision' which enables them to 'overcome the anxieties induced by the glory of their precursors by creatively misinterpreting those Great Originals'.[78] The Romantic tradition from Blake to Hart Crane, as Bloom reads it, is a record of 'creative swerves'.[79] It is an intriguing theory, somewhat overelaborated in *The anxiety of influence* (New York, 1973), but essentially a more faithful account of the young writer's restless and often disingenuous transactions with old masters than we are likely to get from purveyors of parallel passages and their like.

9

Intended meanings

We turn now from assumptions about the structure and genesis of literary works to the third of our main topics, the act of understanding which is prerequisite to literary judgement. How can we be certain that we read correctly, when obviously intelligent readers give conflicting interpretations of the same text, and even cast doubts on the author's ability to know what it means? And how will our judgement be affected if the meaning we arrive at turns out to be unacceptable to other readers? These are problems to be explored in the next three chapters, beginning with the kind of meaning for which a special privilege is claimed because it is the one intended by the author.

The location of intentions

Authorial comments on intentions often appear eccentric. When Johnson says that his intention in writing *Lives of the poets* (1779–81) was 'the promotion of piety', or when Burton says that he wrote *The anatomy of melancholy* (1621) for therapeutic reasons ('one must needs scratch where it itches'), we might well complain of irrelevance, for these are the kind of intentions which concern biographers much more than critics.[1] As such, they can be contested biographically. Did not Johnson write *Lives of the poets* for much the same reason as he compiled his *Dictionary* and edited Shakespeare ('the want of money, which is the only motive to writing that I know of')?[2] It may have been Milton's intention in writing *Paradise lost* either devoutly 'to justify the ways of God to men', or profanely to 'leave something so written to aftertimes, as they should not willingly let it die'.[3] Neither of these intentions, however, is likely to enlighten readers who wonder whether Milton intended to write a poem quite so sceptical of its own doctrines as some critics make it out to be.

If authorial intentions are worth knowing about, where can we find them? Certainly not always in letters, prefaces, diaries, interviews and the like, for the kind of intentions revealed there are likely to be 'purposeful', whereas what we are really in search of is the uniquely 'purposive' intention of each individual work. We seek the intention which is demonstrably 'in' *Paradise lost*, as against all those purposeful intentions which congregate outside it. The distinction now made between purposeful and purposive intentions derives from *A critique of judgement* (1790), where Immanuel Kant argues that there can be 'purposiveness without purpose, so far as we do not place the causes of this form in a will, but yet can only make the explanation of its possibility intelligible to ourselves by deriving it from a will'.[4] The constituent parts of a heterocosm interrelate simply by being in one another's company, and collectively they generate a purposive intention which may not coincide with the purposeful intentions declared by the author: the parts 'intend' their own meaning, no matter what meaning he himself intends. Intentionalists who operate independently of the biographer need concern themselves only with the purposiveness of literature, and feel in no way obliged to square authorial statements about books with the evidence of the books themselves. 'When the work is finished', Wilde observes, 'it has, as it were, an independent life of its own, and may deliver a message far other than that which was put into its lips to say.'[5] Clearly, the idea of purposive intentions is likely to appeal to those who believe that a book is an autonomous heterocosm, containing 'in itself the reason why it is so, and not otherwise',[6] and confidently intending its own meaning. One reason for this is that the art-for-art's sake movement found a stimulus in Kant. Benjamin Constant, for instance, was much taken with Henry Crabb Robinson's work on Kant, especially the idea of '*l'art pour l'art* without purpose, for all purpose perverts art'.[7] Somewhat enigmatically, Constant concludes that 'art attains the purpose that it does not have', which seems another way of saying that art can be purposive without being purposeful.

Because many critics have sensed the distinction which Kant formulates so neatly (without necessarily being aware of Kant's contribution here), various terms have been proposed in the hope of directing intention-seekers away from the author and into his work. Leavis, who believes 'intentions are nothing in art except as realised', has said that 'the deep animating intention (if that is the right word) is something very different from the intention the author would declare'; and Rodway and Lee distinguish a

purposeful 'intention' ('the writer's stated purpose') from a
purposive 'purport' ('the ostensible intention of a work as it
reveals itself to the reader, from the title onwards').[8] Helmut
Hungerland thinks that Alois Riegl's term *Kunstwollen* (introduced
in 1901), which has purposeful and psychological connotations
when translated by Otto Rank as 'will-to-art', refers more
properly to purposiveness, and should be translated therefore as
'artistic intent'.[9] Exactly how we label the distinction is unim-
portant, provided we are able to make it. For it is probable that
much of the critical controversy regarding intentions would never
have occurred if the disputants had been able or willing to
dissociate the purposeful from the purposive. This is not to say
that we should ignore purposeful intentions altogether.

All of this is rather vague, however, for the intentions we hope
to locate in works of literature are no more palpable than those
which earlier critics hoped to locate in authors. Neither sort of
intention leaves a distinctive 'trace'. More recently, however,
attempts have been made to shift the nature of the inquiry away
from books and authors and into language itself. As a result,
'intention' comes to be defined not as a psychological condition
in the writer, nor as an immanent quality in his text, but as a
feature of the linguistic utterances which constitute that text.
Much interest has been aroused by the speech-act theory of
language pioneered by J. L. Austin and developed by John R.
Searle, which defines language as utterance and then classifies
utterances as 'performatives', that is, according to the functions
they perform.[10] To Austin, a performative utterance is a 'locu-
tionary act', and can be one of two basic types: a 'perlocutionary'
act (which achieves what it sets out to do), or an 'illocutionary'
act (which reveals the speaker's attitude towards his utterance).[11]
Austin restricts his inquiries to ordinary language, and has nothing
to say about literary usage. But to a literary critic, his analysis
appears to have an hallucinatory relevance to the way we talk
about books, and therefore interests people who would like to see
literary studies transformed into a science of meanings. Applied
metaphorically to books, Austin's perlocutionary acts constitute
the 'affective' element in literature, and illocutionary acts the
'intentional'. Resemblance, however, is not identity, and the
insights yielded by an illocutionary analysis of ordinary language
are unlikely to be paralleled in the case of literary language, which
contains not utterances but pseudo-utterances. The point is well
made by Graham Hough in connection with Donne's poem, 'Go

and catch a falling star', which amusingly rehearses the conventional complaint that women are fickle. 'The intention to satirise women (because you are indignant at women's frailty)', he notes, 'is not at all the same thing as the intention to write a clever poem satirising women (because you enjoy the literary ingenuity of the performance)'.[12] If poems are not illocutionary acts, but merely imitations of illocutionary acts, the sort of illocutionary analysis which exposes the hidden motives in ordinary language cannot have the same success with literary works. It is not just that Donne's poem is more subtle than the analytic method applied to it, but that we know it to be more subtle, and without benefit of the method. 'To satirise women is the intention of many poems', Hough concludes, but 'to identify this intention cannot tell us much about this particular poem'.[13] What is revealed by an illocutionary analysis of Donne's poem is merely the trace of a pseudo-intention. The intention which led Donne to formulate that pseudo-intention remains obscure.

Intention as a guide to meaning

Even the most straightforward of texts may become enigmatic in tone if the author's intentions are not manifest. Is the writer being serious, we ask, or ironic? Dissenters who read *The shortest way with Dissenters* (1702) denounced it because they did not recognise it as the work of a Dissenter, Daniel Defoe, who was then obliged to publish *A brief explanation* (1703) to the effect that he had intended 'an irony' (whereupon he was imprisoned by anti-Dissenters).[14] What can we do when authorial intentions remain unknown? A definitive interpretation of the last book of *Gulliver's travels* would seem to be out of the question, because we do not know how far Gulliver speaks for Swift, nor what to make of a seemingly false choice between Houyhnhnms and Yahoos.[15] Lacking a purposeful intention, *Gulliver's travels* survives as one of those open-ended texts so much preferred by late twentieth-century critics to closed books with restricted meanings which intentionalism promotes. Another famous example (reported by Beardsley)[16] illustrates very well what can happen when we misjudge the context and so attribute the wrong intentions to the teller. The reader in this case was Frank Harris, and the poem Housman's '1887', written to celebrate Queen Victoria's Jubilee. Harris applauded what he took to be anti-patriotic sentiments in the lines:

> Get you the sons your fathers got,
> And God will save the Queen.[17]

Housman, on the other hand, said that that was not what he meant at all. Was Harris right in standing by what the lines say, rather than what Housman says they say? Seeing that the lines are purposive of the meaning Harris takes from them, his misinterpretation (if that is what it is) must be Housman's responsibility, since it was up to Housman to exercise more vigilance over what he was saying and eliminate such purposive meanings as might embarrass his purposefulness as a patriot. Even so, most readers would find Housman's purposeful intention a more reliable guide to the meaning of '1887' than Harris' interpretation, which focuses perversely on an unintentional meaning.

For as long as we can go on saying that certain meanings are 'unintentional', it will not be possible for us to dispense entirely with purposeful intentions, however troublesome they may prove to formalist critics. We all hope to be understood as having said what we intended to say, and are amused when unintended meanings result from slips of the tongue or ambiguous expressions. We know without being told that *Oh! Calcutta!* connotations were far from Henry Vaughan's mind when he evoked lost childhood with the words, 'How brave a prospect is a bright backside!'[18] And if we choose to ignore the probability that Emily Dickinson is talking about eyes when she celebrates a dying tiger's 'mighty balls', then we do so mischievously, knowing that the writer could not possibly have meant what she seems to say.[19] Tacitly at least, we depend on what we know of Henry Vaughan (seventeenth-century English religious poet) and Emily Dickinson (nineteenth-century American spinster) in order to settle the meanings of 'backside' and 'balls'. Hugh Kenner would say that we are forever making discreet enquiries of this nature in the process of understanding much larger units of meaning. 'It is difficult to discover any objection to a forged Vermeer', he writes,

except that Vermeer did not paint it; to a forged banknote, except that the bank did not issue it; to the *Journal of the plague year*, except that it is not the journal it purports to be, but a fabrication; or to Crusoe's narrative, except that there was no Crusoe. Nor is it easy to decide whether a man who has made a banknote is a government employee, a counterfeiter, or a pop artist, unless we have evidence of how he meant his work to be regarded.[20]

We need to know that some of the more insipid of Blake's *Songs of innocence* were experiments in simplicity, and that the poet who rhymed 'Emily' with 'Ha, Ha, He!' was not as amateurish as he looks.[21] If we were to ignore purposeful intentions, George Watson argues, literary history would become pointless, for it is only by imagining what a writer could possibly have intended (living when he did) that we have any control over possible misreadings of his work.[22] Literary scholarship – especially textual scholarship – is heavily committed to intentionalism, and regards the correction of corrupt texts as an essential step towards the recovery of authorial intentions and therefore of literary meaning.

Intention as a guide to judgement

Purposeful intentions are often called upon as a means of ensuring fairness in judicial criticism, although it is not always recognised that such tolerance is bound to result in the relativistic subversion of judicial procedures. A classic demonstration of judicial intentionalism is to be found in Richard Hurd's 1762 defence of *The faerie queene* on the grounds that Spenser no more intended to write a neoclassical poem than Gothic architects intended to design Grecian buildings: 'Judge of *The faerie queene* by the classic models, and you are shocked with its disorder: consider it with an eye to its Gothic original, and you find it regular.'[23] Here we encounter intentionalism in its most attractive form, with Hurd seemingly the epitome of judicial fairness as he cleverly elaborates a neoclassical argument (memorably expressed by Pope) in order to rout neoclassical objections:

> In every work regard the writer's end,
> Since none can compass more than they intend.[24]

It was in fact Pope himself who said that 'to judge...of Shakespeare by Aristotle's rules is like trying a man by the laws of one country who acted under those of another'.[25]

Judicial intentionalists are prepared to go more than half-way to meet their author, first asking what he set out to do, and then trying to estimate how far he succeeded in achieving his ambition. The fact that we call certain works 'pretentious'[26] must mean that we have some idea (however inadequate) of an intention that has not been made good in the work before us. It is for judicial intentionalists that manifestos are written by authors who believe, as Wordsworth and Coleridge did, that a taste for one's work can be created in advance, and who therefore ignore the rival argument (advanced by Pope) that 'if a book can't answer for itself to the public, 'tis to no sort of purpose for its author to do it'.[27] When the prefatory justification of Davenant's *Gondibert* (1651) appeared in print without the poem itself, a wag wrote:

> A preface to no book, a porch to no house:
> Here is the mountain, but where is the mouse?[28]

But this was a special case, as Davenant himself must have acknowledged, for he was unable to write any more than the first two books of his projected epic. As it now stands, *Gondibert* may well be the earliest English example of the kind of book in which the intention is more impressive than the performance, rather in the way that *Finnegans wake* is more interesting to read about than to read.

Critics of the more antiquarian stretches of English literature often resort to the strategy of consulting putative intentions before commenting upon performances, although in the case of anonymous literature this is by no means easy.[29] Ever ready to compare cheese with butter (as rival versions of milk), historicist critics balk at comparing it with wine, on the grounds that cheese never intended to be wine. A good poem is in these terms one which successfully fulfils its intention, which is all very well until one asks Hirsch's question: 'What difference does it make how well an aim is achieved if it is not a valuable aim?'[30] Hurd's leniency is admirable as an antidote to dogmatism, but it nevertheless paralyses literary judgement. To take into account the purposeful intentions of individual authors before reaching a critical assessment of their work necessarily undermines one's faith in the existence of a comprehensive value-system, for every book comes to constitute a special case requiring special consideration and the waiver of this or that criterion of value.

Objections to intentionalistic arguments

Those who think it pointless to consider purposeful intentions when assessing works of art sometimes do so in the belief that artistic effects are prior to artistic intentions. 'The artist has no idea what the experience is which demands expression until he has expressed it', writes Collingwood.[31] This view of priorities is very much in accord with that of Symbolists who pride themselves on not knowing what they mean until they see what they have said.

A poet may write 'the chestnut's comfortable root', says Auden, and by changing 'comfortable' into 'customary' find himself pleased with something he never intended: 'there is no question of replacing one emotion by another, or of strengthening an emotion, but of discovering what the emotion is'.[32] Here the intention is indeed conterminous with the work, and may continue to be modified as the work grows. 'You write a poem not to say what you think', according to Howard Nemerov, 'but to find out what *it* thinks.'[33] The intention is therefore taken to be a function of the product, rather than an incentive to produce it. Valéry said that if people were to ask what he had wanted to say in a certain poem, he would reply that he 'did not *want to say* but *wanted to make*, and that it was the intention of *making* which *wanted* what [he] *said*'.[34] In other words, Valéry had purposeful intentions to write purposive poems.

Studies of manuscript revisions often support such claims. The intention of Blake's poem 'The tyger', for instance, was evidently uncovered as it was being written, and if the poem is still problematic it is perhaps because Blake never fully discovered what it was intending.[35] We know that the magic casements in Keats's 'Ode to a nightingale' first confronted 'keelless seas' and then 'shipless seas' before finally opening up on 'perilous seas': and here the purposefully privative intention of the poet (as embodied in the suffixes of those provisional adjectives) was obliged to defer finally to the poem's purposively euphonious intention, in so far as a 'perilous' sea is anything but 'peril-less'.[36] The same appears to be true of larger compositional units. To compare novels with notebooks for novels (Dostoevsky's, for instance) is to discover that some of the most striking effects in the finished work are not dwelt upon at all in the notebooks, and were clearly discovered only in the process of writing.[37]

It would appear that writers do not begin with purposeful intentions which are subsequently fulfilled to a greater or lesser degree, but discover something called an intention only in the course of writing, and that this discovered intention is rather more purposive than purposeful. The polar opposite of the Symbolist theory of creation advanced by Auden and Collingwood is the Neoplatonic theory exemplified in the third century by Plotinus, who thought that every artist holds in his head an Idea, a sort of mental blueprint of what it is he wants to do, which he consults all the time he is working.[38] An artifact is said to be finished when it corresponds to this pre-existent Idea, for then the artist knows he has succeeded in achieving what he purposefully intended. 'Construct the whole fabric within the mind's citadel', was Geoffrey of Vinsauf's advice to medieval poets; 'let it exist in the mind before it is on the lips.'[39] Wordsworth said he composed the whole of 'Tintern Abbey' in his head before setting pen to paper; and according to Thackeray, that is how Alexandre Dumas set about writing his novels.[40] Evidently, these are untypical cases. The majority of writers find themselves in agreement with Scott, who said he 'never could lay down a plan – or having laid it down...never could adhere to it' because 'the action of composition always dilated some passages and abridged or omitted others'.[41] But in the Neoplatonic aesthetic, one looks before leaping, thinks before acting, and intends before meaning. On analogy with the *deus artifex*, creative artists are expected to have some prescient awareness of their subsequent creations. The maker who models himself on the Maker, and is a just Prometheus under Jove, is expected to possess Promethean foreknowledge and exercise providential control over all he creates: for does not the name 'Prometheus' mean 'he who knows in advance?'[42] The construction of heterocosms, however, seems to have less in common with Creation than with town-planning, and unforeseen problems have to be dealt with as they crop up, mainly because the best-laid schemes of writers and architects gang aft agley.

The trouble with intentionalistic statements is that they are liable to be made either too soon or too late. Neither forewords nor afterwords yield wholly reliable accounts of what goes on *in medias res*, and we learn to be sceptical of claims made in programmes when attending performances. If the intentionalist statement is premature it may well refer to something the author never got around to achieving. Discrepancies between what we find in *The faerie queene*, and what Spenser's preface to the poem leads us to expect, are easy enough to cope with, because the preface happens to be factually inaccurate and so makes us wary of trusting it absolutely.[43] But intentionalistic prefaces, whether premature or *ex post facto* constructions, may not be so patently unreliable, and if so, they will generate misleading interpretations by readers who try to make the work fit the expressed authorial intentions. 'I do not know who wrote these prefaces', Blake wrote in his copy of Wordsworth's poems: 'they are very mischievous and direct contrary to Wordsworth's own practice.'[44] The same objection can be made to some of Eliot's notes on *The waste land*, especially the one which tells us that the whole poem is written from the point of view of Tiresias ('what Tiresias sees is, in fact, the poem'). To read *The waste land*, however, is to experience a multiplicity of points of view (not unlike the multiplicity of surfaces in a Cubist painting), and to doubt the value of reading it entirely through the eyes of Tiresias. The poem no more manifests a single point of view than a Cubist painting a single perspective.[45]

Obviously, books can depart from intentions as easily as they depart from incepts. Yeats describes how poems prompted by personal anguish would often turn into something quite different as the technical problems they posed became more urgent than the most resolutely purposeful of original intentions: Maud Gonne receded as *The Countess Cathleen* loomed large, just as all politics faded from 'Leda and the swan' as apocalypse came into focus.[46] C. P. Snow may have thought that he 'saw, or felt, or experienced... the outline of the entire *Strangers and brothers* sequence and its inner organisation' in 1935; but it could not have been his intention at that time to write either *The new men* (1954) or *The sleep of reason* (1968), since one is about the atomic bomb which first exploded in 1945, and the other is based on the Moors Murders of 1966.[47] Snow's recollection in 1962 of intentions he had in 1935 seems to be one of those rationalisations after the event whose function is to make the creative process look rather more tidy and controlled than in fact it is. Blake's *Songs of innocence and experience* ('showing the two contrary states of the human soul') was not conceived of as a unity until after *Songs of innocence* had been written, which is why some of the poems of innocence do not quite fit into the scheme subsequently designed for them. In the case of Eliot, *Burnt Norton* (1936) was a poem in its own right before it was chosen to be the first of *Four quartets* (1943), and is rather less schematic than the others because it was not animated originally with the intention which Eliot did not uncover until he was writing what is now the second poem in the sequence, *East Coker* (1940).

Sometimes the expressed intention appears too preposterous to be acceptable. John Wain thinks that Hopkins' theory of 'sprung rhythm' was an *ex post facto* creation, something dreamed up for the benefit of the leading contemporary authority on prosody, Robert Bridges, in the hope of persuading him that every one of Hopkins' amazing poetic effects was systematically calculated.[48] The mischievous iconoclasm of John Donne's youthful *Paradoxes and problems* is not easily reconciled with his later remark that he

designed them as a whetstone of wit. 'If they make you to find
better reasons against them', he told Sir Henry Wotton, 'they do
their office.'[49] And although scholars point out that such an intention is perfectly feasible (for Ortensio Landi makes similar claims
on behalf of his own paradoxes),[50] it is hard to believe that Donne
was only playing the part of devil's advocate in *Paradoxes and
problems*. Yet it sometimes happens that an expressed intention is
signalled flippantly and understood as irony. Nobody believes that
The adventures of Huckleberry Finn (1884) is quite so mindless a book
as Mark Twain makes it out to be, and so nobody takes seriously
his prefatory 'Notice' that 'persons attempting to find a motive
in this narrative will be prosecuted; persons attempting to find a
moral in it will be banished; persons attempting to find a plot in
it will be shot'[51] – unless, perhaps, to wonder whether this is not
a roundabout way of letting us know that this seemingly guileless
novel contains a motive and a moral and a plot.

Books are capable of resisting interpretations put on them by
their authors, and not surprisingly so, for the more autonomous
the heterocosm, the more expressive it will be of its own purposive
intention, and the less tolerant of purposeful violations of its
sovereignty. Robert B. Heilman has drawn attention to discrepancies in *The mayor of Casterbridge* (1886) between the way Hardy's
characters behave and the kind of remarks Hardy makes about
them. Susan Henchard, for instance, is made out to be simple and
dull to the point of stupidity, but tends to behave shrewdly and
resourcefully. It is as if there were two Hardys at work, says
Heilman: one of them tells complex tales for their own sake, while
the other purposefully forces upon us a dour view of oppres-
sive circumstances. Miraculously, *The mayor of Casterbridge* escapes
Hardy's purposeful intention: 'had he actually made his characters
conform to his doctrines, they would hardly have life enough
to survive as long as this'.[52] And of course readers of D. H.
Lawrence soon discover that Lawrence's novels survive as novels
only when the characters in them are able to escape Lawrence's
intentions, as Paul Morel's father escapes them in *Sons and lovers*
(1913) to emerge as a much more sympathetic character than the
Oedipal scheme would allow. 'Never trust the artist', Lawrence
wrote. 'Trust the tale.'[53] And in his case especially we do precisely
that.

There is much to be said, then, on behalf of the view that
intentionalistic statements promote misreadings by encouraging us
to make our experience of the work conform to authorial *obiter*

dicta, and that writers are sometimes too deeply involved in details to comprehend the larger significance of their work. Whatever may be said in defence of Miltonic irony, it is still arguable that certain effects of *Paradise lost* are not wholly consonant with the intentions it proclaims.[54] For although Milton intends us to find Adam weakly uxorious and therefore culpable in falling with Eve, his poem insists that Adam's love for Eve is a noble and positive thing, which makes it emotionally right for him to stand by her as he does in a time of crisis. Here, even more so than in *The mayor of Casterbridge*, we experience a compelling tension between purposeful and purposive claims.

The kind of intentions which come under severe attack in Wimsatt and Beardsley's provocative essay of 1946 on the 'intentional fallacy'[55] are primarily purposeful ones which lead us away from textual certainties into biographical speculations, and so ensnare us in the biographical fallacy. The term 'fallacy' – with its connotations of strictly logical deduction and demonstration – is rather honorific than logical in such contexts;[56] for no matter which side one finds oneself on in the controversy instigated by Wimsatt and Beardsley's essay, there is no doubt that the issue is not nearly so clear-cut as it was made out to be at the time, and that logic has played none too prominent a part in what was mainly a polemical attempt to take the criticism of literature out of the hands of literary historians and biographers and all such people as are allegedly willing to do anything with a text except read it as it stands and judge it accordingly. Yet in 1968, when Wimsatt came to review various objections to their original arguments he concluded that its theoretical basis needed neither revision nor emphasis.[57] Intentionalism is still treated in this retrospective essay as a genetic issue concerning literary processes, and therefore quite irrelevant to literary products, which are what they are regardless of whatever they were intended to be. But the anti-intentionalism which was so very heterodox when it first appeared in the 1940s ('against a background of triumphantly prevalent genetic studies in various modes')[58] fast became a new orthodoxy of a triumphantly prevalent formalism, and is now opposed by critics who claim that the intentional fallacy is itself symptomatic of the formalist mistake of treating literature as something much more pure and autonomous and tidy than it really is. So we now hear about 'the fallacy of the intentional fallacy',[59] and can afford to reconsider the whole problem of intention without having to fear (thanks to the formalist purge of literary studies) that to do so is to risk handing over literature once again to the speculative biographer.

Unconscious intentions

A wise old Yeats concluded that 'man can embody truth but he cannot know it'.[60] Can he therefore create literary effects of which he is equally unconscious? Probably. We know that the painter Henri Rousseau had no intention of becoming a Primitive as he laboured under the handicap of an imperfect technique to produce canvases meant to have a photographic accuracy of detail. Presumably he was sometimes satisfied with what he did, but never consciously intended to produce the starkly candid effects for which his paintings are admired. Literary examples are rather more complicated. If *The turn of the screw* (1898) is not quite the Freudian fantasy which Edmund Wilson made it out to be,[61] it is certainly something more than a run-of-the-mill ghost story. Yet it is clear from the published notebooks that James's conscious intention was to write a ghost story.[62] Did *The turn of the screw* acquire Freudian overtones of which James was unconscious, or did he consciously abandon his original intention in the course of exploring possibilities which make the tale what it now is? 'What Wilson could, and should, have argued', writes Dorothea Krook, 'was that *The turn of the screw* was an example of the triumph of intentions never entertained'.[63] Or again, think of the first part of Richardson's *Pamela* (1740). Did Richardson intend to portray with uncanny accuracy the unconsciously sexual and masochistic fantasies of a teenage girl, or are we to read in all those scenes of predatory sexuality an unconscious revelation of Richardson's own lubriciousness?[64] Whether we find Richardson's intentions conscious or unconscious will depend on whether we choose to regard him as a sophisticated psychologist or as a mere amateur who happened to be present at the birth of the text. The problem is unlikely to be resolved by a close reading of the novel, so dependent are we on our prior assumption about the kind of writer Richardson was. It is indeed disturbing to discover how often our response to literary effects is determined by prior assumptions about whether or not they could have been intended. The assessment of metrical irregularity in the poems of Wyatt, for instance – is it the subtlety of a master prosodist, or the bungling of a beginner[65] – depends largely on whether or not we believe that early sixteenth-century poets would ever have dreamed of departing from standard metrical schemes for special effects.

Although *Moby Dick* (1851) is a novel which sometimes groans under the weight of allegory it trundles along, Melville gave Hawthorne's wife to understand that the allegorical details she was pleased to find in the book had not been put there intentionally:

> Your allusion for example to the 'Spirit Spout' first showed to me that there was a subtle significance in that thing – but I did not, in that case, *mean* it. I had some vague idea while writing it, that the whole book was susceptible of an allegoric construction, and also that *parts* of it were – but the speciality of many of the particular subordinate allegories, were first revealed to me, after reading Mr Hawthorne's letter, which, without citing any particular examples, yet intimated the part-and-parcel allegoricalness of the whole.[66]

What could Melville stand to gain by saying such a thing unless (believe it or not) it happened to be the truth? There is no reason why a mind habituated, as a novelist's is, to those patterning processes which result in form should not achieve such proficiency in its operations as to structure the data it encounters without needing conscious directions to do so. Much of what is said to be 'there' in *Lord of the flies* (1955) was not consciously put there by William Golding, who complains that his novel has been overread.[67] As a novelist of deeply ingrained allegorical habits, however, Golding is in no position to arbitrate on the part-and-parcel allegoricalness of his novel, although it is certainly interesting to learn which meanings he was conscious of and which not. Plausibility is no criterion in such matters. The author of *Lady Chatterley's lover* (1928) tells us that he made Clifford Chatterley a cripple long before he 'recognised that the lameness of Clifford was symbolic of the paralysis, the deeper emotional or passional paralysis, of most men of his sort and class today'.[68] Again, why should we disbelieve this? Why not accept what Lawrence says as true, but with the un-Lawrentian qualification that what a writer does unconsciously he may also do badly?

IO

Apparent meanings

Much of what passes for literary criticism is less concerned with problems of value than with problems of interpretation (hermeneutics). Explicatory rather than judicial in emphasis, it draws attention to meanings overlooked, and corrects other people's so-called misreadings. The aim of such exercises is to transcend the uncertainties generated by conflicting interpretations. Critics who are determined to show us what a book is really about often take a 'monistic' attitude towards meaning, in so far as they believe there is only one correct meaning in any book, and the critic's business is to identify it. But some hermeneutic critics offer their new interpretations not with a view to discrediting the old, but in the hope of revealing further facets of complex works whose purposive intent is to generate many meanings, some of them perhaps mutually contradictory. Such readers take a 'pluralistic' attitude towards meaning, and bring to literature rather different expectations from those of monists, with whose assumptions and methods we now begin.

The monistic theory of meaning

The monistic theory of meaning rests on the hypothesis that although ordinary language itself is ambiguous, literary language is not, because literary language is under the control of an author who makes it mean precisely what he wants it to mean. In its parodic form, this is the attitude of that belatedly medieval nominalist, Humpty Dumpty, who tells Alice:' When I use a word it means just what I choose it to mean – neither more nor less.'[1] And what is true of the word is true of the work to critics of this persuasion. It was Pope who spoke out against those commentators on Homer who 'fancy two meanings for want of knowing one'; and Fielding once wrote that 'when two meanings of a passage can in the least balance our judgements which to prefer, I hold it a matter of unquestionable certainty that neither of them is worth a farthing'.[2] The critical task is made much easier if one can believe that a good writer has a single meaning to communicate, and the skill to communicate it unambiguously.

'The poem is a statement in words about a human experience', writes that most rational of twentieth-century theorists, Yvor Winters.[3] If such an approach might seem feasible in the case of eighteenth-century didactic verse, it would appear to be impossible in the case of deliberately obscure work, but in fact it has been taken to Mallarmé by Robert Greer Cohn, who believes that 'there is only *one* meaning to a Mallarmé poem, or any other authentic poem'.[4] Cohn admits the existence of complexities created by linguistic ambiguity and the presence of possibly unconscious meanings, but is not hindered by them. Adhering to 'the basic condition of *integrity*, or authenticity, or inner harmony', he works to a theory of consonance, according to which the true meaning of a poem is the one which harmonises all available interpretations.

Ways of establishing the correct meaning

Cohn's theory of consonance is but one of several tactics adopted by those who believe they would be failing in their duty as critics, and misrepresenting the authors they discuss, if they were to concede the possibility that literature is fundamentally ambiguous. A common way of eliminating ambiguity and preventing the spread of conflicting interpretations is to try to make the work as a whole mean what the author wants it to mean, making due allowance for the fact that authorial statements about meaning are likely to be intentionalistic in form and therefore open to objections already discussed. This approach to meaning – dispensed with as naive in formalist criticism – is defended at some length by E. D. Hirsch, on the anti-formalist grounds that 'the doctrine of the autonomy of a written text is the doctrine of the indeterminacy of meaning',[5] and that the interpretation of literature must be in some sense the restoration of authorial meaning, however one defines it. This, of course, is roughly what people were inclined to believe before Symbolist poets and formalist critics persuaded them otherwise. When James Bridie was asked what one of his plays was about, he replied: 'How should I know? I am the last person you should ask. I am only the author.'[6] Whether one finds this remark despairingly cynical, or the epitome of critical wisdom, will depend on how far one believes in the semantic autonomy of literary texts.

'The ultimate goal of the hermeneutic process', wrote Wilhelm Dilthey, 'is to understand an author better than he understood himself.'[7] This may look like arrogance, but the ambition is not impossible. 'I did not explain my own meaning so well as you', Pope told Warburton, who had written on Pope's *Essay on man* (1733–34). 'You understand me as well as I do myself, but you express me better than I could express myself.'[8] The supposition that writers themselves are always capable of settling disputes over the interpretation of their own work is neatly parodied in one of Auden's academic graffiti:

> T. S. Eliot is quite at a loss
> When clubwomen bustle across
>   At literary teas
>   Crying:- 'What, if you please,
> Did you mean by *The Mill on the Floss?*'[9]

Eliot himself was unusually vulnerable to inquiries of this sort, although he learned to say that in writing 'three white leopards sat under a juniper tree' he had meant no more than that three white leopards sat under a juniper tree.[10] Conveyed in appropriately bland tones of assurance, such information may have been less vexatious to mid-century inquirers than corresponding replies from a number of other writers, who were never quite sure what it was they meant. 'I have just written a superb poem', Mallarmé once told Heredia, 'but I do not quite know what it means, and I have come to see you so you can explain it to me.'[11] W. B. Yeats, looking hard at 'the bright hearts of those long dead', years after writing these words, had to confess: 'I do not remember what I meant.'[12] When this happens, the author becomes merely another reader of his own work, as Valéry predicted, with no special insight into what he has written. He is therefore not much use to literalists who want to know why the long dead should have *bright* hearts, or why there should be *three* leopards (and white ones at that) under a juniper tree. As merely another reader of his own work, the writer too is capable of responding differently at different times. 'The poem has always meant a great deal to me', Yeats said of 'Cap and bells', 'though... it has not always meant the same thing.'[13] Here the monist needs to be on his guard, for the one person he would like to believe knows best about his own meaning appears to be supporting the pluralists' claim that works

of literature contain many meanings. The monistic answer to this
is to say that what Yeats is talking about here is not 'meaning'
but 'significance': *meaning* is 'what the author meant by his use
of a particular sign sequence', writes Hirsch, whereas *significance*
'names a relationship between that meaning and a person, or a
conception, or a situation'.[14] It was not the meaning of Yeats's
poem which changed, but the significance of that meaning to
Yeats.

Monists who are convinced that the author knows best are
further troubled by the problem of authorial meanings which
appear to be inferior to those preferred by sympathetic and
intelligent readers. 'The reader's interpretation may differ from
the author's and be equally valid', Eliot once wrote: 'it may even
be better.'[15] The problem was well illustrated some years ago in
a series of exchanges about the meaning of the famous prefatory
poem to Blake's *Milton*, especially the lines about 'dark Satanic
mills' and the need to build Jerusalem in England's green and
pleasant land.[16] The authorial meaning here is inaccessible to
readers unacquainted with the rest of Blake's writings, where
'Jerusalem' is not a city but something like 'sexual liberty', and
'mills' symbolise that discursive form of intellect which Blake
identified with Newton and Locke, and loathed. It can be argued,
however, that we make better sense of the poem by ignoring
Blake's private vocabulary, interpreting 'mills' in the industrial
sense, and reading the poem as an indictment of the Industrial
Revolution.[17] Or again, consider that little song of experience in
which Blake contrasts a clod of clay (much trampled upon, but
willing to make a heaven out of existential hell) with a pebble
which 'builds a hell in heaven's despite'.[18] Should we read this
poem as a Christian parable concerning the moral superiority of
clods, or should we read it in the private 'infernal' sense it acquires
in the context of Blake's *Proverbs of Hell* or *Urizen*, and conclude
that 'value resides with the Pebble, who makes a revolutionary
hell out of heaven, not with the Urizenic Clod, who makes a
conventional heaven out of hell?'[19]

Here indeed the evidence suggests a plurality of meanings. Once
again, Hirsch intercedes with characteristic subtlety to distinguish
'textual meaning' from 'meaning experience' before opposing the
idea of equating the 'best' reading with the correct one, on the
grounds that the preferred reading may not be the author's.[20] We
would all like to believe that Nashe's most exquisite lyric begins
with the words, 'Brightness falls from the air'; but reluctantly we

have to settle for an inferior meaning-experience if we are to accept the textual meaning enforced by McKerrow's emendation of 'air' to 'hair' ('which gives a more obvious, but far inferior, sense').[21] In these terms, a meaning-experience which does not coincide with a textual meaning is necessarily erroneous, and of no interest except to such people as prefer their own misreadings to the poems actually written by Nashe and Blake.

Accurate texts are essential to monists. 'A knowledge of the true text is the basis of all criticism', Greg wrote, 'and textual criticism is thus the root from which all literary science grows.'[22] Editors such as A. E. Housman believe that there is only one correct solution to a textual crux, and that this can be arrived at by a thorough study of textual transmission from the author's manuscript to the printed copy. Textual scholars like to believe that their work is wholly restitutional, and that in emending texts they are simply removing errors introduced accidentally by printers or wilfully by unscrupulous earlier editors – errors which (to the amusement of Fredson Bowers and associate bibliographers) are sometimes admired by textually naive critics.[23] Every editor is bound to admit, however, that his text is the result of editorial decisions which, though consistent with one another, may not coincide with what the author himself actually wrote. Textual scholarship received a slight jolt only a few years ago with the discovery that the sole surviving holograph of a poem by John Donne is textually so different from what scholars have come to expect that it might have been 'rejected...as worthless testimony' (according to A. J. Smith) 'were it not indisputably in the author's hand'.[24] Monists must therefore hope that their editor has not unwittingly remodelled the text by projecting on to it his own meaning-experiences in the form of editorial emendations.

Once the monist has acquired a correct text, he can then support his interpretation of it by appeals to semantics, in accordance with Geoffrey Tillotson's view that 'the original meaning of a word in a great poem is the only one worth attending to', and that 'to read later emotions here and there into a poem is a tedious error in criticism'.[25] History, therefore, determines meaning, and the original meaning of a work is its proper meaning for all time. Anything else is a mere interpretation. You can talk about racism in *Othello* if you like, or study *The tempest* for insights into colonialism, but on the clear understanding that such interpretations are quite irrelevant to the meaning of either play, controlled as it is by the Renaissance meanings of the words which constitute it. The key to meaning is therefore philology, in the broader sense understood by Leo Spitzer: 'the modern commentator is enabled, by his training and studiousness, to approximate and, perhaps, restore the original "meaning" of a work of art composed at another time and place'.[26] Monists advise us to treat with caution any seemingly modern element in older literature. So when Sidney's Astrophil is told by his Muse to 'look in [his] heart and write', we are directed to suppress romantic connotations of the phrase and remember that '"heart" refers to the mind in general, the seat of all the faculties' (and that what Astrophil might expect to see on looking into his heart is made clear in a later poem by Thomas Carew:

> Rip up my heart, oh then I fear
> The world will see thy picture there).[27]

Unwisely mistaking the 'usages' listed in the *O.E.D.* for 'meanings', a monist often imagines contemporary reactions to a play, telling us (for instance) what a Jacobean audience would have thought of *Measure for measure*. The original answer to Shylock's 'If you prick us, do we not bleed?' would have been a resounding 'No!' thinks George Boas.[28] After Auschwitz, gentile guilt makes us flinch at the probability, and so the scholar's 'construct audience' enables us to get things in their proper perspective. 'The meaning of a poem', F. W. Bateson argues, 'is the meaning that it had for the ideal representatives of those contemporaries of the poet to whom the poem, implicitly or explicitly, was originally addressed.'[29] Background books which introduce us to abstractions like 'the Elizabethan World Picture' set out with the laudable ambition of assembling the commonplaces from which a truly distinguished mind will invariably depart, but may end up promoting the most crippling kind of antiquarianism. For they encourage the placing of any book at the apex of some pyramidal 'age', such that the range of meanings possible in the apex is controlled by the range of meanings permitted in the base. In this way, any interpretation of Hamlet's state of mind is suspect if it ignores Renaissance opinions on melancholy. Such a procedure is open to serious objections. In the first place, it can be argued that the opinions of any writer's contemporaries are largely irrelevant, because his true audience is always an ideal one. 'The reader addressed, or the listeners urged to "heed well"', Alice S. Miskimin observes of Chaucer, 'are reflexive of the speaker and imagined by the poet as the third dimension of the fiction.'[30] To mistake the inhabitants of fourteenth-century England for the imaginary audience addressed in Chaucer's poems is therefore as erroneous as to confuse Chaucer with the 'Chaucer' who appears in The Canterbury tales. Secondly, the 'construct audience' theory invites the objection that any literary work which is capable of speaking to people outside the situation in which it was originally produced cannot be constrained by that situation.[31] Shakespeare's plays, as Wilson Knight has laboured to show, transcend the age in which they appeared: suspended from their apices, they are very much more than projections from some hypothetically Renaissance base. Thirdly, the work of any writer who finds himself opposed to contemporary fashions is unlikely to be illuminated by contemporary opinion. 'To include me in an anthology of the Nineties', Housman once wrote, 'would be just as technically correct, and just as technically inappropriate, as to include Lot in a book on Sodomites.'[32] As the published correspondence of Henry James and H. G. Wells reveals, even highly intelligent contemporaries are quite capable of misunderstanding one another.[33] 'To imagine what [Blake's] poetry would have meant to his contemporaries', writes Theodore M. Gang, 'we should have to ask ourselves what it would have signified to a man in every way like Blake.'[34]

In short, the monistic approach to meaning aims at stabilising literary interpretation. It is understandably obnoxious to pluralists, who see no reason for proscribing the variety of meaning-experiences in the interests of something as arbitrary as an allegedly correct meaning which imprisons a book forever in the historical moment of its creation, and denies authors the opportunity to speak to any but their own contemporaries without the mediation of historical scholarship. 'The words of a dead man / Are modified in the guts of the living', writes Auden in his elegy on Yeats.[35] And if this is how our classics survive, we need a more dynamic theory of meaning than the monist is prepared to allow us.

The pluralistic theory of meaning

Ordinary language is said to be 'polysemous' because it enables several meanings to be present at the same time. Ambiguities occur mainly at the lexical level, partly because of homophones ('right' and 'write'), and partly because of homonyms ('my right' may be something I am entitled to, or the opposite side to my left).[36]

Whether this seems a good thing or not depends on whether one wants to use language for analytic or evocative purposes. Traditionally, philosophers have treated ambiguity as a disease of language: 'the imperfection of words', Locke declared, 'is the doubtfulness of their signification'.[37] Poets, on the other hand, look upon ambiguity as a usefully expressive device for evoking the ambivalence of human experience. What hinders the philosopher actually helps the poet, who can capitalise on the 'weaknesses' of his medium instead of trying to eradicate them.

What semantics is to the monist, ambiguity is to the pluralist, especially in the wake of William Empson's *Seven types of ambiguity* (London, 1930), which shows time and again that the glory of words is the doubtfulness of their signification. Empson is accused of many academic sins, ranging from over-ingeniousness in unravelling ambiguities of his own devising from inaccurate texts, to an arbitrary and apocalyptic choice of categories; and from having a philosophically untenable conception of ambiguity, to displaying an unhistorical concern with 'amphibolies' (that is, the use of an unrepeated word in at least two senses, as in a *double entendre*).[38] But taking all this into account, there is no doubt that a copy of Empson's book (suitably re-titled '*N*' *types of plurisignation*, to quieten one sort of objector) can do more than any comparable study to convince one of the sheer unlikelihood that any work of literature can have one meaning and one meaning only. To a pluralist, the nuclear model for literature is not the clear and distinct axiom but the open-ended aphorism which may mean different things to different people at different times.

An eloquent statement of the pluralist point of view is to be found in Shelley's *Defence of poetry* (1820), with its transcendental theory that great poetry is 'infinite' and therefore inexhaustible in meaning:

Veil after veil may be undrawn, and the inmost naked beauty of the meaning never exposed. A great poem is a fountain for ever overflowing with the waters of wisdom and delight; and after one person and one age has exhausted all its divine effluence which their peculiar relations enable them to share, another and yet another succeeds, and new relations are ever developed, the source of an unforeseen and unconceived delight.[39]

Looked at from this perspective, *Hamlet* is not a play exceptionally vulnerable to the meaning-experiences of egocentric readers, but rather a cornucopia of inexhaustible meanings. The immense body of commentary it has attracted proves that *Hamlet*, like all masterpieces, is polysemous.

'The meaning of the poem as a whole', writes Eliot, in a Shelleyan moment, 'is not exhausted by any explanation, for the meaning is what the poem means to different sensitive readers.'[40] Generalising from such statements, Wellek and Warren define 'the total meaning of a work of art' as 'a process of accretion, i.e. the history of its criticism by its many readers in many ages'.[41] Meanings accrue to literary works over the years. 'All the connotations that can be found to fit are to be attributed to the poem', writes Beardsley: 'it means all it *can* mean, so to speak.'[42] Authors themselves are sometimes reluctant to comment on the meaning of their work for fear of inhibiting speculation or circumscribing the infinite. 'If an author interprets a poem of his own he limits its suggestibility', said Yeats.[43] 'My verses have the meaning attributed to them', said Valéry, who even attended Gustave Cohen's lecture on 'Le cimetière marin' to learn more about a poem he himself had written.[44] Unlike Eliot, Valéry was never placed in the position of having objectionable meanings attributed to his poems; for Eliot's permissiveness with regard to interpretation came abruptly to an end with the publication of John Peter's reading of *The waste land* as a poem about homosexual love.[45] All meanings are permissible except impermissible meanings. 'Whatever good meanings are in the book', Lewis Carroll once remarked of *The hunting of the Snark*, 'I'm glad to accept as the meaning of the book'.[46] 'Bad' meanings, like Empson's Freudian reading of *Alice in Wonderland*, are another matter altogether.[47] Clearly, infinity is not without its hazards, but writers who pride themselves on being able to say more than they intend cannot justifiably object to the revelation of meanings they find offensive.

Meaning as projection

It is sometimes said that what enables a writer to lay claim to more meanings than he is aware of is the complicity of readers who attribute such meanings to his work. The pluralities of meaning do not 'inhere' in the text but are 'projected' on to it by readers:

> The only meaning inherent in things
> Is that there is no meaning inherent in things.[48]

To read alertly involves projecting on to the text one interpretation after another, each of which has to be modified by unpredictable elements in the text.[49] Projections are necessary because (in a more literal sense than perhaps Gide intended),[50] books supply answers to questions not yet formulated, and a critic is judged by the acuteness of the questions he asks of the works he confronts. Studies in the psychology of perception demonstrate conclusively that we think before we see. What Ruskin knew as the 'innocent eye' is in fact no such thing, and if it were, it would see nothing: for every act of perception is the result of certain problem-solving activities discussed by R. L. Gregory in *The intelligent eye* (London, 1970). E. H. Gombrich applies similar findings to the visual arts in *Art and illusion* (London, 1960), and Gombrich's approach is directed towards literary studies by Geoffrey N. Leech in *A linguistic guide to English poetry* (London, 1969). Theoretically, a wild hypothesis will always be falsified by recalcitrant data in the work it is supposed to explain. We all know from personal experience, however, the difficulty of surrendering a hypothesis we have grown fond of. Corroborative 'evidence' emerges all too easily, as A. C. Hamilton amusingly illustrates in his mock interpretation of the opening book of *The faerie queene* (1590), in which a proletarian Red Cross Knight manages to slay the dragon of Capitalism with the aid of the Spirit of Communism (Una) and a Comintern agent called Arthur.[51] Hamilton's interpretation fits the poem as closely as some other 'straight' readings which uncover a detailed allegorical treatment of the Reformation and its aftermath; and it exposes the pointlessness of circular explanations in which the 'facts' are constituted by the hypothesis which seeks to explain them. At the same time, it has to be admitted that a contemporary of Spenser's would have found Hamilton's interpretation less absurd than he intended it to be.[52] For anybody who can bring himself to believe that The Revelation of St John is a Protestant Apocalypse (which is what Reformation polemicists believed, Spenser among them) is unlikely to find it wholly improbable that a text written in 1590 could glance at greater matters over three centuries later, and in another country.

To judge from comments made by Sandys on Ovid, and by Harington on Ariosto, it did not much matter to Elizabethan readers whether an author had actually put into his work the meanings one took out of it, provided such meanings were felt to be in some way 'appropriate'.[53] Modern explicators, on the other hand, know how very easily a 'projective' explanation can become a pseudo-creative activity, in which the meaning taken out of a book is more important to the taker than any meaning put into it by the author. The reader then becomes a secondary creator of 'deutero-creations', as Geoffrey Hartman calls them;[54] in more down-to-earth terms, a manufacturer rather than a consumer of meanings.

In a sense, this is always the case, if we think of the words which make up the sentences, the sentences the paragraphs, the paragraphs the chapters, and the chapters the book, as discrete fragments in need of assembly by those skilled operators we call competent readers. Some literary forms, such as the essay, are designedly pieces of unfinished business: two early essayists, Robert Johnson (1601) and William Mason (1621), actually subtitled their books 'imperfect offers', in the Shakespearian expectation of attracting readers willing to piece out such imperfections with their thoughts.[55] It is a notably Protestant activity, as Rosalie L. Colie observes, 'to call upon a reader's ever-revived capacity to contribute to his own revelation'.[56] It is a much less cerebral activity than might appear, for affectivist versions of the theory turn up in the literature of sensibility. 'A true feeler always brings half the entertainment along with him', Sterne wrote in 1768. 'His own ideas are only called forth by what he reads, and the vibrations within, so entirely correspond with those excited, 'tis like reading *himself* and not the *book*.'[57] The word 'reader' (with its associations of arm-chair passivity) seems less than adequate in such circumstances, which is why Norman N. Holland suggests we use the term 'literent' (meaning 'one who responds to – re-creates – literature') and the analogous forms 'novelent', 'dramatent', 'poetent', and so forth.[58]

The rival view has always been that any writer who solicits our assistance is simply shirking his duty – 'trying to make us imagine for him', as Virginia Woolf said damningly of Arnold Bennett.[59] The shift of emphasis in modernist writing from art-as-product to art-as-process has forced readers to work much harder than they used to, because poems or stories are often so fragmentary that we cannot avoid being forced into the role of deutero-creators. 'The author today proclaims his absolute need of the reader's cooperation, and active, conscious, *creative* assistance', writes Robbe-Grillet. 'What he asks of him is no longer to receive a ready-made world completed, full, closed upon itself, but on the contrary to participate in a creation, to invent in his turn the work – and the world – and thus to learn to invent his own life.'[60] Art of this kind holds up the mirror to the audience in a new way, and subsequent performances are as good or as bad as we ourselves make them. Value judgements are pointless, because no two people reconstruct the work in the same way, which means that everybody ends up talking about a construct of his own invention.

Tendencies so often deplored in literary criticism nowadays are clearly in line with redefinitions of the consumer's role in process-art. Saul Bellow complained some years ago that professors of literature 'are not interested in poetry but only in what can be said about it', and that they treat books as raw materials in the manufacture of a much more precious commodity, critical discourse.[61] It is true that the most ambitious achievement of the deutero-creator (Wilde's 'critic as artist') is to make criticism an end in itself. Instead of dissipating his energies in explaining and evaluating other people's books, he uses them as ingredients in a system of his own devising, as Northrop Frye does in his dazzling display of the metacritic as artist, *Anatomy of criticism* (Princeton, 1957), a book which attempts to treat the whole of literature as a coherent system in which everything has its place.

The more moderate position is to concede that although the business of interpretation is beset with difficulties, it is worth persevering with. Identifying a meaning does not call for quite the precision a monist seems to expect. Meaning is 'like the square root of two or like pi', writes Wimsatt: 'criticism of poetry is like 1.414 or 3.1416, not all it would be, yet all that can be had and very useful'.[62] It can be conceived of as a calculus of variables, rather in the manner of I. A. Richards' four-point tension between sense, feeling, tone and intention.[63] But if meaning is in the eye of the beholder, it is surely much less so in literature than in the visual arts, because words are referentially much more specific than shapes and colours. Somewhere between the extremes marked out by the meticulous monist and the self-indulgent deutero-creator stands the ideal reader Saul Bellow would like to write for, who is gifted not with 'perfect understanding, which is Cartesian' but 'approximate understanding, which is Jewish'.[64] Although books clearly have 'meaning' rather than 'a meaning', we must agree with Sheila Dawson that some interpretations are 'permanent *im*possibilities', and that 'there is a limited range of possible meanings even though there is not one cut-and-dried *correct* meaning'.[65] This being the case, we are perhaps better employed in working out hierarchies of probability among the meanings we identify than in constructing elimination procedures in the hope of reaching some chimerical state of correctness in our interpretations.

The irrelevance of meaning

Playing around with a calculus of variables or a hierarchy of probabilities is not everybody's idea of a worthwhile response to literature. And indeed if we find ourselves impatient with the minuter discriminations and apparent hair-splitting which form the staple of hermeneutic criticism, we may well wish ourselves rid of the problem of meaning altogether. In this we are encouraged by attempts on the part of various writers since the late nineteenth century to liberate language from its bondage to meaning by developing it in the direction of non-discursive modes, such as music or abstract painting. The shift from language-as-lens to language-as-texture (in the interests of creating an autonomous world of words which refer to nothing outside themselves) encourages belief in the possibility of a verbal language which has objective existence but no meaning. Words on the page then become things, patterned things, whose only purpose is to be what they are, as they are: 'A poem' (in Archibald MacLeish's aphorism) 'should not mean/But be'.[66] The Dadaist 'sound-poem' (Lautgedicht) was an early attempt by a group of multi-national emigrés to create an international poetry free of meaning; and the more recent Orghast experiment, in which actors were invited to fit vowels of their own choice to consonants supplied by Ted Hughes, was a deliberate attempt to bypass 'semantic athleticism' by showing that 'the sound of the human voice, as opposed to language, is capable of projecting very complicated mental states'.[67] In such experiments, language is guided towards music in its flight from meaning. And when language is pushed the other way, in the direction of the visual arts, the result is concrete poetry, in which words are uprooted from their semantic contexts and presented as typographical objects, bold and enig-matic 'presences' which mean nothing and solicit no interpretation (although by no means safe from the attentions of deutero-creators ever ready to piece out presumed imperfections with their thoughts). 'A poem need not have a meaning', writes Wallace Stevens, 'and like most things in nature often does not have.'[68] He has in mind an analogy between poetry and modern non-representational art. 'Picasso expresses surprise', he notes, 'that people should ask what a picture means and says that pictures are not intended to have meanings. This explains everything.'[69] Does it really? Most readers would be reluctant to surrender meaning so easily, and would agree with Graham Hough that 'it is only through its meaning that a poem can be at all'.[70] From this perspective, concrete poetry is not poetry but graphic design, and sound-poems are musak.

Those who accept the Absurdist premise that life itself is meaningless might be supposed sympathetic to a literature which tries to get beyond meaning, and come mimetically close to life conceived of in Absurdist terms. Purists, however, suspect that even the Absurd is a compromising doctrine, in so far as to believe in the meaninglessness of everything is to make a meaning of meaninglessness and so evade the essential bleakness of things.[71] 'The world is neither significant nor absurd', Robbe-Grillet finds. 'It simply *is*.'[72] Sections of his novels attempt to replicate is-ness without veering off into the twin evasions of explanation or speculation, because that is how things are. When 'presentation' supplants 'representation', the old representational characteristics have to be dispensed with to allow for the emergence of what Ronald Sukenick calls 'bossanovan' fictions, which have 'no plot, no story, no character, no chronological sequence, no verisimilitude, no imitation, no allegory, no symbolism, no subject matter, no "meaning"'.[73] They aspire to be things-in-the-world rather than comments upon it. 'None of us confronted with a frog, the Crab Nebula, or plankton, can say what it means', writes Paul West. 'We are here to witness, not interpret.'[74] Concrete poems exist to be witnessed, not interpreted, and therefore call for a new kind of criticism fully emancipated from its traditional concern with meaning. And those most alert to this problem would like to see the new criticism-without-meanings applied to the whole of literature, and not just to that relatively small part of it which is designedly meaningless. 'The function of criticism should be to show *how it is what it is*, even *that it is what it is*, rather than to show what it means', writes Susan Sontag. 'In place of a hermeneutics we need an erotics of art.'[75]

Perhaps so, and tentative moves in that direction have been made by Roland Barthes in *Le plaisir du texte* (Paris, 1973). But by far the most striking manifestation of the flight from meaning and its interminable wrangles over points of interpretation has been the emergence of a structuralist approach to literature, promoted by theorists who hope to develop a kind of 'descriptive' criticism along the lines of descriptive linguistics as developed by

Ferdinand de Saussure. 'The critic is not responsible for reconstructing the work's message', says Roland Barthes, 'but only its system, just as the linguist is not responsible for deciphering the sentence's meaning but for establishing the formal structure which permits this meaning to be transmitted.'[76] The structuralists' decision to ignore the meanings of individual books, and to concentrate instead on the rules of the literary 'system' which enables meaning to be communicated, indicates their ambition to move literary study in the direction of the sciences by giving it as firm a methodological foundation as descriptive linguistics. In a typically 'systemic' analysis, linguistic terms are applied metaphorically to literary texts, on the grounds that because literature is made out of language, any key which unlocks the secrets of language will also unlock the secrets of literature. The metalanguages developed by descriptive linguists accordingly become the meta-metalanguages of literary structuralists, and this one of the reasons why reading systemic criticism can be as arduous an activity as the writing of it. Methodologically, structuralists have a right to insist that the semantic component in a text is not especially privileged,[77] although to devise a type of literary study which plays down the importance of meaning must strike the average reader as being as perverse an achievement as a music criticism based on the premise that audibility is not a privileged component. For as long as understanding continues to play an important part in our reading experience, we shall have to go on concerning ourselves with hermeneutic problems.

II

Truth and credibility

Writers as liars

What Plato was already calling 'the long-standing quarrel between poetry and philosophy' (*Republic*, x 606) is still with us, and concerns the truth-claims made on behalf of imaginative literature. Are its meanings (so difficult to determine) really worth having, when much more reliable modes of cognition are available? Plato was inclined to think not, and favoured Socratic dialectic as an alternative. His remedy was new, although his diagnosis was not, because opposition to the unveraciousness of imaginative literature is recorded as early as the sixth century BC, when Solon complained that poets tell many lies.[1] So began the durable slander that poets are 'liars by profession', in David Hume's phrase.[2] What was thought to make their mendacities exceptionally dangerous was that poets, by their suasive skills, manage to disguise untruths as truths and so corrupt the unsuspecting. Poetic lies are insidious because 'verisimilar': 'lies that resemble truth' (*Odyssey*, XIX 203). Tradition lays the blame partly on poets themselves and partly on their Muses, who warned Hesiod that the truths they dispense are mingled sometimes with 'lies which counterfeit true speech' (*Theogony*, 22–23). The result may be something like Shakespeare's history plays, which present a Tudor view of Tudor history so compellingly that efforts by historians to correct such a bias meet with popular resistance. For hundreds of years, readers were willing to be teased with the Senecan tag with which George Crabbe prefaces one of his poems: 'mingling the false with the true'.[3] Even to Dante, allegorical poetry was a 'beautiful lie'.[4] Consequently, one of the traditional tasks for defenders of poetry is to show that its beauties outweigh its lies, a task which involves rehearsing many of the arguments assembled by Boccaccio in that section of his *Genealogia deorum gentilium* subtitled 'Poets are not liars'.[5]

The literary activities of imaginative writers were sanctioned traditionally by what came to be known as 'poetic licence', a carte blanche which disemburdens the professional tale-teller of that fidelity to the way things are (or were) which characterises the historian. In comparison with history, said Lucian, 'poetry enjoys unqualified freedom' because 'its sole law is the poet's will'.[6] So although the Younger Pliny had to admit that poets are notorious liars, he was obliged to add that they are in a sense licensed to lie (*poetis mentiri licet*), licensed to produce what Huckleberry Finn called 'stretchers'.[7] As long as the Christy Mahons of this world can be made to remember that 'there's a great gap between a gallous story and a dirty deed',[8] there will always be room for the enjoyment of gallows stories as tall tales, the taller the better.

Poets had much more freedom than orators. Cicero might legislate what was and what was not permissible in public disputations, but saw no way of controlling 'the freer utterances of the poet's licence'; and subsequently Dryden was to deplore the nonsense written in the name of what Ovid called 'creative licence' (*fecunda licentia*).[9] Like any other form of discourse, poetic lying developed its characteristic figures of rhetoric: hyperbole for exaggeration, litotes for understatement, irony for saying the opposite of what is meant, and so on.[10] In addition, exigencies of form (such as rhyme and metre) frustrate truth-telling ambitions. Joseph Spence, for instance, complained in 1755 about the way poets intermingle Biblical and pagan materials, 'just as the humour takes, or as the verse demands. If two syllables are wanting, it is Satan; but if four, you are sure of meeting with Tisiphone.'[11] If Spence's religious objection anticipates Johnson's strictures on *Lycidas*, his technical explanation of how such iniquities come about is reminiscent of a passage in Quevedo's 'Complaint of the poets in Hell':

> Oh, this damned trade of versifying
> Has brought us all to Hell for lying!
> For writing what we do not think,
> Merely to hear the verse cry clink;
> For rather than abuse the metre,
> Black shall be white, Paul shall be Peter.[12]

Here the literary medium itself is suspected of sabotaging truth by making exorbitantly formal demands on expression. And there is always the possibility that much larger units of meaning are at the mercy of formal restraints. Racine would have changed

Phèdre's character, Valéry told Gide, rather than write a bad
line.[13]

This can be so dispiriting an experience to those obsessed with
truth-telling as to tempt them to follow Laura Riding's example
and give up writing altogether, on the grounds that the 'inveterate
unveraciousness' of poetry as a verbal medium makes it totally
unsuitable for the production of 'simulacra of truth'.[14] For some
thirty years Laura Riding did what she could to prevent the spread
of untruth in the world by refusing permission to reprint her
poems; and when she finally relented and allowed a small selection
of her poems to be republished, it was only with the intransigent
reminder that 'truth begins where poetry ends'.[15]

Facts and fictions

A familiarity with literary biography reveals that if writers are
neither more nor less untruthful than non-writers, they certainly
lie more impressively, and sometimes (like Ford Madox Ford)
pathologically.[16] Do writers become liars as a result of spending
their lives making up stories, or are they liars by nature (like Keith
Waterhouse's Billy Liar) who avoid more obviously criminal
careers by writing fiction? To talk about authors in such terms is
to assume that a book is true if it 'corresponds' to things in the
world, past or present. Implicitly, novelists are compared to
historians, whose ability to reconstruct events that actually happened set them apart in ancient times from dramatists or novelists,
who dwell upon purely imaginary matters; briefly, historians deal
in facts, which are true, whereas poets market fictions, which are
not. The defence of poetry, therefore, becomes a defence of fiction
against fact. 'What is in question is not man's right to sing', notes
C. S. Lewis, explaining the origin of formal defences of poetry,
'but his right to feign, to make things up.'[17] This is why Scott
could think of historical novels as mere enticements to study the
'real' history on which they were based.[18]

When writers themselves come to believe that the only kind
of truth which really matters is truth-of-correspondence, various
tactics are tried in the hope of closing the gap between historical
fact and poetic fiction. Time after time, Daniel Defoe demonstrated
that the authenticity laid claim to by historians is a verbal illusion
easily counterfeited and capable of being applied to wholly
imaginary events. Nothing then separates history from fiction
except the writer's intention, especially if the first-person singular

is employed to vivify an eye-witness account. *Robinson Crusoe* (1719) and *A journal of the plague year* (1722) at first looked too authentic not to be true; *Memoirs of a cavalier* (1720) was not proven conclusively to be fictitious until 1961; and *A true relation of the apparition of one Mrs Veal* (1706) was first taken to be fact, then as fiction (the first English ghost-story), and is now regarded as a factual report of allegedly psychic phenomena.[19] 'The counter-feit', Hugh Kenner points out in a brilliant book on such problems, 'does not claim a reality it does not possess, but only an origin – that is, an authorisation.'[20] It is relatively easy to fake the kind of authorisation we associate with historical documents or historical writings (whose correspondence with reality is in any case problematic), because both are verbal in form, like a fictitious memoir, and therefore only an account of things, and not the things themselves.

But why bother to fake a document when historical documents are so readily available? Why invent an imaginary nuclear scientist with imaginary moral qualms about military abuses of his research when the records of an actual case are there for the taking? *Le dossier Oppenheimer* (1964), by Jean Vilar, is a 'document-play' which takes its materials directly from transcripts made at Oppen-heimer's trial in 1954 before the Personal Security Board in Washington, and thus disables the old objection that imaginative works are untrue.[21] In a similar spirit, Peter Weiss condensed *The inquiry* (1965) from transcripts of the 1964 trial of former Auschwitz officials; and Rudolph Hochhuth wrote *The deputy* (1966) on the ambiguous role of the papacy during the Second World War. A related phenomenon is what Truman Capote has called the 'non-fiction novel', of which his own book *In cold blood* (London, 1966) is a well-known example, although one could find earlier experiments *avant la lettre* in this mode, such as Ernest Hemingway's *Green hills of Africa* (New York, 1935). Norman Mailer's account of the 1967 march on the Pentagon by protesters against American involvement in the war in Vietnam, *The armies of the night* (New York, 1968), is subtitled 'History as a novel, novel as history', and overrides traditional distinctions between fact and fiction in claiming to be a form of fiction truer than truth. And his creative fantasy on the life of Marilyn Monroe draws frequently on what he calls 'factoids', that is, matters not based on fact but felt to be fact by those who transmit them.[22]

Despite the apparent double-talk here, a preoccupation with documentary reality might well be interpreted as a loss of faith in the imagination, and a corresponding belief that truth is stronger than fiction. Fears that this would happen were already being voiced during the heyday of realism, when readers first experienced a concerted attempt to establish documentary accuracy as the gateway to truth in literature. 'There is sure to be someone', Leopoldo Alas wrote prophetically in 1883, 'who will plan a political novel, naturalistic as well, in which with the idea of making the protagonist a deputy he will set down the electoral laws and the census.'[23] But what seemed bizarre to Alas is quite unremarkable to admirers of Allen Drury's *Advise and consent* (New York, 1959), or James A. Michener's *Centennial* (London, 1974) or any other of those monumentally 'researched' novels by Irving Stone, such as *The passions of the mind* (London, 1971), which is about Freud.

The use of documentary materials is one way of bridging the gap between verifiable fact and unverifiable fiction. The alternative is at once less troublesome and more bold, namely, to question the historian's right to use words like 'fact' and 'truth' of his own writings. 'History would be an excellent thing', said Tolstoy, 'if only it were true.'[24] For to the extent that historical reconstruction is provisional, it is the product of a speculative imagination, and what passes consequently for an objective fact may be no more than a contingency of speculations given substance by expediency and force of habit. This is the argument of one of Robert Graves's poems:

> Truth-loving Persians do not dwell upon
> The trivial skirmish fought near Marathon.[25]

Nor should they, seeing that they have their own report of what went on there – the Persian version – which must be taken notice of if we accept A. J. P. Taylor's definition of history as 'a version of events'.[26] In *Joseph Andrews* (1742), Henry Fielding makes fun of so-called historians who metamorphose into romance-writers when called upon for anything more demanding than the location of events and the addresses of those who took part in them (Bk III, ch. 1). For what historians deal with are not facts but meanings: able to tell us *who* Napoleon was, they have no way of showing us *that* he was, and are therefore obliged to enter into competition with the author of *The history of Tom Jones* (1749).[27] Historian and poet, formerly divided by a false distinction between fact and fiction, are reunited in Fielding's theory of the novel, and English distinctions between 'story' and 'history' blur in the profound ambiguities of *histoire*, which means both. It then becomes possible to claim, as Taine did in 1863, that 'a great poem, a fine novel, the confessions of a superior man, are more instructive than a heap of historians with their histories.'[28]

Non-assertion theories of truth

Feeling inferior to historians is not the least problem faced by poets and novelists; justifying their fictions to the more positivistic brands of philosopher can be a much more harrowing experience. A typical bugbear is Jeremy Bentham, who (in John Stuart Mill's account) believed that 'all poetry is misrepresentation' because it perverts words from their proper office, which is the conveyance of 'precise logical truth'.[29] A concern for 'logical truth' involves setting up a system of verification by which statements have to be framed propositionally so that they can be judged true or false. Anything which is not declarative in a propositional manner exists in a limbo of non-verifiability. It is generally assumed that poems are non-propositional, and to many poetry readers this is one of their strengths: 'you can refute Hegel', said Yeats, 'but not...the Song of Sixpence'.[30] But Yeats's own poems contain many statements which look like propositional truth claims, notably his verdict on twentieth-century politicians:

> The best lack all conviction, while the worst
> Are full of passionate intensity.[31]

In literary works we commonly encounter propositional statements which look refutable. Some famous novels begin with a proposition ('Happy families are all alike; every unhappy family is unhappy in its own way'); others begin with a counter-proposition ('All happy families are more or less dissimilar; all unhappy ones are more or less alike'); and others begin with an ironical proposition ('It is a truth universally acknowledged, that a single man in possession of a good fortune, must be in want of a wife').[32] Curiously, we tend to treat them as pseudo-propositions which require a provisional assent rather than outright acceptance or rejection. 'Whether life, compared to a dome of coloured glass, does or does not stain the white radiance of eternity, is a question no one asks', writes Dorothy Walsh.[33] Literature contains interrogatives we are not obliged to answer ('Did he who made the lamb make thee?'), and declaratives we are not obliged to accept ('The world is charged with the grandeur of God').[34] Its performative utterances are neither illocutionary nor perlocution-ary, but constitute rather what Marcia Eaton calls 'translocu-tions', which are neither true nor false because they function in purely imaginary situations.[35] What would happen to literature if its pseudo-propositions were taken seriously is amusingly suggested in Housman's redrafting of Wordsworth's lines 'To the cuckoo' as an examination question:

> O cuckoo shall I call thee bird
> Or but a wandering voice?
> State the alternative preferred
> With reason for your choice.[36]

Positivistic objections to the truth-claims of literature can be side-stepped by arguing that propositional criteria determine only one kind of truth, and that seemingly declarative statements in literature are not really declarative at all. 'The poet', says Sidney, 'nothing affirms, and therefore never lieth', because although 'he recounteth things not true, yet because he telleth them not for true, he lieth not'.[37] Sidney's explanation provides a model for all later non-assertion theories of literary truth, from Ben Jonson's observation that the

> poet never credit gained
> By writing truths, but things (like truths) well feigned,

to Northrop Frye's perception that poets are like mathematicians in saying 'not "this is so"', but "let this be"'.[38] Symbolist attempts to treat poems as 'presences' which simply exist (rather than as representations which aspire to resemble something else) are therefore conducive to Justus Buchler's view that literature is far more 'exhibitive' than 'assertive' of ideas and attitudes.[39]

Nomenclature is a problem. I. A. Richards notes that although it is not necessarily the poet's business to make true statements, 'poetry has constantly the air of making statements, and important ones', which we ought to call 'pseudo-statements'. 'A pseudo-statement is "true"', he says, 'if it suits and serves some attitude or links together attitudes which on other grounds are desirable.'[40] Analogous dissociations spring to mind. John Hospers, for instance, thinks literature contains 'implied' truths, whereas Dorothy Walsh interprets literary truth as a form of 'revelatory disclosure' which we are able to apprehend only by submitting to those virtual experiences embodied in books.[41] Others defend literature on purely subjective grounds and produce sophisticated reworkings of that emotionalist theory of truth ('felt' truth) which we associate with the Romantic poets, but which is clearly discernible in Augustan criticism, such as Johnson's strictures on Addison's *Cato* as an unconvincing play whose 'hopes and fears communicate no vibration to the heart'.[42] It was Shelley who said that '*reason* can never either account for, or prove the truth of feeling'; and Keats believed that the only kind of truth worth bothering about in the long run is one which has been 'proved upon our pulses'.[43] The non-assertionist is never less assailable than when reporting truths proved on his pulses. 'It is said, I know', wrote Hazlitt, 'that truth is *one*; but to this I cannot subscribe, for it appears to me that truth is *many*.'[44] What possible answer is there to that? Romantics treasure their private truths because they are personal and therefore more valuable than abstractions. It is not a very satisfactory way of going about things, as different readers find when they try to compare their sense of the 'true'. Anything more ambitious, however, results in the word 'truth' being boxed in inverted commas to indicate that it is something in need of protection against those verificatory procedures by which 'true' truths are tested.

Truth of coherence

Creators of word-worlds which are not designed to match an outside world are understandably unhappy with a theory which interprets truth correspondentially and classifies as false anything which is demonstrably not *adequatio ad rem*. Much more promising is the rival theory which makes 'coherence' the criterion of truth, and obliges the constituent parts of a literary work to be true not to a world beyond themselves but merely to one another. 'Information is true if it is accurate', writes E. M. Forster. 'A poem is true if it hangs together.'[45] The coherential view is that 'one poem proves another and the whole' (Wallace Stevens).[46] If beauty is the product of aesthetic coherence, then 'beauty is truth, truth beauty', for Keats believed that 'what the imagination seizes as beauty must be truth'.[47] Coherential theorists define truth as a relation of parts within a whole. Neither the cosmology nor the eschatology of *The divine comedy* needs to be true correspondentially, provided they are true with respect to what goes on in the poem.[48]

Like the non-assertion theory of truth, truth-of-coherence makes for a double standard of truth, and is able to protect literature from the wrong kind of probings only by placing it in a special category where such probings are strictly forbidden. Is this worth doing? Should we try to preserve a special truth-value for heterocosms by sealing them off hermetically from external reality, and never expecting them to venture outside the cocoons of their own coherence? Or should we value only those which appear to correspond to the way things are? The trouble with trying to preserve two different sorts of truth is that people always believe one is more true than the other. Historically, the problem is first raised for English readers by Bacon's dissociation of the truth of science from the truth of religion, which left religion 'true' in a merely figurative sense; and it was Bacon also who, with equally disastrous consequences for literature, separated the procedures of reason (which 'doth buckle and bow the mind unto the nature of things') from those of literature, which commits the correspondential mistake of 'submitting the shows of things to the desires of the mind'.[49] By the middle of the seventeenth century there seemed good reason to believe that the future of literature was in jeopardy if its veridical claims were to go on being undermined by the new experimental science, which was correspondentially more true than any literature ancient or modern. Thomas Sprat felt that contemporary writers ought to keep an eye on Royal Society experiments and concern themselves with empirically established facts, because 'truth is never so well expressed or amplified, as by those ornaments which are true and real in themselves'.[50] And this dream of an eventual alliance between science and literature – an event which might terminate that long-standing quarrel between poets and philosophers – was still being entertained when Wordsworth speculated that 'the remotest discoveries of the chemist, the botanist, or mineralogist' might become 'proper objects of the poet's art' if only they could be shown to be 'manifestly and palpably material to us as enjoying and suffering beings'.[51] Half a century later, Edward Fitzgerald saw that science has really no need of such literary embellishments because its discoveries are themselves acts of imagination. 'It is not the poetical imagination', he wrote, 'but bare science that every day more and more unrolls a greater epic than the *Iliad*'.[52]

If Sprat's proposal appears naive, and Wordsworth's conjecture far-fetched, both are timely reminders that the only kind of truth which gains general acceptance without benefit of special pleading is truth-of-correspondence:

> O how much more doth beauty beauteous seem
> By that sweet ornament which truth doth give.[53]

It would simplify matters considerably if we could agree to call true only those things which are true in a correspondential sense, and to use some other word altogether for such things as non-assertive truths and truth-of-coherence. For such is the prestige of correspondential truth that we are pleased when books believed to be true only in a coherential sense turn out to be true correspondentially. An example is the theory of involuntary memory on which Proust based *A la recherche du temps perdu*. This was confirmed a few years ago at the Montreal Neurological Institute, when it was demonstrated that electrodes placed on various parts of the brain can induce patients to recollect in great detail certain experiences they think they have forgotten.[54] Neurosurgical verification makes not the slightest difference to the novel as a novel, but significantly alters its relation to reality, and for the better. Conversely, the knowledge that people do not explode (no matter how much alcohol they drink) discredits the death of Mr Krook in *Bleak House* (1853) from 'spontaneous combustion', which Dickens believed to be scientifically authenticated.[55] It is a singular triumph to be able to write a novel like Upton Sinclair's *The jungle* (New York, 1906), which represented the contemporary condition of Chicago stock-yards so accurately as to provoke Theodore Roosevelt into setting up a commission of inquiry whose findings corroborated practically everything the book alleged.[56] And it is to Shelley's credit that a coherential preoccupation with the internal harmonies of an ode to the west wind did not weaken his ability to describe a thundercloud with a correspondential accuracy which later meteorologists have scarcely matched.[57] But we should let an acknowledged master of the coherential mode, Henry James, have the last word on the lure of correspondence: 'The only reason for the existence of a novel is that it does attempt to represent life.'[58]

Factual error and honest lying

Fear of arousing disbelief in otherwise acquiescent readers encourages most writers to aim at factual accuracy whenever possible. Tennyson declined to publish 'Anacaona' – a poem which exploits the musical resources of exotic names (rhyming 'liana' with 'anana', 'guava fruit' with 'yuccarout', etc.) – on the grounds that it 'would be confuted by some midshipman who had been in Hayti latitudes and knew better about tropical vegetables and fruit'.[59] And there is evidence elsewhere in his collected poems of a desire to get things exactly right, even if it means attending to a manic precisionist like Charles Babbage, who pointed out that a couple of lines in 'The vision of sin' –

> Every minute dies a man,
> Every minute one is born –

give the misleading impression that the death-rate is exactly proportional to the birth-rate, whereas the correct proportion is 1:1.167, and that this fact could be conveyed more accurately if the lines were revised to read:

> Every moment dies a man
> And one and a sixteenth is born.[60]

What is interesting is not so much Tennyson's refusal to contaminate his verse with vulgar fractions as his decision to change the chronologically specific 'minute' into the poetically vague 'moment'. One cannot imagine Jonathan Swift being nearly so patient with the objection that his Lilliputians are much too small to have the necessary number of brain-cells to make them human.[61]

Errors have to be unusually striking before they trouble readers. Even then, they have by no means so detrimental an effect in literary as in expository works. Whether or not the medieval castle in Keats's 'Eve of St Agnes' could ever have had a carpet to flap in the draught, or whether it should be Balboa instead of 'stout Cortez' who first glimpses the Pacific in another poem, or whether Grecians ever had urns on which odes might be written, are questions which do not normally occur to us as we read.[62] They can be made to look serious only when taken out of context, as in the following objection to the 'Ode to a nightingale': '"Thou wast not born for death, immortal bird", was true, to Keats's knowledge: it is simply silly to a modern student. Nightingales will be fossils a million years from now.'[63] How a writer reacts when given the opportunity to correct an error depends on what he feels about the function of details, particularly if truth-of-correspondence clashes with truth-of-coherence, as it does notably at one point in Coleridge's 'Rime of the ancient mariner'. In the first version of 1798,

> The breezes blew, the white foam flew,
> The furrow follow'd free;

but when Coleridge reprinted the poem in 1817 he altered 'follow'd' to 'stream'd off', pointing out in a note that the wake only seems to follow a ship if one happens to be watching it from the shore or some other vessel, whereas when observed by someone actually on the ship, 'the wake appears like a brook flowing off from the stern'. Correspondentially accurate as a mariner's eye-view of things, the revised lines founder on alliterative, assonantal and rhythmical infelicities:

> The fair breeze blew, the white foam flew,
> The furrow stream'd off free.

So when Coleridge reprinted the poem for the last time in 1834, truth-of-coherence triumphed over truth-of-correspondence, and the original and nautically incorrect version was restored.[64]

Assessments of correspondential truth in literature cannot be conducted, therefore, on the assumption that truth of this kind is invariably intended or desired. 'All poems are lies', says George Barker, 'but they are lies native to a country in which the truth does not conclusively exist', the *pays du mensonge*.[65] Explorers go there in the Shakespearian belief that the truest poetry is the most feigning.[66] 'What makes it difficult for a poet not to tell lies', said Auden, 'is that, in poetry, all facts and all beliefs cease to be true or false and become interesting possibilities.'[67] Literature conceived of as the pursuit of the possible is so far beyond mere correspondence that its points of contact with reality seem merely coincidental. Travellers in the *pays du mensonge* learn to domicile themselves there, but tourists find it harder to do so because they keep remembering that 'real' world they have just left behind. Differences between travellers and tourists raise what is known in literary criticism as 'the problem of belief'.

Incredibility

'We are affected only as we believe', said Johnson;[68] and seeing that many readers judge only as they are affected, judicial criticism has had to find room for the affectivist criterion of belief. It is generally assumed that readers will rate more highly something they believe in than something they do not. On the one hand, therefore, we encounter readers like that nurse Robert Graves met, who objected to Blake's poem 'Infant joy' because it expects us to believe that babies can smile when only two days old, whereas every nurse knows that they have to be at least two weeks old before they can do that.[69] On the other hand we have T. S. Eliot assuring us from personal experience that Dante's line *la sua voluntate è nostra pace* ('His [God's] will is our peace') is much more beautiful and pleasurable to Christians who accept what it says than it can ever be to agnostics who merely appreciate its mellifluousness.[70] Coleridge thought an appreciation of George Herbert's poetry quite beyond non-Christian readers who rely entirely on their 'cultivated judgement, classical taste, or even poetic sensibility'.[71] The next step is to say (as George Watson does) that agnostic readers who appreciate Dante's poetry 'aesthetically' probably misread it by focusing on stylistic features which Dante would have regarded as merely instrumental to the terminal business of promulgating Christian doctrine.[72]

Agnostic admirers of *The divine comedy*, however, are not put down so easily, and may reply that Dante's brand of Christianity is no more an obstacle to literary appreciation than any other obsolete mythology. 'Good religious poetry', wrote Housman, 'is likely to be most justly appreciated and most discriminatingly relished by the undevout.'[73] The problem is familiar to anybody who ventures into the more antiquarian stretches of literature and acquires the habit of reading, as it were, bifocally – keeping his own convictions separate from those embodied in whatever happens to engage his serious attention. When we read a medieval romance it is not with the innocence of Don Quixote, for whom reading was believing, but rather in the spirit of John Dryden, who advises us to be 'pleased with the image, without being cozened by the fiction'.[74] Ever since the Enlightenment discovery that a good deal of Europe's finest literature is based on superstition and ignorance, Dryden's advice has been followed either unconsciously or deliberately. Nor is it only authors remote from us in time who elicit such a bifurcated response. The 'ideas' of Lawrence or Blake or Yeats are very often taken *cum grano* even by well-disposed critics. But this is not always the case. Douglas Bush, for instance, finds *The divine comedy* flawed because it contains an *Inferno* so devoid of 'ethical humanity' as to condone the eternal punishment of sinners; and Erich Heller objects to aestheticist readings of Rilke's poetry which never question what Rilke is actually saying there.[75] 'We cannot fully appreciate the poetry without being at least *tempted* to accept the beliefs as well', Heller insists. And if we happen to find the beliefs unacceptable, it may be necessary to say so as bluntly as John R. Harrison does in his book *The reactionaries* (London, 1966), which assails the authoritarian politics of such founding fathers of Anglo-American modernism as Ezra Pound, T. S. Eliot, D. H. Lawrence and Wyndham Lewis.

Traditionally, writers have tried to achieve what Trevor Eaton calls 'affidence',[76] cultivating verisimilitude of action and character in the expectation of wooing audiences with their plausibility. If truth is indeed stranger than fiction, it is not much use to those who write for readers who are affected only as they believe. *Vraisemblance* is preferable to *vérité* in the Aristotelian tradition, where literature is linked with rhetoric, the aim of which (said Aristotle) is to induce belief.[77] From this perspective, narrative is a spell-binding art, and therefore to draw attention to the fictitiousness of one's fiction (as Fielding and Trollope do) is a suicidal act in the opinion of spell-binders like Henry James and Sir Walter Scott.[78] Yet the non-fiction novel, in revealing the limitations of Aristotelian plausibility, questions the importance of 'belief' in our reading experience. *The green hills of Africa* capitalises on those very implausibilities that make it more 'real' than Aristotelian fictions, which always try to have a good excuse for everything that happens in them, and never risk episodes like the one in which Hemingway meets in the African wilderness a man who likes to talk about Rilke and is an admirer of Hemingway's contributions to *Der Querschnitt*.[79] 'Too fantastic', Hemingway comments; but the anecdote belongs nevertheless in that capacious category of non-Aristotelian fictions which include the majority of the world's myths, legends, frontier-tales, fairy-tales, ghost-stories and the like.

The enjoyment of wonder may be naive, but we cannot assume that tellers of tall tales either believe them or expect to be believed, nor that they tell them only because they lack the sophistication to recount more plausible stories. Folklorists report that 'the bearers of legend tradition do not always believe in the truth of their story', and that 'attitudes towards belief range from absolute acceptance to absolute rejection through many intermediary stages'.[80] Credibility is such a relative term as to tempt ironists to play with it instead of trying to induce it – which is what Cervantes does in *Don Quixote*, a novel which is forever inviting us to disbelieve its ingenious nonsense, and shattering its own illusions.[81] If Eliot is correct in arguing that poets do not so much *think* as make poetry out of *thought*,[82] it is probable that they do not *believe* either, but make poetry out of *beliefs*, as Milton made poetry out of the Ptolemaic model of the universe without being a Ptolemaicist. Impersonalists profess to be interested less in the content than in what Beckett calls 'the shape of ideas'.[83] If writing is the art of delineating the shapes of ideas, then reading must become the art of appreciating the shapes of ideas thus delineated. Neither Beckett's own beliefs (whatever they may be) nor the widely divergent beliefs of his audience can be said to play an important part in such a transaction. This is to assume, however, that the proper response to literature is one of detached contemplation, and that everybody is capable of tracing the trajectory of despair in Beckett's work without experiencing despair or questioning Beckett's analysis of the human condition. Such readers, if indeed they exist, leave their beliefs behind them before embarking on a book, and therefore avoid the entanglements and *ad hoc* solutions of more ordinary readers.

'Suspension of disbelief'

It is said that when Caelia stepped naked into a cold bath it immediately became so hot as to give off steam. Such a story is 'to be believed with a poetical faith' in the opinion of Robert Burton, who was not thereby dissuaded from repeating it.[84] 'Poetical faith' is as necessary to readers as poetic licence is to writers. 'To many things', Ben Jonson said, 'a man should owe but a temporary belief, and a suspension of his own judgement, not an absolute resignation of himself, or a perpetual captivity.'[85] This is particularly true of theatrical experience. The neoclassical 'unities' of time and place in drama were the invention of people apparently embarrassed by the fact that the same stage could represent different places in the same play, and that sixteen years could be said to elapse in the course of an afternoon's performance. But as Johnson perceived, the unities try to solve problems which audiences are not normally troubled by. If we are willing to grant in the first place that a stage located geographically in London 'is' Alexandria in act one, it is no trouble to imagine it as Rome in act two.[86] Theatrical illusion calls for a special kind of fideism on the part of spectators, who do not have to believe in the objective existence of the thing represented in order to judge whether it is represented well or badly. A belief in ghosts is not obligatory among theatre audiences who believe in Hamlet's ghost for the duration of his appearance on stage: it still makes 'the hair stand on end', said Lessing, 'whether it covers a believing or unbelieving brain'.[87] Does something similar occur when we read?

Coleridge thought so, and produced by far the most influential if somewhat cautious formulation of a principle adumbrated by so many critics when he spoke of 'that willing suspension of disbelief for the moment, which constitutes poetic faith'.[88] He was thinking particularly of poems on supernatural themes like 'The rime of the ancient mariner', which were contrived with sufficient semblance of truth to overcome an anticipated resistance to the improbable. His conception of the phenomenon is misleadingly negative, for he assumes that something has to be switched off rather than switched on (disbelief suspended, rather than belief conferred). So it is salutary for George Barker to remind us that for every suspension of disbelief there must be 'simultaneously an act of interpretive credence', a positive and welcoming curiosity such as Chaucer described long before the reading of tall tales became problematic:

> On bokes for to rede I me delyte,
> And to hem yive I feyth and ful credence,
> And in myn herte have hem in reference.[89]

There is much to be said for regarding literary works as self-justifying presences which the reader has no alternative but to accept or ignore. We have to take on trust what is given us because we have no way of knowing what we might have been given instead; the *don du poème* is to be accepted gracefully, or cast aside. Reading imaginative literature is an act of faith. It is not a matter of believing *that* such and such is the case, but of believing *in* it: the sea-voyage in 'The rime of the ancient mariner', Walter Ong argues, is something we believe in differently from the way we believe that two and two make four.[90] We 'assent' to the sea-voyage in the manner Eliot suggests when he dissociates 'philosophical *belief*' from 'poetic *assent*' in the act of reading.[91] I. A. Richards would persuade us that belief is never a problem when we are reading well, and that if it becomes so, 'either through the poet's own fault or our own, we have for the moment ceased to be reading poetry and have become astronomers, or theologians, or moralists, persons engaged in quite a different type of activity.'[92] 'Belief' is a non-problem to Richards because, in his opinion, poems contain only pseudo-statements, and are therefore incapable of saying anything at all or upsetting anybody's beliefs. This is a characteristic feature of other attempts to circumvent the same problem. Delmore Schwartz, for example, applies to the poetry of Thomas Hardy a subtle theory of belief not unlike the theory of purposive intentions. He suggests that we should keep Hardy's beliefs securely inside Hardy's poetry, and instead of worrying whether Hardy was duly or unduly pessimistic, ascertain how many of his poems actually embody the beliefs they purvey.[93] But the kind of reader who can distinguish Hardy's beliefs from the beliefs in Hardy's poetry is already well beyond the innocent stage at which disbelief might hinder his apreciation and evaluation of literature. Besides, the kind of response Schwartz recommends is not what Hardy himself would have wanted. He wrote for readers of much less Olympian detachment who are ready to quarrel with what they read, but who might eventually see things his way as a result of prolonged exposure to a powerful rhetoric in the service of a vivid imagination. By comparison, 'suspension of disbelief' is a much more cerebral activity, an elaborate form of self-deception which in the end fools nobody, least of all ourselves. 'The "problem of belief"', Jeremy Hawthorne observes, 'only arises for those who assume that there should ideally be an absolute, aesthetic response to any given piece of literature'.[94] For those who do not, a book is unlikely to appear any more credible as a result of our willingness to grant it provisional assent. Disbeliefs cannot be suspended indefinitely; and when they are reinstated, truthfulness will still concern us.

—

12

Evaluation

In electing to write about this rather than that, authors make qualitative selections from an inconceivably wide range of possibilities, and compel their readers to take a correspondingly evaluative interest in what is offered and the manner in which it is presented. A concern with literary values is therefore unavoidable, since even the decision to avoid value-judgements is itself a value-judgement. Judicial criticism is therefore a troublesome inevitability, 'perpetually necessary', as Allen Tate once remarked, 'and perpetually impossible'.[1] Why this should be so is our final subject of inquiry.

Aesthetic and non-aesthetic values

To the extent that we all prefer some books to others, everybody is a judicial reader, whether he simply knows what he likes, or tries to admire what is said to be admirable. Yet although we all read evaluatively, we lack an 'axiology' or theory of value which is comprehensive enough to grade the enormous variety of literary experiences. Instead, we have at our disposal a number of systems invented to satisfy particular needs in certain kinds of reader, or to justify the existence of certain books or styles of writing. Claimed to be universally valid, critical systems begin invariably as doctrines of special instances; thus new criticism derives from Donne to the extent that myth criticism derives from Blake, and structuralism from Mallarmé. Axiologies fall into two main categories, depending on whether or not books are believed to have 'artistic' qualities which must be given preference over other considerations. On the one hand there are 'aestheticist' theories of value which focus on so-called intrinsic phenomena such as style and form, and treat books as autonomous objects for leisurely contemplation; and on the other hand there are various 'affectivist' theories of value which treat books as powerful forces with social consequences, and therefore question the moral calibre, mental health and political affiliations of writers, as manifest allegedly in their books.

The assumption that books are treated most fairly if judged primarily on their 'aesthetic' merits is a relatively recent development, perhaps no older than the eighteenth century, when Baumgarten published his book on aesthetics.[2] Originally, the Greek term 'aesthesis' denoted sense experience in general. Baumgarten was the first to use the word 'aesthetic' in its current sense, that is, as referring exclusively to the experiences we get from the arts. The whole controversy as to whether the arts are distinct from life or conterminous with it (and whether or not they are to be judged by a special set of values) rests on our ability to make Baumgarten's distinction. Once we have made it, we can dissociate the moral values we choose to live by from the aesthetic values we happen to admire in literature, and see nothing odd in being able to say that a certain book is morally repulsive in content but extremely well written.

This is very different from the traditional view of such matters endorsed by Kant when he concludes that 'the beautiful is the symbol of the morally good'.[3] In ancient times, a distinction between morality and aesthetics was semantically unlikely, given the tendency of certain Greek and Roman words to mean both 'good' and 'beautiful': the Latin word *bellus* ('beautiful'), for example, derives from *benulus*, an archaic diminutive form of *bonus* ('good'). The durably Platonist equation of goodness with beauty and evil with ugliness (challenged long ago in Shakespeare's sonnets) was made an issue of in Baudelaire's provocative title, *Les fleurs du mal* (1857), with its tacit claim that beautiful poems can be made out of unsavoury subject-matter. In order to recapture the outrage first provoked by such speculations, we need only recall the publicity they received at the trial of Oscar Wilde, the man who had prefaced *The picture of Dorian Gray* (1891) with Huysmans' statement that 'there is no such thing as a moral or an immoral book. Books are well written, or badly written. That is all.' Counsel for the prosecution was highly suspicious. 'I take it', said Carson, 'that no matter how immoral a book may be, if it is well written, it is, in your opinion, a good book?' Wilde agreed, provided the book were 'well written so as to produce a sense of beauty, which is the highest sense of which a human being can be capable. If it were badly written, it would produce a sense of disgust.' So Carson pressed forward to ask whether 'a well-written book putting forward perverted moral views may be a good book' – which Wilde countered with the non-assertion argument that 'no work of art ever puts forward views' because 'views belong to people who are not artists'.[4] The poet nothing affirms, and therefore never offendeth.

Among the various revelations afforded by this wilful display of mutual incomprehension is the manifest tenuousness of aesthetic criteria in cases where a book contravenes the social *mores* of its time. People condone the autonomy of literature except when it appears to threaten the status quo. As soon as this happens, books are stripped of their aesthetic wrapping and rough-handled as subversive propaganda. While littérateurs find this deplorable, the primacy of aesthetic over social values is by no means self-evident, and certainly not so on historical grounds. To the Carsons of this world, aesthetic values are best treated as means rather than as end, in so far as social responsibility is a more worthwhile ideal than the manufacture of allegedly beautiful objects whose truth to themselves is achieved only at a price which society should not be expected to pay. 'Aesthetic evaluation' becomes therefore an inconsequential game played with non-controversial texts, a suitable pastime for harmless dilettanti who compare (shall we say) the sonnets of Sidney with those of Petrarch, or wonder whether Swinburne's lyric voice is purer than Shelley's. But in matters of import the game stops, and 'real' values are brought to bear. As subject-matter becomes the centre of attention, treatment tends to be ignored, and critics reach back to those moral certainties which preceded the demarcation of aesthetic from social values. A writer who believes that writing badly is the worst thing he can be accused of suddenly discovers the primitive strength of non-aesthetic value-systems, and finds his books being used as evidence that he himself is socially a misfit, morally obnoxious, and of questionable sanity. Just as Johnson could censure the profanities in Shakespeare's plays on the grounds that 'there are laws of higher authority than those of criticism',[5] socially vigilant critics are not convinced that aesthetics constitutes the highest court of appeal in literary verdicts.

Literature and moral responsibility

There is no denying the ubiquity of moral criteria in the history of judicial criticism. 'The essential function of art is moral', said D. H. Lawrence, reaffirming for twentieth-century readers an assumption which the nineteenth-century *l'art pour l'art* movement had set out to destroy, but which nevertheless has dominated discussions about literature since the fifth century BC, when Xenophanes first complained that Homer and Hesiod were morally reprehensible in crediting the gods with shameful behaviour.[6] In a central text for moralistic critics, Horace's *Ars poetica*, we learn that the writer 'who has managed to blend profit with delight [*utile dulci*] wins everyone's approbation' (l. 343). Writers are treated as ethical teachers who make morality palatable by coating it with sweet poesy: poetry is like honey smeared on a cup of unpleasantly tasting medicine, says Lucretius, so that children might be 'deceived for their own good'.[7] According to this theory of teaching-by-delighting (*delectando docere*), literature is unrivalled in its effectiveness as a moral agent because it teaches (as Christ did) by parable rather than precept, and thus circumvents our resistance to straight doctrine. 'A verse may find him, who a sermon flies', was George Herbert's maxim: it was for this reason that Milton could call Spenser 'a better teacher than Scotus or Aquinas'.[8]

The humanist defence of literature rests on a faith that reading good books is a morally enlightening experience from which the young and impressionable student will emerge, like the Ancient Mariner, a wiser and a better man. Literary study is thus absorbed into moral education, and the analysis of selected texts enables students to rehearse roles to be taken when confronted by moral problems in their own lives. The faith was still strong in English Departments in British universities as recently as 1972,[9] despite difficulties in maintaining it. For in the first place, it fosters the assumption that literary works are reducible to the moral lessons they embody – as though the purpose of reading *Paradise lost* were to learn, like Adam, that 'to obey is best' (XII 561). And secondly, it places on teachers of literature the intolerable burden of being morally better informed (and, by implication, morally better) than carpenters or electrical engineers or others who perform socially constructive tasks without being called upon to act as custodians of social values. For despite their familiarity with the classics, professors of literature do not appear to lead better lives than other people, and frequently display unbecoming virulence on the subject of one another's shortcomings.

This is worth bearing in mind because a traditional corollary of the moralistic theory of value is that only a good man can write a good book, and that nobody (to use Sartre's example) could ever write a good novel in praise of antisemitism.[10] 'The goodness of a poet is not like that of a carpenter or a smith', wrote Strabo at the very end of the pagan era. 'Theirs has nothing grand or noble about it; the poet's is linked with the man's – one cannot be a good poet without first being a good man.'[11] The association of poetry with rhetoric strengthened this conviction, since it was fear of demagogic powers which led Cicero and Quintilian to link rhetoric with ethics: 'if oratorical ability is added to the armoury of evil', Quintilian said, 'nothing would be more dangerous, whether publicly or privately, than eloquence'.[12] Stylistic features consequently take on the semblance of symptoms, and moral squalor oozes out of artistic flaws. 'A bad novel is ultimately seen to fail', according to Q. D. Leavis, 'not because of its method but owing to a fatal inferiority in the author's make-up'; and her husband once claimed that 'the formal perfection of *Emma*...can be appreciated only in terms of the moral preoccupations that characterise the novelist's peculiar interest in life'.[13]

In spite of such wishful thinking, aesthetic traits stubbornly persist in being morally neutral, no matter how skilfully a moralising analyst tries to evade the naturalistic fallacy of inter-preting facts as values. It is only by bringing to literary works a preconceived set of moral-aesthetic equations that such critics can operate at all. Sentimental verses like Wordsworth's 'We are seven' are aesthetically bad only to someone who has decided beforehand that sentimentality is an undesirable emotion, and that undesirable emotions are aesthetically bad. It is not a matter of starting with aesthetic traits and then working inductively towards the moral syndrome from which they stem, but of inspecting aesthetic traits through moralistic lenses. An antisemite would have no difficulty at all in naming a good antisemitic novel.

At the same time, books designed with a moral purpose ought not to have that purpose overlooked. Some writers think of themselves as the moral conscience of their times, and devote their energies to the exposure of vice and folly. Traces of this reprimanding function remain in the etymology of various words signifying 'poet', such as *skald* and *scop*, which are cognate with 'scold' and 'scoff'.[14] As the bad conscience of civilisation, the scolding scoffer claims a moral right

> To undo the folded lie,
> The romantic lie in the brain
> Of the sensual man-in-the-street

> And the lie of Authority
> Whose buildings grope the sky.[15]

Tolerated more often than heeded (for there is something pleas-
antly purifactory in being abused every now and then for
perpetrating a life-style one has no intention of changing), the
overt moralist is intent on ensuring that justice is seen to be done.
Nothing riles him more than to have his message muffled by
readers who admire his work on purely aesthetic grounds. 'I show
men their plain duty', Ruskin complained, 'and they reply that
I have a beautiful style.'[16] Style, he felt, is properly instrumental
to those moral purposes without which art is trivial.

Moralists have left their mark on literature most indelibly by
inventing and fostering 'poetic justice', shaping their plots in such
a way that vice is punished and virtue rewarded, with the result
that our aesthetic pleasure in a well-told tale is indistinguishable
from our moral satisfaction at witnessing the heroine's triumphant
escape from death or such fates as are said to be worse. Insufficient
respect for poetic justice was one of the things which provoked
Plato's objections to imaginative literature. 'Poets and prose-
writers are guilty of the most serious misstatements about human
life', he says, 'making it out that wrongdoers are often happy and
just men miserable; that injustice pays, if not detected.'[17] In an
idealistic aesthetic, it is a writer's duty to make his heterocosm
function more justly than that fallen world we inhabit, whose
history is a dispiriting record of cruelty and injustice. Retribution
is an authorial prerogative.

A famous case which brought the matter to a head was the death
of Cordelia in *King Lear*, an event 'contrary to the natural ideas
of justice, to the hope of the reader, and...to the faith of the
chronicles', in the opinion of Samuel Johnson.[18] It was to rectify
Shakespeare's gross moral error here that Nahum Tate rewrote
the ending of the play so that Cordelia could marry Edgar and
live happily ever after, for the Johnsonian reason that (all other
things being equal) an 'audience will...always rise better pleased
from the final triumph of persecuted virtue'.[19] The trouble with
Shakespeare, Johnson notes, is that 'he seems to write without any
moral purpose' and 'makes no just distribution of good or evil',
leaving Angelo unpunished at the end of *Measure for measure*, for
instance, in spite of the sufferings he has inflicted on Isabella and
Claudio.[20] Two distinct issues merge in the concept of poetic
justice. On the one hand, it satisfies an escapist desire for

happy-ever-after endings, as Dickens did when he rewrote the ending of *Great expectations* (1860–61), abandoning the one required by the plot in favour of the one expected by romantic readers (and it is this sort of poetic justice which Addison denounces as having 'no foundation in nature, in reason, or in the practice of the Ancients').[21] On the other hand, poetic justice has metaphysical and religious sanctions to those who believe that life is not just a tale told by an idiot. 'Poetic justice would be a jest', wrote John Dennis, 'if it were not an image of the divine':[22] however banal in practice, it is a recognition by the author of providential vigilance over human affairs, and an acknowledgement that there are laws of higher authority than those of criticism.

Whenever an admired book is not explicitly moral, moralistic critics often take it upon themselves to show that it is much more moral than we suspect. Historically, this tactic has been invaluable, for if literature could be shown to be fundamentally moral, it justified its existence by being socially beneficial. For centuries, allegory was instrumental in the discovery of pious fables in unlikely places, perhaps nowhere more strikingly than in a pagan love poem known to us as The Song of Solomon, and interpreted by Origen as an allegory of Christ's mystic marriage with the Church. Allegorists are at pains to show us that things are not what they seem, and that we must discard the fallacious surfaces of what we read in order to uncover the 'real' meaning underneath. Superficially, Ovid's poetry is erotic, but duly 'moralised' it taught spiritual truths to medieval readers.[23] And in our own century, learned witnesses have testified in a court of law that *Lady Chatterley's lover* (1928) only looks like an immoral book: deep down, it is fiercely puritanical.[24] Until late in the seventeenth century it was possible (and sometimes expedient) for writers to profess pious intentions in works seemingly lascivious to the untutored, who might be forgiven for suspecting that there are more efficient ways of denouncing vice than by delineating vicious practices exquisitely and condemning them 'implicitly'. Dryden's prologue to *Love triumphant* (1694) betrays a certain cynicism about the didactic efficacy of an entertaining play with a covert moral:

> The fable has a moral too, if sought:
> But let that go; for upon second thought,
> He fears but few come hither to be taught.[25]

Implicit morality has been the kind most favoured in literature since the advent of Romantic critics, as is illustrated in Lamb's complaint to Wordsworth about those 'many modern novelists and modern poets who continually put a sign post up to show where you are to feel'.[26] Wordsworth failed to discredit such objections by insisting that 'every great poet is a teacher', and that he himself wished 'either to be considered as a teacher, or as nothing'.[27] Hazlitt felt on the contrary that 'the most moral writers...are those who do not pretend to inculcate any moral'; and even a professed moralist like Nathaniel Hawthorne said that 'to impale the story with its moral' is like 'sticking a pin through a butterfly'.[28] In the Romantic tradition, a good writer is one who shows rather than tells. 'We don't want a man with a wand going about a gallery and haranguing us', was George Eliot's reaction to *Westward ho!* (1885): *Middlemarch* was to be a moral book, but not in Kingsley's way.[29] And this has been the rule ever since. If you think that people undervalue the imagination, you are not advised to say so explicitly in a novel, but you may well get away with a scene like the one in Janet Frame's *Owls do cry* (Christchurch, 1957) where some children find a book of fairy-tales at a local rubbish-dump. Anything more obviously hortative you may live to regret, as Coleridge came to regret 'the obtrusion of the moral sentiment so openly on the reader' of 'The rime of the ancient mariner'.[30] For the moralistic theory of literature which Arnold and Leavis were later to defend was seriously challenged in 1850, when Poe described 'the heresy of *The Didactic*' as having 'accomplished more in the corruption of our poetical literature than all its other enemies combined'; and in its Baudelairean form, *l'hérésie de l'enseignement* was influential in the shaping of *poésie pure*, uncontaminated by such extrinsic matters as an unambiguous moral stance.[31]

A major problem for those who defend the implicit morality of literature is to account for the fact that a number of highly esteemed books are superficially immoral or amoral, either in part or in whole. For the morality of literature is neither a formalist nor an intentionalist issue, but an affectivist one, which is the point made by Socrates in Plato's *Republic*. 'A child cannot distinguish the allegorical sense from the literal', he says, 'and the ideas he takes in at that age are likely to become indelibly fixed; hence the great importance of seeing that the first stories he hears shall be designed to produce the best possible effect on his character.'[32] Literature for adults needs to be screened also, in case it panders to undisciplined emotions and tempts us to forget our civic duties.

Censorship is believed to be inevitable in case we read books for the wrong reasons (the commercial success of *Lady Chatterley's lover* does not betoken a widespread interest in Lawrentian puritanism).[33] Because good intentions are powerless to curb abusive effects, moralists conclude that certain subjects are taboo, since they cannot be written about without engendering the wrong kind of response. But if so, then all subjects are taboo, because even the most innocent of texts is capable of being misconstrued: 'Ding dong bell' has to go on to a list of proscribed nursery rhymes in case it incites children to drop pussies into wells.[34] The more correct complaint to make about literature is not that some of it is immoral but that all of it is ineffectually moral. This is a theme expounded by George Steiner, who notes that administrators of Nazi concentration-camps were frequently well-educated men with cultivated tastes in the arts, and concludes that the humanities do not necessarily humanise anybody, because the moral values we encounter in books are unlikely to determine the way we live.[35]

This is a much more radical critique than earlier moralists cared to make, for it casts doubt on literature as an instrument of moral edification. In the past, people assumed that some books are above suspicion, and settled down to the business of clarifying dubious cases. The projectionist defence, for example, is that books are more often moral than not, and that immorality is in the eye of the beholder. 'There is nothing unclean of itself', St Paul learnt from Christ; 'but to him that esteemeth any thing to be unclean, to him it is unclean' (Romans, 14:14). Unto the pure, all things are pure: there are no such things as dirty words, wrote Sir John Harington (three centuries before D. H. Lawrence), but only people with 'base minds, filthy conceits, or lewd intents'.[36] The realist defence, on the other hand, is that some books are immoral but inevitably so if the aim of art is to mirror the times. 'Is it [the writer's] fault if ugly people have passed in front of the mirror?' asks Stendhal.[37] Evidently not: 'the nineteenth-century dislike of Realism', said Wilde, 'is the rage of Caliban seeing his own face in a glass'.[38] Such writers claim 'a kind of *benefit of clergy*' which George Orwell (thinking of Salvador Dali) finds indefensible, because it makes artists 'exempt from the moral laws that are binding on ordinary people'.[39] Orwell's objection would apply equally well, of course, to the impersonalist defence that the moral habits of authors are not deducible from their books. 'I write wantonly but live decently', said Martial of his scurrilous epigrams, thus prompting the Reverend Robert Herrick to close a substantial collection of poems in praise of wine, women and song with the apology:

> To his book's end this last line he'd have placed,
> Jocund his Muse was; but his life was chaste.[40]

Style is certainly not the man to impersonalists. Théophile Gautier thought it 'as ridiculous to say that somebody is a drunkard because he describes drinking, a debauchee because he writes about debauchery, as to pretend somebody is virtuous because he has written a book about morality'.[41]

None of this impresses those who believe with Tolstoy that we are 'infected' by what we read, and therefore susceptible to being depraved and corrupted by books, as Wilde's Dorian Gray was 'poisoned' by Huysmans' *A rebours* (1884).[42] Invariably, moralists themselves claim personal immunity, but express concern on behalf of less experienced people (presumably relatives of Mr Podsnap's blush-prone 'young person') who are alleged not to have built up the necessary number of antibodies: everybody is susceptible to corruption, apparently, except ourselves. The farcical results of such anxieties, recorded in minute detail in transcripts of 'obscenity-trials' held during the 1960s,[43] point to the difficulty of trying to ground literary criticism in codes of moral behaviour which are themselves subject to change. Some other validation of literature seems called for.

Absolute values and the classics

We have inherited from Renaissance humanists the idea that Greek and Roman literature embodies a set of values well-worth preserving, not merely in grateful memory of their stimulating effect on northern Europeans who would otherwise have remained (in Milton's opinion) mere Goths and Jutlanders,[44] but because of their continuously benign influence on western civilisation. Richards' description of the arts as 'our storehouse of values'[45] is a persuasive if untested formulation of what most readers hope is true of literature in particular. And when English literature was introduced in the nineteenth century as a subject fit for study in English universities (as against something which any educated man would pick up casually by way of light relief from more demanding disciplines such as law or classics), it was instituted in the belief that it contains a corpus of texts comparable in value to those of the two ancient literatures, a set of canonical works which are indisputably the 'classics' of English literature.[46]

One of the functions of a classic is to be normative: its existence stabilises standards and enables front-line readers (bombarded by new and newer books) to tell the difference between stinking fish and good red herring; and it is a constant admonishment to wayward readers with a predilection for the picayune. Ever since Swinburne responded to the *Pall Mall gazette*'s request for the titles of the hundred best books,[47] we have been offered numerous consumer-guides, ranging from handy reprints in Everyman's Library and the World's Classics series, to Cyril Connolly's naming of the hundred 'key books' which make up *The modern movement* (New York, 1966). We have also had the obverse of such ventures, *Fifty works of English literature we could do without* (New York, 1968), by Brigid Brophy, Michael Levey and Charles Osborne.

Excellence is held to be the only quality common to the diverse books which constitute our canon of literary classics, and those who refer to such canons are usually better at damning non-classics than at defining the 'classic' quality of classics. It is commonly assumed, however, that classics are works which withstand the test of time and achieve their elevation by common consent: Daunty, Gouty and Shopkeeper are elected by a *consensus gentium* which is the judgement of the ages, whereas Blight, Mildew and Smut will never even be nominated.[48] *Consensus facit legem*, in the words of the old legal principle; and in judicial criticism, *consensus gentium* means the verdict of that elusive though much respected custodian of common sense, the Common Reader. For the final arbiter in literary judgements, writes Johnson, must always be 'the common sense of readers uncorrupted with literary prejudices, after all the refinements of subtlety and the dogmatism of learning'.[49] There is no point, of course, in consulting the *consensus gentium* synchronically, unless one happens to be interested in best-sellers and literary fashions. What Johnson envisages is a diachronic *consensus* which has accumulated over the ages and relieves us of the irksome task of sifting the classic from the bogus. Time is therefore essential to the judicial process: a good book is a book which lasts. 'What has been longest known has been most considered', writes Johnson, 'and what is most considered is best understood.'[50]

The association of value with permanence is strongly marked in the literary tradition, nowhere more noticeably than in those 'eternising' conceits familiar in love-poetry since the time of

Theognis, who was using them some two thousand years before Shakespeare wrote the lines:

> So long as men can breathe or eyes can see,
> So long lives this, and this gives life to thee.[51]

Spenser celebrated his marriage with a poem which was to be 'short time's endless monument'; and the 1590 dedication to *The faerie queene* is set up typographically in the form of a well-wrought urn to consecrate the memory of Elizabeth I until the end of time. Such works, as Jonson said of Shakespeare's, were intended to be 'for all time',[52] written in anticipation of never ending esteem by a *consensus gentium*. The expectation was substantiated by Gutenberg's printing-press, which conferred the stability of print on what for oral poets like Homer had been intangibly winged words, turned the sonnet into 'a moment's monument', and was therefore (E. M. Forster notes) 'mistaken for an engine of immortality'.[53]

For as long as permanence is accepted as a defining characteristic of the best literature, prophets without honour in their own century are tempted to address themselves to posterity, in the Miltonic belief that 'fame is no plant that grows on mortal soil'.[54] Petrarch accordingly begins his *Familiar epistles* with one addressed to posterity, just as Ovid had addressed 'readers of the future' in his *Tristia*.[55] Always, the judgement of posterity is assumed to be favourable and infallible. 'I shall dine late', wrote Landor, expecting no popular acclaim for years spent conducting dialogues with the dead, 'but the dining-room will be well lighted, the guests few and select.'[56] For all this, the test-of-time theory leaves much to be desired. Quite apart from the fact that it turns criticism into a prognosticatory art, it is cold comfort for a writer to be told that only future generations can decide whether or not his work is any good. Moreover, it evades the very problem of value which it pretends to solve, since there is nothing to prevent a masterpiece from sinking without trace in the great shipwreck of time. In a manuscript culture, survival is a hazardous affair at best, having no more to do with merit than biological survival has to do with fitness. All that can be said of survivors is that they have survived, and often as fortuitously as a Sapphic fragment, two lines preserved from an otherwise lost marriage poem because they happened to catch the eye of some ancient collector of metrical specimens:

> To what, dear bridegroom, may I well compare you?
> To a slender sapling I compare you above all.[57]

In the case of printed books, Robert Escarpit reckons that 80% are forgotten within a year of publication, and 99% within twenty years; and among the 1% which remains, a significant proportion will be what Alfred Andersch calls *Trivialromanen*, like *The woman in white* (1860) and *Ben Hur* (1880).[58] These are books which never make the canon of 'serious' literature, although they are undoubtedly the ones selected by the *consensus gentium*, and continue to be read (unlike highbrow classics) whether critics denounce or merely ignore them. In this respect, they are considerably more robust than some of the classics kept alive in the intensive care wards of university English departments.

The trouble with posterity is that we do not know who they will be. Nobody has yet taken up Pope's ironic challenge to 'fix the year precise/When British bards begin t'immortalise'.[59] Are we ourselves already someone else's posterity? 'In the final analysis', runs the critical cliché, *x* will be judged superior to *y*, as though criticism were like Christianity, with a Judgement Day placed at the end of time. The truth is that no analysis is final. 'Works of art which "withstand the test of time"', Boas writes in a controversial essay on the continuing popularity of the Mona Lisa, 'change their natures as the times change'.[60] Where Vasari marvels at Leonardo's technical mastery of *trompe l'œil* techniques, Pater thrills to the depiction of a *femme fatale*, and Freud sees an unconscious revelation of the Oedipus Complex (Duchamp, however, sees only a visual cliché, and reacts accordingly by placing over the Gioconda smile a pair of Laughing Cavalier moustaches taken from an equally famous visual cliché). Authors undergo comparable transformations. The Chaucer we admire is unrecognisable as Caxton's fifteenth-century 'noble great philosopher' or Dunbar's sixteenth-century 'rose of rhetoricians'; nor does Leigh Hunt's Romantic Spenser (a painter of gorgeous scenes of chivalry) resemble either the sage and serious poet Milton studied with pleasure, or the erudite iconographer and numerologist familiar to twentieth-century critics.[61] Try as we may, we get no closer to authors than our conceptions of them, and have no grounds for believing that later critics will do any better.

How the classics of our literature attain that eminence is therefore something of a mystery. Even after reaching it, their tenure is far from permanent, for their status is likely to be questioned whenever a new book attracts sufficient attention to compel revaluation of the old, thus creating that retroactive phenomenon first described by T. S. Eliot and labelled by Kubler the 'Eliot-effect':[62]

The existing monuments form an ideal order among themselves, which is modified by the introduction of the new (the really new) work of art among them. The existing order is complete before the new work arrives; for order to persist after the supervention of novelty, the *whole* existing order must be, if ever so slightly, altered; and so the relations, proportions, values of each work of art toward the whole are readjusted.

Absolutists who apply prescriptively a set of criteria deduced from a body of writings known to be classic have a much easier task than others whose response to the new entails regular revision of the canons by which they judge it. Unless absolutists are willing to contravene their own rules – as Addison did in admiring *Chevy Chase*, or Johnson Shakespeare ('there is always an appeal open from criticism to nature') – they are likely to end up as narrow-minded as Max Beerbohm's tourist, 'who takes a home-made tuning-fork about with him and condemns the discords'.[63] Matthew Arnold called his tuning-forks 'touchstones': eleven fragments from Dante (3), Homer (3), Milton (3) and Shakespeare (2), all offered as quintessential examples of greatness in literature.[64] They were to constitute (writes Leavis) 'a tip for mobilising our sensibility; for focusing our relevant experience in a sensitive point; for reminding us vividly of what the best is like'.[65] On closer inspection, however, they turn out to be surprisingly Arnoldian in their tone of melancholy resignation, and not at all the objective criteria they are made out to be. The absolutist's show of impartiality when applying the so-called classic criteria prescriptively is rarely convincing. Nobody is ever going to achieve that somewhat ludicrous state of mind deemed necessary in the ideal observer: 'fully informed, and vividly imaginative, impartial, in a calm frame of mind, and otherwise normal'.[66] Yet critics continue to reinvent the Joycean spectre of an 'ideal reader suffering from an ideal insomnia', such as Lowry Nelson's 'optimum reader' and Michael Riffaterre's 'superreader'.[67] Understandably, a recent investigator of the normative fallacy concludes that 'absolute evaluation, the measuring of a work of art against some universally accepted norm, is not a valid function of criticism'.[68] And if that is so, our only alternative is to abandon absolutism for some form of relativism.

The subjectivity and relativity of values

Pythagoreans believed beauty to be an objective property which we discover in the course of observing the nature of things; Sophists, on the contrary, believing with Protagoras that man is the measure of all things, saw beauty as a subjective experience in the beholder.[69] 'Beauty is no quality in things themselves', David Hume observed in 1757; 'it exists merely in the mind which contemplates them.'[70] Similarly, literary values do not reside in literary works, but are projected on to them by readers.[71] Moreover, we cannot quantify such qualitative experiences, which is why we find it amusing to invent imaginary machines for doing precisely that, like Keats's 'pleasure thermometer'.[72] We have nothing comparable to the Richter scale to help us calibrate the seismic experience of reading. Consequently, the precise gauging of literary excellence has never been more than a makeshift affair heavily disguised with pseudo-scientific terminology.

If value resides in the eye of the beholder (and there is nothing either good or bad but thinking makes it so), evaluation becomes a solipsistic activity. All value-judgements are relative to the people who make them and therefore the expression of personal taste. *De gustibus non est disputandum*: there is no disputing tastes, and certainly not with the tasteless. The historicist version of this argument is to treat all values as relative to the era or culture in which they are found, and therefore to assess individual achievement in terms of contemporary value-systems, as Hurd does when insisting that Spenser should be judged by 'Gothic' rather than 'Grecian' standards.[73] Critical relativists are strongly historicist, and come under attack for this very reason. They are accused of subverting the critical endeavour by parading their weakness as a strength, notably in their cultivation of an eclecticism which entails liking different things for different reasons, and therefore nothing for the right reason. 'The man who sees both sides of a question, is a man who sees absolutely nothing at all', wrote Wilde. 'It is only an auctioneer who should admire all schools of art.'[74] Although the house of fiction contains many mansions, absolutists imagine it as being more like Sainte-Beuve's selective 'temple of taste' than André Malraux's *musée imaginaire*, to which everything reproducible is admitted.[75]

Relativists are also accused of being tacitly absolutist in distributing their enthusiasms over a wide variety of works generally held in high repute. 'Relativists always shirk the issue of thoroughly bad poetry', Wellek complains; and they do so, according to Wimsatt, 'by moving steadily in a realm of great and nearly great art'.[76] Certainly, the relativist position is not without its paradoxes. The very decision to judge things on their own terms, John Passmore observes, is an absolute decision: 'even more difficult is the attempt to maintain, as a timeless philosophical truth, that there are no timeless philosophical truths'.[77] To 'profess' relativism is therefore theoretically as bizarre as Blake's generalisation that 'to generalise is to be an idiot'.[78] Instead of contesting the theoretical issue, however, relativists point to the history of critical reputations as exemplified in E. E. Kellett's reconstruction of the whirligig of taste.

A Cowley takes the world by storm: a generation passes, and Pope asks, 'Who now reads Cowley?' Pope himself becomes the *ne plus ultra* of genius, and the *Essay on man* is the height of the sublime. Half a century after his death it is seriously debated whether he is a poet at all. Byron's *Cain*, said Scott in 1821, 'certainly matches Milton on his own ground'; in 1860 people did not stop to consider such a judgement –[79]

because by then the greatest poet was Tennyson, who was regarded as old-fashioned when Kellett published these reflections (1928), and is currently read much more sympathetically now that the great Victorians are remote enough in time to invite historical interest.

The opening-up of new areas of literary study – black, working-class, feminist, commonwealth, and so on – has lent further support to relativists by drawing attention to problems which arise when people take the criteria deemed appropriate to one type of literature and apply it to other types. Eurocentric pundits ('Better fifty years of Europe than a cycle of Cathay') are less prominent than they used to be, and no longer have the nerve to confront a newly emergent literature quite so arrogantly as Sydney Smith did when he asked readers of the *Edinburgh review* in 1820: 'In the four quarters of the globe, who reads an American book?'[80] Nevertheless, teachers of the newer literatures written in English face serious problems of evaluation if they reject the 'double standard' which rates (say) Ursula Bethell a major New Zealand but minor English poet.[81] Inevitably, arguments about performances come down to arguments about criteria. The bolder defenders of alternative literatures call for new scales of value. Afro-American writing, they insist, has qualities not measurable by WASP standards; and feminist writing is said to be discriminated against by tacitly androcentric criteria in exactly the same way as working-class literature is disparaged by a tacitly middle-class scale of values.[82] The usual remedy is to invent 'relevant' criteria which issue from the works themselves, on the grounds that Afro-Americans are Afro-Americans and not non-WASPs, just as women are women and not non-men. Each group decides what books it wants to call literature, and then agrees on ways of talking about them. It is a striking vindication of John M. Ellis's view that texts are not inherently literary but are 'made into literature by the community', and that 'assertions of value refer primarily not to the structural properties of texts, but to their performance as literary texts'.[83]

Relevance is the most common manifestation nowadays of so-called 'interest' theories of value, which are resorted to by relativists who admit that they do not really invent fresh criteria every time they read a new book. Boas defines value as 'the satisfaction of any interest'.[84] Genuine interest-values are often obscured as a result of our reluctance to face up to the fact that we like some things more than others, and for reasons we would rather not go into. We may not know much about art, but at least we know what we like. If this sounds like the quintessence of philistinism, it is at least the philistinism of Henry James, who thought that 'nothing... will ever take the place of the good old fashion of "liking" a work of art or not liking it: the most improved criticism will not abolish that primitive, that ultimate test'.[85]

Criticism appears to be the art of persuading other people that one's own likes and dislikes are worth emulating. This is done by inventing reasons coherent with one another, and supporting them by reference to carefully selected texts. A judicial end is thus achieved by rhetorical means. Those seminal figures we call great critics (Dryden, Johnson, Coleridge, Arnold, Eliot) have always known what they liked at the time of writing, even if they sometimes lived long enough to modify or disavow the tastes of their salad days. Powerful rhetoricians, they tried to make universal laws out of their personal tastes. If their achievements are still exemplary, it is because they show us there are different ways of being right about books. Faced with the authoritative subjectivity of their different styles of criticism, is it surprising that so many readers nowadays prefer the accommodations of relativism to the exclusiveness of absolutism?

Writers as critics

A venerable tradition holds that criticism is dispensable with because the wrong kind of people practise it. One could no doubt compile a whole bestiary of abuse levelled at professional critics, from the Elizabethan 'viperous critic' assailed by Samuel Daniel to Tennyson's designation of Churton Collins as 'a louse upon the locks of literature'.[86] At the root of the matter is Aristotle's opinion that you cannot be a good judge of something you yourself are unable to do: 'to judge of poets is only the faculty of poets', wrote Ben Jonson, 'and not of all poets, but the best'.[87]

The critic is commonly accused of being fundamentally a writer manqué, whose envy of his betters comes out in sour comments on their work. The 'malignant critic', Shelley told Byron, is 'that second degree in the descending scale of Disappointed Authors'.[88] Non-malignant critics receive the same diagnosis. It was T. S. Eliot who described the criticism of Ruskin and Pater as 'etiolated creation', 'the satisfaction of a suppressed creative wish', and in this respect akin to the criticism of Sainte-Beuve, who was 'certainly...a failed creative writer'.[89] Even critics sometimes perpetuate this myth. 'When he looks back, the critic sees a eunuch's shadow', writes George Steiner,[90] although not very convincingly, in so far as his own criticism displays a virtuosity which must surely persuade our more pedestrian poets and novelists that a life spent playing Leporello to someone else's Don Juan is not exactly devoid of compensations.

As a parasitic activity, criticism is held to be naturally inferior to creative work: 'even a bad verse', Gray told Mason, is 'as good a thing or better, than the best observation, that ever was made upon it'.[91] Moreover, critics are condemned for trying to lay down the law to people who see it as their business to make and break such laws. For if to criticise is to judge (which is what the etymology of the word insists), then authors constitute the accused in the judicial relationship, and feel entitled to demand with Shelley that 'the jury which sits in judgement upon a poet...must be composed of his peers'.[92] Judicial critics seek guidance from those precedents they call classics, and do so in the hope of preventing a lowering of standards. But to young writers (who usually receive rough justice from such a system), reliance on prescriptive criteria is rear-vision driving at its worst, and can only result in a disastrous collision with the present. Rather than wrangle with self-appointed arbiters of taste, confident writers prefer to live outside the law, as Fielding did in writing *Tom Jones* (1749): 'as I am, in reality, the founder of a new province of writing, so I am at liberty to make what laws I please therein'; or in the more aggressive style of William Carlos Williams: 'I'll write whatever I damn please, whenever I damn please and as I damn please.'[93]

The continuing existence of a cold war between writers and critics, interrupted every now and then by open hostility, is a curious phenomenon perhaps unique to the business of criticism. In most other disciplines, a clear-cut distinction is drawn between students and their subject of study. If it is true that 'aesthetics is for the artist as ornithology is for the birds',[94] it is equally true that birds do not make the best ornithologists. 'You *may* abuse a tragedy', Johnson told Boswell, 'though you cannot write one. You may scold a carpenter who has made you a bad table, though you cannot make a table. It is not your trade to make tables.'[95] Critics must always feel free to say, as Francis Jeffrey did of Wordsworth's *The excursion* (1814), 'this will never do'.[96] To writers, however, such remarks must always appear exasperatingly negative. E. M. Forster said he 'nearly always found criticism irrelevant' because it never told him what to do but only what not to do.[97] Judicial criticism is a continual rewriting of Ezra Pound's 'A few don'ts for Imagists', with the scope widened to include dramatists and novelists.[98] More often querulous than approbatory, it appears to confirm the popular view that to criticise something is to find fault with it. And so its fastidious exclusiveness is neatly mocked in Randall Jarrell's definition of a novel as 'a prose narrative of some length that has something wrong with it'.[99]

'Let such teach others who themselves excel': like Jonson before him, Pope believed that only the best writers are capable of producing the kind of judicial criticism from which others can benefit.[100] Unfortunately, their record is more disappointing than might be expected, and certainly not untainted by professional malice of the sort displayed in Robert Graves's *The crowning privilege* (London, 1955). In criticising their own work they are frequently very impressive, as notebooks and worksheets testify; but their comments on fellow practitioners are scarcely characterised by that 'disinterested' curiosity which Matthew Arnold recommended to critics.[101] Emerson could see no more value in Hawthorne or Poe than Eliot or Pound could see in Emily Dickinson.[102] While Byron thought Keats spoilt his poetry with 'the fantastic fopperies of his style', Keats spoke of *Don Juan* as 'Lord Byron's last flash poem';[103] and so on. Nevertheless, publishers and editors continue to hire the services of poets and novelists as reviewers and anthologists. Yet although D. H. Lawrence's *Studies in classic American literature* (New York, 1923) is still regarded as the best in its field, it is a remarkable exception to the rule. For on the whole, criticism by a practising writer tends to be a justification of his own practice at the time of writing, a declaration (in Auden's phrase) of 'what he should do next and what he should avoid'.[104] Pragmatic in emphasis, it is likely to be just as self-centred in its own way as the work of any professional critic with an axe to grind. When Eliot argued in 1920 that the only genuine criticism is that of the poet-critic who is 'criticising poetry in order to create poetry', he betrayed interests which led him to disparage Milton in 1921 and reinstate him in 1947, for the selfish reason that Milton had much less to contribute to *The waste land* (1922) than to *Little Gidding* (1942).[105] Scholars and critics have not always taken Eliot's advice and treated his essays as 'workshop criticism'.[106] Some, like Basil Willey and F. R. Leavis, have adduced historical and critical support for his theory that in the seventeenth century there occurred a 'dissociation of sensibility' which has made the writing of poetry inordinately difficult ever since.[107] Nowadays, in the wake of a penetrating critique of this theory by Frank Kermode, it is tempting to go to the other extreme and treat Eliot's famous dicta as true only of local instances in the Eliot oeuvre – to read his remarks on the dissociation of sensibility as a gloss on 'Whispers of immortality', for example, or to approach 'Rhapsody on a windy night' (1915) by way of the *Hamlet* essay (1919) on 'objective correlatives', or to consider the 1942 essay on 'The music of poetry' as a guide to *Four quartets* (1943).[108]

The changing fortune of Eliot's criticism illustrates some of the drawbacks of allowing a major poet to dictate the terms in which criticism is to be conducted. What Wordsworth had to say about Gray in 1800 illuminates largely Wordsworth's own difficulties in trying to assert himself in a milieu of stale Augustanisms: Wordsworth had no creative use for the style of Gray, so was obliged to dismiss it.[109] Yet surely one of the ways in which a writer demonstrates his superiority is by seeming to exhaust all the possibilities of the mode in which he works. It is no more to Gray's discredit that he left nothing for Wordsworth to do in that particular mode, than that Wordsworth himself is culpable for having perfected a poetic idiom to be avoided at all costs by Tennyson and Browning, whose own styles were in turn to provide fresh obstacles to the young Eliot and Pound. There is much truth in Helen Gardner's observation that 'the critic or scholar has a different function from that of the artist or original thinker', because 'his humble task is to protect his betters from the corruptions of fashion'.[110] By contrast, the criticism of any self-assured writer is bound to be revisionary. Unlike the critic, who may suspect something has gone wrong but does not know what would make it go right, the poet-critic tends to wonder what he himself would have done with the same materials. The result of Pound's celebrated excisions from *The waste land* was to make a more Poundian poem of Eliot's original version by heightening the effects of juxtaposition with which Pound was already experimenting in *The cantos*.[111] And the effect of reviewing George Eliot's *Middlemarch* (1871–72) was to enable Henry James to discover an abortive Jamesian novel in it. 'Dorothea was altogether too superb a heroine to be wasted', thought James.

She is of more consequence than the action of which she is the nominal centre. She marries enthusiastically a man whom she fancies a great thinker [Casaubon], and who turns out to be but an arid pedant. Here, indeed, is a disappointment with much of the dignity of tragedy; but the situation seems to us never to expand to its full capacity.[112]

Almost as if to remedy this deficiency, James went on to write *The portrait of a lady* (1881), in which the heroine, Isabel Archer, marries enthusiastically a man whom she fancies to be an embodiment of European culture, Gilbert Osmond, but who turns out to be an arid dilettante. And James sees to it that the tragedy of Isabel's situation is expanded to its full capacity.

As his prefaces reveal, James was very good on Jamesian novels, but rather less reliable on other people's, which makes it unwise to take his views as exemplary to the extent that Percy Lubbock did in *The craft of fiction* (London, 1921). Self-centred in his genius, James was puzzled by novels based on different premises from his own, such as those of H. G. Wells and D. H. Lawrence. A reading of *Sons and lovers* (1913) – 'that rather sickly and morally unintelligible book', as T. S. Eliot was to call it – convinced James that Lawrence hung 'in the dusty rear' of Hugh Walpole, Gilbert Cannan and Compton Mackenzie; and he thought equally unfavourably of *The rainbow* (1915), although predictably so according to Lawrence, who deliberately avoided that 'subtle conven-

tional design' to which James was partial.[113] Set a thief to catch
a thief, so they say: but to ask one writer to judge another is to
multiply the variables without any guarantee of improving the
assessment.

A powerful impediment to the development of a literary
axiology is a widespread suspicion that there are much better
things to do with books than evaluate them. Cast in the role of
reputation-mongers, evaluative critics are accused of degrading
literature into a Stock Exchange commodity:

> Joyces are firm and there there's nothing new.
> Eliots have hardened just a point or two.
> Hopkins are brisk, thanks to some recent boosts.
> There's been some further weakening in Prousts.[114]

'The practice of pitting works of art against each other', André
Malraux complains, 'is at the opposite pole from the mood of
relaxation which alone makes contemplation possible.'[115] Evaluation is reductive. 'Don't you see', John Cage asks, 'that when
you get a value judgement, that's all you have? They are
destructive to our proper business, which is curiosity and
awareness.'[116] The alternative envisaged by Northrop Frye in his
Anatomy of criticism (Princeton, 1957) is a generic approach to
literature which enables us to group together books which
resemble one another, without indulging in the wasteful activity
of prematurely setting up elimination-procedures by which the
good is eclipsed by the major and the major by the great, or trying
to sort out terminological farces such as whether a badly written
great novel like Theodore Dreiser's *An American tragedy* (1925) is
better than a well-written minor novel like Ken Kesey's *One flew
over the cuckoo's nest* (1962). Frye's categories are mytho-poetic, and
his whole approach is deutero-creative, but he has mapped out the
only comprehensive 'placement' theory of value to rival the older
hierarchical models which are nowadays in such disrepute. And
he has been more successful than any other literary theorist in
persuading us that the supreme critical act is not evaluation but
recognition.

Notes

Abbreviations

BJA	British journal of aesthetics
CE	College English
CL	Comparative literature
EIC	Essays in criticism
ELH	ELH: journal of English literary history
ES	English studies
HudR	Hudson review
JAAC	Journal of aesthetics and art criticism
JEGP	Journal of English and Germanic philology
JHI	Journal of the history of ideas
JP	Journal of philosophy
MLR	Modern language review
MP	Modern philology
NLH	New literary history
PMLA	Publications of the Modern Language Association of America
PPR	Philosophy and phenomenological research
PQ	Philological quarterly
SP	Studies in philology
SR	Sewanee review
TLS	Times literary supplement
UTQ	University of Toronto quarterly
YCGL	Yearbook of comparative and general literature
YR	Yale review

Notes to chapter 1

1. Abraham Cowley, 'The muse [1668]', *Poems*, ed. A. R. Waller (Cambridge, 1905), p. 185.
2. The Earl of Shaftesbury, *Characteristics of men, manners, opinions, times* [1711] (3 vols., Birmingham, 1773), vol. 1, p. 207.
3. Alexander Gottlieb Baumgarten, *Reflections on poetry* [*Meditationes philosophicae de nonnullis ad poema pertinentibus*, 1735], trans. K. Aschenbrenner & William B. Holther (Berkeley, 1954), para. 51–53.
4. Thomas G. Pavel, '"Possible worlds" in literary semantics', *JAAC*, 34 (1975–76), 165–76.

5. H. Winston Rhodes, 'The moral climate of Sargeson's stories', *Landfall*, 9 (1955), 25–41; Rosette C. Lamont, 'The topography of Ionescoland', *Modern occasions*, 1 (1971), 536–46.

6. J. R. R. Tolkien, 'On fairy-stories', in *Essays presented to Charles Williams*, ed. C. S. Lewis (New York, 1947), p. 70.

7. J. Middleton Murry, *Countries of the mind* (London, 1931).

8. Wallace Stevens, *The necessary angel* (London, 1960), pp. 57–58; John Press, *The chequer'd shade* (London, 1958), ch. 7; Andrei Voznesensky, *Antiworlds*, ed. Patricia Blake & Max Hayward (London, 1967), p. 40.

9. P. N. Furbank, *Reflections on the word 'image'* (London, 1970), pp. 113–24.

10. E. M. Forster, *Aspects of the novel* [1927] (London, 1949), p. 12.

11. Dorothy Walsh, *Literature and knowledge* (Middletown, Conn., 1969), p. 57.

12. Heinrich Wölfflin, *The sense of form in art*, trans. Alice Muehsam & Norma A. Shatan (New York, 1958).

13. Letter dated 5 August 1844, *The correspondence of Thomas Carlyle and Ralph Waldo Emerson 1834–72*, ed. Charles Eliot Norton (2 vols., London, 1883), vol. 2, p. 66.

14. Edward W. Said, *Beginnings* (New York, 1975), p. 81.

15. Terry Eagleton, 'Marxist literary criticism', in *Contemporary approaches to English studies*, ed. Hilda Schiff (London, 1977), p. 96.

16. James Joyce, *Finnegans wake* (London, 1939), p. 118.

17. Henry Adams, *The education of Henry Adams* [1918], intro. D. W. Brogan (Boston, 1961), p. 451.

18. George Boas, *The heaven of invention* (Baltimore, 1962), p. 281.

19. 'To...Sir Robert Howard, on his excellent poems [1660]', *The poems of John Dryden*, ed. James Kinsley (4 vols., Oxford, 1958), vol. 1, p. 13.

20. Anton Ehrenzweig, *The hidden order of art* (London, 1967).

21. Max Wertheimer, 'Über Gestalttheorie [1924]', trans. in *History of psychology*, ed. William S. Sahakian (Itasca, Ill., 1968), p. 417.

22. Hermann Rorschach, *Psychodiagnostik* [1921], trans. in *History of psychology*, ed. Sahakian, p. 350.

23. Monroe C. Beardsley, 'Order and disorder in art', in *The concept of order*, ed. Paul G. Kuntz (Seattle & London, 1968), p. 194.

24. 'Song [from *The silent woman*, 1609]', *Poems of Ben Jonson*, ed. George Burke Johnston (London, 1954), p. 272; 'Delight in disorder [1648]', *The poetical works of Robert Herrick*, ed. L. C. Martin (Oxford, 1956), p. 28.

25. Jonathan Culler, *Flaubert* (London, 1974).

26. Rudolf Arnheim, 'Information theory and the arts', *JAAC*, 17 (1958–59), 501.

27. Rudolf Arnheim, *Entropy and art* (Berkeley, 1971), p. 13.

28. Louis T. Milic, 'Information theory and the style of *Tristram Shandy*', in *The winged skull*, ed. Arthur H. Cash & John M. Stedmond (London, 1971), pp. 237–46.

29. 'The man with the blue guitar [1937]', *The collected poems of Wallace Stevens* (London, 1945), p. 165.

30. Hugh Kenner, *Flaubert, Joyce and Beckett* (London, 1964), p. 53.

31. Anthony Trollope, *An autobiography* [1883], intro. Charles Morgan (London, 1946), p. 144; 'My first book – *Treasure island* [1894]', *The works of Robert Louis Stevenson*, intro. Andrew Lang (25 vols., London, 1911–12), vol. 16, p. 339.

32. W. B. Stanford & J. V. Luce, *The quest for Ulysses* (London, 1974), p. 118.

33. John D. Boyd, *The function of mimesis and its decline* (Cambridge, Mass., 1968); Ernst Robert Curtius, 'The ape as metaphor', *European literature and the Latin Middle Ages*, trans. Willard R. Trask (New York, 1953), pp. 538–40.

34. Shakespeare, *Hamlet*, III ii 26; Stendhal, *Le rouge et le noir* [1830], ed. Henri Martineau (Paris, 1960), p. 76.

35. Victor Erlich, 'Limits of the biographical approach', *CL*, 6 (1954), 137.

36. Marianne Moore, 'Poetry [1921]', *Collected poems* (New York, 1951), p. 41.

37. W. H. Hunt, *Pre-Raphaelitism and the Pre-Raphaelite Brotherhood* (2 vols., London, 1905), vol. 1, p. 150; Charles Baudelaire, 'Éloge du maquillage [1863]', *Oeuvres complètes*, ed. Y.-G. Le Dantec & Claude Pichois (Paris, 1961), p. 1185.

38. Sir Philip Sidney, *An apologie for poetry*, ed. Geoffrey Shepherd (London, 1965), p. 100; John M. Steadman, *The lamb and the elephant* (San Marino, 1974).

39. *The grounds of criticism in poetry* [1704], *The critical works of John Dennis*, ed. Edward Niles Hooker (2 vols., Baltimore, 1939–43), vol. 1, p. 336.

40. Baudelaire, 'Salon de 1859', *Oeuvres complètes*, ed. Dantec & Pichois, pp. 1037–38.

41. 'Annotations to "Poems" by William Wordsworth [1826]', *The complete writings of William Blake*, ed. Geoffrey Keynes (London, 1957), p. 783; 'A descriptive catalogue [1810]', *ib.*, p. 600.

42. 'The poetic principle [1850]', *The works of Edgar Allan Poe*, ed. John H. Ingram (4 vols., 1899), vol. 3, p. 202.

43. Vladimir Nabokov, *Pale fire* (London, 1962), p. 130.

44. M. H. Abrams, 'What's the use of theorising about the arts?' in *In search of literary theory*, ed. Morton W. Bloomfield (Ithaca & London, 1972), pp. 44–45.

45. René Wellek, *A history of modern criticism: 1750–1950* (5 vols., New Haven & London, 1955–), vol. 1, pp. 229–30.

46. Jerome Stolnitz, 'On the origins of "aesthetic disinterestedness"', *JAAC*, 20 (1961–62), 131–43.

47. A. C. Bradley, *Oxford lectures on poetry* (London, 1909), p. 5.

48. Virginia Woolf, 'Mr Bennett and Mrs Brown [1924]', *Collected essays* (4 vols., London, 1966–67), vol. 1, pp. 326–27.

49. 'La Mélinite: Moulin Rouge [1895]', *Poems by Arthur Symons* (2 vols., London, 1921), vol. 1, pp. 99–100; G. Ingli James, 'The autonomy of the work of art: modern criticism and the Christian tradition', *SR*, 70 (1962), 313.

50. Stéphane Mallarmé, 'Quant au livre [1895]', *Oeuvres complètes*, ed. Henri Mondor & G. Jean-Aubry (Paris, 1945), p. 378.

51. A. C. Howell, '*Res et verba*: words and things', *ELH*, 13 (1946), 131–42.

52. Letter dated 22 September 1800, *Collected letters of Samuel Taylor Coleridge*, ed. Earl Leslie Griggs (6 vols., Oxford, 1956–71), vol. 1, p. 626.

53. 'An ordinary evening in New Haven [1950]', *The collected poems of Wallace Stevens*, p. 473.

54. Conversation dated 3 July 1833, *The table talk and omniana of Samuel Taylor Coleridge*, ed. T. Ashe (London, 1884), p. 238.

55. Ford Madox Ford, *Joseph Conrad* (London, 1924), p. 186.

56. 'Introduction', *The principles of human knowledge* [1710], *The works of George Berkeley*, ed. A. A. Luce & T. E. Jessop (9 vols, London, 1948–57), vol. 2, p. 40.

57. Samuel Johnson, 'Cowley', *Lives of the English poets* [1779–81], intro. L. Archer-Hind, Everyman's Library (2 vols., London, n.d.), vol. 1, p. 39.

58. 'Preface to *Troilus and Cressida* [1679]', *Essays of John Dryden*, ed. W. P. Ker (2 vols., Oxford, 1900), vol. 1, p. 204.

59. 'Style, iv [1841]', *The collected writings of Thomas De Quincey*, ed. David Masson (14 vols., London, 1896–97), vol. 10, pp. 229–30.

60. 'Essay upon epitaphs [no. iii, 1812]', *The prose works of William Wordsworth*, ed. W. J. B. Owen & June Worthington Smyser (3 vols., Oxford, 1974), vol. 2, p. 84; *The prelude*, III 515–16.

61. Ovid, *Metamorphoses*, X 86–144; Gerald L. Bruns, *Modern poetry and the idea of language* (London, 1974).

62. 'The song of the happy shepherd [1885]', *The collected poems of W. B. Yeats*, 2nd edn (London, 1950), p. 7.

63. Richard Poirier, *A world elsewhere* (New York, 1966); cf. Tony Tanner, *City of words* (London, 1971).

Notes to chapter 2

1. M. H. Abrams, *The mirror and the lamp* (New York, 1953); G. N. G. Orsini, *Organic unity in ancient and later poetics* (Carbondale, 1975).

2. Rudolf Wittkower, 'The changing concept of proportion', *Daedalus* (Winter 1960), 199–215.

3. George E. Duckworth, *Structural patterns and proportions in Vergil's 'Aeneid'* (Ann Arbor, 1962), p. 13.

4. Guy Le Grelle, 'Le premier livre des *Georgiques*, poème pythagoricien', *Les études classiques*, 17 (1949), 139–235.

5. Matthew Arnold, 'On the study of Celtic literature [1866]', *Lectures and essays in criticism*, ed. R. H. Super (Ann Arbor, 1962), p. 345.

6. Colin Robert Chase, 'Panel structure in Old English poetry', *Dissertation abstracts international*, 32 (1972), 6965; Bernard F. Huppé, *The web of words* (Albany, 1970), p. xvi; Eugène Vinaver, 'The poetry of interlace', *The rise of romance* (Oxford, 1971), pp. 68–98.

7. *The poems of John Milton*, ed. John Carey & Alastair Fowler (London, 1968), p. 445; Christopher Butler, *Number symbolism* (London, 1970); R. G. Peterson, 'Critical calculations: measure and symmetry in literature', *PMLA*, 91 (1976), 367–75.

8. Douglas Bush, *Engaged and disengaged* (Cambridge, Mass., 1966), p. 65; *The poems of John Milton*, ed. Carey & Fowler, p. 441.

9. Joseph Frank, 'Spatial form in modern literature', in *The widening gyre* (New Brunswick, 1963), pp. 3–62; 'Spatial form: an answer to critics', *Critical inquiry*, 4 (1977–78), 231–52.

10. Berjouhi Bowler, *The word as image* (London, 1970); Thomas Hobbes, 'Answer to Davenant's preface to *Gondibert* [1650]', in *Critical essays of the seventeenth century*, ed. Joel L. Spingarn (3 vols., Oxford, 1908–09), vol. 2, p. 57.

11. G. Wilson Knight, *The wheel of fire* [1930] (London, 1949), pp. 14–15; Barbara Herrnstein Smith, *Poetic closure* (Chicago, 1968), p. 36.

12. 'Shakespeare's judgement equal to his genius [1813]', *Coleridge's literary criticism*, intro. J. W. Mackail (London, 1908), p. 186.

13. 'Prolegomena [1912]', *Literary essays of Ezra Pound*, ed. T. S. Eliot (London, 1954), p. 9.

14. Edmond Duranty, '[Review of] *Madame Bovary* [1857]', in *Documents of modern literary realism*, ed. George T. Becker (Princeton, 1963), p. 98.

15. M. H. Abrams, 'Archetypal analogies in the language of criticism', *UTQ*, 18 (1948–49), 321.

16. W. K. Wimsatt, 'Organic form: some questions about a metaphor', in *Organic form*, ed. G. S. Rousseau (London, 1972), p. 70.

17. S. T. Coleridge, *Biographia literaria* [1817], ed. J. Shawcross (2 vols., London, 1907), vol. 2, p. 56; 'Hints towards the formation of a more comprehensive theory of life [1848]', quoted in Owen Barfield, *What Coleridge thought* (Middletown, Conn., 1971), p. 50; James Benziger, 'Organic unity: Leibniz to Coleridge', *PMLA*, 66 (March 1951), 24–48.

18. Peter Salm, *Drei Richtungen der Literaturwissenschaft* (Tübingen, 1970), p. 47.

19. Ezra Pound, *Guide to kulchur* (London, 1938), p. 152.

20. Letter dated 5 June 1914, *The letters of D. H. Lawrence*, ed. Aldous Huxley (London, 1932), p. 199.

21. Dionysius, *De compositione verborum*, 20, in *Ancient literary criticism*, ed. D. A. Russell & M. Winterbottom (Oxford, 1972), pp. 335–37.

22. F. R. Leavis, *Revaluation* (London, 1936), pp. 55, 263–64.

23. John Donne, 'Satire iii', *The satires, epigrams and verse letters*, ed. W. Milgate (Oxford, 1967), p. 13.

24. William T. Moynihan, 'The auditory correlative', *JAAC*, 17 (1958–59), 93–102; 'An essay on criticism [1711]', *The poems of Alexander Pope*, ed. John Butt (London, 1963), p. 155.

25. Samuel Johnson, *Rambler*, no. 94 (9 February 1751), *The rambler*, ed. W. J. Bate & Albrecht B. Strauss (3 vols., New Haven & London, 1969), vol. 2, p. 139.

26. Johnson, *Idler*, no. 60 (9 June 1759), '*The idler*' and '*The adventurer*', ed. W. J. Bate, *et al.* (New Haven & London, 1963), p. 189.

27. Yvor Winters, *In defence of reason* (Denver, 1947), p. 41.

28. Antonio Minturno, *L'arte poetica* [1564], in *Literary criticism: Plato to Dryden*, ed. Allan H. Gilbert (New York, 1940), p. 278; Richard Hurd, *Letters on chivalry and romance* (London, 1762), pp. 65–66.

29. *Encounters*, ed. John Dixon Hunt (London, 1971), plate 30.

30. William Holtz, 'Typography, *Tristram Shandy*, the aposiopesis, etc.', in *The winged skull*, ed. Cash & Stedmond, pp. 247–57.

31. Coleridge, *Biographia literaria*, ed. Shawcross, vol. 2, p. 36.

32. Robert Martin Adams, *Strains of discord* (Ithaca, 1958), pp. 13, 202.

33. Quoted in G. Jean-Aubry, *Joseph Conrad: life and letters* (2 vols., New York, 1927), vol. 2, p. 68.

34. D. H. Lawrence, 'Introduction to *New poems* [1920]', *Selected literary criticism*, ed. Anthony Beal (London, 1955), p. 85; *Sons and lovers* [1913], intro. Anthony Beal (London, 1963), p. 152.

35. Letter dated 5 June 1914, *The letters of D. H. Lawrence*, ed. Huxley, p. 198.

36. Lawrence, 'Introduction to *New poems* [1920]', *Selected literary criticism*, ed. Beal, pp. 85, 87.

37. Jon Stallworthy, *Between the lines* (Oxford, 1963).

38. Adams, *Strains of discord*, pp. 13–14; D. F. Rauber, 'The fragment as Romantic form', *Modern language quarterly*, 30 (1968), 212–21.

39. Paul Valéry, 'Concerning "Le cimetière marin" [1933]', *The art of poetry*, trans. Denise Folliot, intro. T. S. Eliot (London, 1958), pp. 140–41.

40. Jane Austen's unfinished novel, *The Watsons*, was begun in 1803 and published posthumously in 1871. It was 'concluded' by L. Oulton (London, 1923) before being 'completed in accordance with her intentions by Edith (her great grand-niece) and Francis Brown' (London, 1928); and it has since been 'continued and completed' by John Coates (New York, 1958) and by 'Another' (London, 1977).

41. Max Beerbohm, 'Quia imperfectum [1918]', *The incomparable Max*, intro. S. C. Roberts (London, 1962), p. 259; Albert R. Corns & Archibald Sparke, *A bibliography of unfinished books in the English language* (New York, 1969).

42. Kathleen Freeman, *The pre-Socratic philosophers*, 2nd edn (2 vols., Oxford, 1949), vol. 2, pp. 113–14.

43. Samuel Johnson, *The history of Rasselas* [1759], ed. Geoffrey Tillotson & Brian Jenkins (London, 1971), p. 21; Helmut Hungerland, 'Consistency as a criterion in art criticism', *JAAC*, 7 (1948–49), 93–112.

44. André Gide, *The counterfeiters* [1925], trans. Dorothy Bussy (New York, 1927), p. 311.

45. Walt Whitman, 'Song of myself', *Leaves of grass* [1855], ed. Harold W. Blodgett & Sculley Bradley (New York, 1965), p. 88.

46. R. W. Emerson, 'Self-reliance', *Essays* (Boston, 1941), p. 47; *The wit and humour of Oscar Wilde*, ed. Alvin Redman (New York, 1959), p. 207.

47. Sermon preached 1618, *The sermons of John Donne*, ed. George R. Potter & Evelyn M. Simpson (10 vols., Berkeley & Los Angeles, 1953–62), vol. 2, p. 50; Coleridge, *Biographia literaria*, ed. Shawcross, vol. 1, p. 15; Monroe C. Beardsley, 'The concept of economy in art', *JAAC*, 14 (1955–56), 370–75.

48. Virginia Woolf, *A writer's diary*, ed. Leonard Woolf (London, 1953), p. 139.

49. Henry James, 'Preface [1907] to *The tragic muse*', *The art of the novel*, intro. Richard P. Blackmur (New York & London, 1934), p. 84; letter dated 19 May 1912, *Selected letters of Henry James*, ed. Leon Edel (London, 1956), p. 202.

50. Forster, *Aspects of the novel*, p. 148.

51. Donald Barthelme, *Snow White* (New York, 1967), p. 106.

52. Catherine Lord, 'Organic unity reconsidered', *JAAC*, 22 (1963–64), 265.

53. Ruth Crosby, 'Oral delivery in the Middle Ages', *Speculum*, 11 (1936), 88–110; Bruce F. Kawin, *Telling it again and again* (Ithaca & London, 1972).

54. Trollope, *An autobiography*, intro. Morgan, p. 213.
55. Ford Madox Ford, *It was the nightingale* [1934], quoted in Miriam Allott (ed.), *Novelists on the novel* (London, 1959), p. 236.
56. 'Lecture ix: Sterne [1818]', *Coleridge's miscellaneous criticism*, ed. Thomas Middleton Raysor (Cambridge, Mass., 1936), p. 126.

Notes to chapter 3

1. Arnold, 'On the study of Celtic literature [1866]', *Lectures and essays in criticism*, ed. Super, p. 362.
2. *Troilus and Criseyde*, Proem to Bk III, *The works of Geoffrey Chaucer*, ed. F. N. Robinson, 2nd edn (London, 1966), p. 421.
3. 'Il penseroso [1631]', *Paradise lost*, III 380, *The poems of John Milton*, ed. Carey & Fowler, pp. 144, 583; 'The night [1650]', *The works of Henry Vaughan*, ed. L. C. Martin (London, 1957), p. 523.
4. A. S. Palmer, *The folk and their word-lore* (London & New York, 1904), pp. 163–65.
5. *The letter-book of Gabriel Harvey* [1573–80], ed. Edward John Long Scott [1884] (New York, 1965), p. 123; Samuel Purchas, *Purchas his pilgrimage* [1613], quoted in Palmer, *The folk and their word-lore*, p. 164.
6. 'The new obscurity in poetry [1889]', *Literary criticism of Oscar Wilde*, ed. Stanley Weintraub (Lincoln, Nebraska, 1968), p. 110.
7. T. S. Eliot, 'The Metaphysical poets [1921]', *Selected essays*, 3rd edn (London, 1951), p. 289.
8. *Gabriel Harvey's marginalia*, ed. G. C. Moore Smith (Stratford-upon-Avon, 1913), p. 161.
9. Millar MacLure, 'The learned poet', *George Chapman* (Toronto, 1966), ch. 2; Arnold Stein, 'Donne's obscurity and the Elizabethan tradition', *ELH*, 13 (1946), 98–118.
10. Scaliger quoted in H. B. Charlton, *Castelvetro's theory of poetry* (Manchester, 1913), pp. 77–78.
11. James Spedding, *An account of the life and times of Francis Bacon* (2 vols., Boston, 1880), vol. I, p. 56; 'Preface to notes and observations on *The Empress of Morocco* [1674]', *The works of John Dryden*, ed. Sir Walter Scott, 2nd edn (18 vols., Edinburgh, 1821), vol. 15, p. 411.
12. Letter dated April 1797, *Collected letters of Samuel Taylor Coleridge*, ed. Griggs, vol. I, pp. 320–21.
13. 'Epistle to J. Lapraik...April 1st, 1785', *The poems and songs of Robert Burns*, ed. James Kinsley (3 vols., Oxford, 1968), vol. I, p. 87.
14. Lycophron, 'Alexandra', *Callimachus, Lycophron, Aratus*, trans. A. W. & G. R. Mair (London & Cambridge, Mass., 1955), pp. 320–443; T. S. Eliot, 'Mr Eliot's Sunday morning service [1918]', *Collected poems 1909–1962* (London, 1963), pp. 57–58.

15. Coleridge, *Biographia literaria*, ed. Shawcross, vol. 1, p. 61.

16. Oliver Wendell Holmes, 'Aestivation', *Poems* (London, 1886), p. 289.

17. Allen Tate, 'Horatian epode to the Duchess of Malfi [1928]', *Poems 1920–1945* (London, 1947), p. 29.

18. W. H. Auden, 'Shorts', *New York quarterly*, 1 (1970), 14.

19. 'Nuns fret not at their convent's narrow room [1807]', *The poetical works of William Wordsworth*, ed. E. de Sélincourt & Helen Darbishire (4 vols., Oxford, 1940–47), vol. 3, p. 1.

20. O. B. Hardison, 'The rhetoric of Hitchcock's thrillers', in *The way it is*, ed. Douglas A. Hughes (New York, 1970), pp. 489–98.

21. H. J. Chaytor, *From script to print* (Cambridge, 1945), pp. 67–72.

22. André Gide, *Journal des faux-monnayeurs* (Paris, 1927), p. 53.

23. *Writers at work*, ed. Malcolm Cowley (New York, 1959), p. 134.

24. St Augustine, *De doctrina christiana*, Bk II, ch. 6, para. 8; Mark Pattison, *Milton* [1879] (London, 1909), p. 215.

25. Victor Shklovsky, 'Art as technique [1917]', in *Russian formalist criticism: four essays*, trans. Lee T. Lemon & Marion J. Reis (Lincoln, Nebraska, 1965), pp. 4, 12–13; R. H. Stacy, *Defamiliarisation in language and literature* (Syracuse, NY, 1977).

26. 'Poeta fit, non nascitur', *The complete works of Lewis Carroll*, intro. Alexander Woollcott (New York, 1936), p. 881; 'A vision', *The poems English and Latin of Lord Herbert of Cherbury*, ed. G. C. Moore Smith (Oxford, 1923), p. 24.

27. 'Timber, or discoveries [1640]', *Ben Jonson's literary criticism*, ed. James D. Redwine (Lincoln, Nebraska, 1970), p. 171.

28. *Ib.*, p. 173.

29. Percy Simpson, 'King James on Donne', *TLS*, no. 2073 (25 October 1941), 531.

30. Mayne quoted in Robert Lathrop Sharp, 'Some light on Metaphysical obscurity and roughness', *SP*, 31 (1934), 505.

31. Oscar Wilde, *Lady Windermere's fan* [1893] (London, 1913), p. 17.

32. Letter dated 23 January 1882, *Letters of Robert Browning*, ed. Thurman L. Hood (New Haven, 1933), p. 208.

33. Empson, 'Note on notes [1940]', quoted in Press, *The chequer'd shade*, p. 41.

34. Wallace Stevens, *Opus posthumous*, ed. Samuel French Morse (London, 1959), p. 171.

35. W. H. Auden, 'Squares and oblongs', in *Poets at work*, intro. Charles D. Abbott (New York, 1948), pp. 176–77.

36. Nerval quoted in Henri Peyre, *Writers and their critics* (Ithaca, 1944), p. 217.

37. Mallarmé, 'Sur l'évolution littéraire [1891]', *Oeuvres complètes*, ed. Mondor & Jean-Aubry, p. 869; Krishna Rayan, *Suggestion and statement in poetry* (London, 1972).

38. Letter dated 13 May 1878, *The letters of Gerard Manley Hopkins to Robert Bridges*, ed. Claude Colleer Abbott (London, 1935), p. 50.

39. P. B. Medawar, 'Science and literature', *Encounter*, 32 (January 1969), 19.

40. Letter dated 3 March 1865, *Letters of Matthew Arnold 1848–1888*, ed. George W. Russell (2 vols., London & New York, 1901), vol. 1, pp. 289–90.

41. Michaċ. Polanyi, *The tacit dimension* (London, 1967), pp. 3–25; F. R. Leavis, *Nor shall my sword* (London, 1972), pp. 21–24.

42. D. P. Walker, 'Esoteric symbolism', in *Poetry and poetics from ancient Greece to the Renaissance*, ed. G. M. Kirkwood (Ithaca, 1975), p. 223.

43. Mallarmé, 'Hérésies artistiques: l'art pour tous [1862]', *Oeuvres complètes*, ed. Mondor & Jean-Aubry, pp. 257–60.

44. J. W. Saunders, 'The stigma of print', *EIC*, 1 (1951), 139–64.

45. Dylan Thomas, 'Letter to my aunt discussing the correct approach to modern poetry [1934]', *The poems*, ed. Daniel Jones (London, 1971), p. 84.

46. 'Proclamation', *transition*, nos 16–17 (June 1929), 13.

47. *Boccaccio on poetry*, trans. Charles G. Osgood (Princeton, 1930), p. 62; Matthew, 7:6.

48. Letter dated 23 August 1799, *The complete writings of William Blake*, ed. Keynes, p. 793; 'Advertisement' to 'Epipsychidion [1821]', *Shelley*, ed. A. S. B. Glover (London, 1951), p. 529.

49. Baldassare Castiglione, *The book of the courtier* [1528], trans. Sir Thomas Hoby [1561], intro. W. H. D. Rouse (London & New York, 1928), p. 51.

50. 'An essay of dramatic poesy [1668]', *Essays of John Dryden*, ed. Ker, vol. 1, p. 52.

51. Coleridge, *Biographia literaria*, ed. Shawcross, vol. 1, p. 15.

52. Julian Symons, 'Obscurity and Dylan Thomas', *Kenyon review*, 2 (1940), 61–70.

53. Calvin S. Brown, 'Difficulty and surface value', in *The disciplines of criticism*, ed. Peter Demetz et al. (New Haven & London, 1968), p. 54; G. Steiner, 'On difficulty', *JAAC*, 36 (1977–78), 263–76.

54. R. D. Havens, 'Simplicity, a changing concept', *JHI*, 14 (1953), 4.

55. Teilhard de Chardin, *The phenomenon of man* (London, 1959), p. 60; Arthur Koestler, *The roots of coincidence* (London, 1972), p. 60.

56. Bertrand Russell, 'Logical atomism', in *Logical positivism*, ed. A. J. Ayer (Glencoe, Illinois, 1959), p. 44.

57. Lawrence Richard Holmes, 'The mystery of "the simple" in poetry', *Mankato studies in English*, 3 (1968), 28.

58. C. S. Lewis, *Studies in words* (Cambridge, 1960), p. 170.

59. Richard F. Jones, 'The moral sense of simplicity', in *Studies in honour of Frederick W. Shipley* (St Louis, 1942), pp. 265–87.

60. George Orwell, *Nineteen eighty-four* [1949] (Harmondsworth, 1954), p. 45; Howard Fink, 'Newspeak: the epitome of parody techniques in "Nineteen eighty-four"', *Critical survey*, 5 (1970–72), 155–63.

61. David Hume, 'Of simplicity and refinement in writing [1742]', *Of the standard of taste*, ed. John W. Lenz (Indianapolis, 1965), p. 47.

62. Fanny Burney quoted in Chauncey Brewster Tinker, *Nature's simple plan* (Princeton, 1922), p. 82.

63. 'Elegy written in a country church yard [1751]', *The complete poems of Thomas Gray*, ed. H. W. Starr & J. R. Hendrickson (Oxford, 1966), p. 39; Robert Southey, *The lives and works of uneducated poets* [1831], ed. J. S. Childers (London, 1925).

64. Coleridge, *Biographia literaria*, ed. Shawcross, vol. 2, pp. 105–06.

65. Letter dated 20 April 1786, *The letters of Robert Burns*, ed. J. De Lancey Ferguson (2 vols., Oxford, 1931), vol. 1, p. 26.

66. Havens, 'Simplicity, a changing concept', p. 28.

67. 'Wordsworth and Kipling [1912]', *Collected essays papers &c of Robert Bridges* (London, 1933).

68. Pound quoted in Noel Stock, *The life of Ezra Pound* (London, 1970), p. 112.

69. *The poems and songs of Robert Burns*, ed. Kinsley, vol. 3, pp. 1454–55; *Robert Burns' commonplace book* (Edinburgh, 1872), p. 3.

70. 'An essay of dramatic poesy [1668]', *Essays of John Dryden*, ed. Ker, vol. 1, p. 92.

71. Mary Ellen Rickey, *Utmost art* (Lexington, 1966).

72. David Craig, *The real foundations* (London, 1973), p. 263.

Notes to chapter 4

1. Quoted in Neville Rogers, *Shelley at work*, 2nd edn (Oxford, 1967), p. 1.

2. Norman Fruman, *Coleridge, the damaged archangel* (New York, 1971), pp. 3–12; *The poems of Samuel Taylor Coleridge*, ed. Ernest Hartley Coleridge (London, 1912), p. 296; Lilian Furst, 'Spontaneous', *Romanticism in perspective* (London, 1969), pp. 244–75.

3. John Ch. Simopoulous, 'The study of inspiration', *JP*, 45 (1948), 36–37; Rosamond E. M. Harding, *An anatomy of inspiration*, 3rd edn (London, 1967); Allott (ed.), *Novelists on the novel*, pp. 111–58.

4. *The first folio of Shakespeare* [1623], prepared by Charlton T. Hinman (London, 1968), p. 7; 'On Shakespeare [1630]', *The poems of John Milton*, ed. Carey & Fowler, p. 123.

5. 'An essay of dramatic poesy [1668]', *Essays of John Dryden*, ed. Ker, vol. 1, p. 52; Johnson, *Idler*, no. 77 (6 October 1759), '*The idler' and 'The adventurer*', ed. Bate, p. 239.

6. 'Clio's protest [1771]', *The plays and poems of Richard Brinsley*

Sheridan, ed. R. Crompton Rhodes (3 vols., Oxford, 1928), vol. 3, p. 117.

7. Samuel Butler, 'A small poet [1667–69]', *Characters*, ed. Charles W. Daves (Cleveland & London, 1970), p. 83.

8. J. A. Sutherland, *Thackeray at work* (London, 1974).

9. 'An epistle to Robert Lloyd, Esq. [written 1754]', *The poetical works of William Cowper*, ed. H. S. Milford (London, 1911), p. 267.

10. *Menaphon* [1589], *The life and complete works in prose and verse of Robert Greene*, ed. Alexander B. Grosart (15 vols., London, 1881–86), vol. 6, p. 11.

11. 'Adam's curse [1902]', *The collected poems of W. B. Yeats*, p. 88.

12. Rogers, *Shelley at work*, pp. 207, 209.

13. W. B. Yeats, *A vision* (London, 1937), p. 8.

14. Richard Aldington, *Life for life's sake* [1941] (London, 1968), p. 302; Graham Balfour, *The life of Robert Louis Stevenson*, 13th edn (London, 1913), p. 161.

15. *George Eliot's life*, ed. J. W. Cross (New York, 1884), p. 724.

16. Jerome Beaty, 'Visions and revisions: chapter lxxxi of *Middlemarch*', *PMLA*, 72 (1957), 662–79.

17. E. M. Forster, 'The raison d'être of criticism in the arts [1947]', *Two cheers for democracy* (London, 1951), p. 123.

18. Ernst Kris, *Psychoanalytic explorations in art* (London, 1953), pp. 292–94.

19. Auden, 'Squares and oblongs', in *Poets at work*, intro. Abbott, p. 174.

20. Stanley Burnshaw, *The seamless web* (London, 1970), pp. 177, 308.

21. Roland Barthes, 'To write: an intransitive verb?' in *The languages of criticism and the sciences of man*, ed. Richard Macksey & Eugenio Donato (Baltimore & London, 1970), pp. 134–45.

22. B. L. Skinner, 'On "having" a poem', *Saturday review* (15 July 1972), 35.

23. 'A defence of poetry [1821]', *Shelley*, ed. Glover, p. 1055.

24. 'On personality, grace and free will [1881]', *The sermons and devotional writings of Gerard Manley Hopkins*, ed. Christopher Devlin (London, 1959), p. 158.

25. Jeremiah, 23:9; Isaiah, 21:3; Abraham Anvi, 'Inspiration in Plato and the Hebrew prophets', *CL*, 20 (1968), 53–63.

26. R. A. Knox, *Enthusiasm* (Oxford, 1950), pp. 41–42.

27. Geoffrey Grigson, *The harp of Aeolus* (London, 1947), pp. 24–46.

28. 'A defence of poetry [1821]', *Shelley*, ed. Glover, p. 1024.

29. Mallarmé, 'Don du poème [1865]', *Oeuvres complètes*, ed. Mondor & Jean-Aubry, p. 40.

30. Monroe C. Beardsley, 'On the creation of art', *JAAC*, 23 (1964–65), 291.

31. Valéry, 'Concerning "Adonis" [1921]', *The art of poetry*, trans. Folliot, p. 18.

32. Siegfried Mandel, *Rainer Maria Rilke* (Carbondale & Edwardsville, 1965), p. 92.

33. Valéry, 'Reflections on art [1935]', *Aesthetics*, trans. Ralph Manheim, intro. Herbert Read (London, 1964), p. 171.

34. Allen Wade, *A bibliography of the writings of W. B. Yeats*, rev. Russell K. Alspach (London, 1968), p. 67; Yeats, *The cat and the moon* (Dublin, 1924), p. 37.

35. 'De finibus [1862]', *The Oxford Thackeray*, intro. George Saintsbury (17 vols., London, n.d.), vol. 17, p. 597.

36. George Kubler, *The shape of time* (New Haven, 1962), p. 49.

37. Sermon preached 26 April 1625, *The sermons of John Donne*, ed. Simpson & Potter, vol. 6, p. 281.

38. Henry More, *Enthusiasmus triumphatus* [1662], intro. M. V. DePorte (Los Angeles, 1966), p. xvii; Susie I. Tucker, *Enthusiasm* (Cambridge, 1972).

39. Jonathan Swift, *A tale of a tub* [1704], ed. Herbert Davis (Oxford, 1939), p. 95.

40. Ernest Jones, 'The Madonna's conception through the ear', *Essays in applied psychoanalysis* (2 vols., London, 1951), vol. 2, p. 292.

41. E. R. Dodds, *The Greeks and the irrational* (Berkeley, 1951), p. 8.

42. *Chapman's Homer*, ed. Allardyce Nicoll (2 vols., London, 1957), vol. 2, p. 6.

43. Roscommon, 'An essay on translated verse [1684]', in *Critical essays of the seventeenth century*, ed. Spingarn, vol. 2, p. 306.

44. Lily Bess Campbell, 'The Christian muse', *Huntington Library bulletin*, 8 (1935), 60–63; William Kerrigan, *The prophetic Milton* (Charlottesville, 1974).

45. Robert J. Clements, 'Iconography on the nature and inspiration of poetry in Renaissance emblem literature', *PMLA*, 70 (1955), 792; Mary Barnard, *The mythmakers* (Athens, Ohio, 1966), p. 20.

46. 'October', *The shepherd's calendar* [1579], *Spenser's minor poems*, ed. Ernest De Sélincourt (Oxford, 1960), p. 100.

47. François Rabelais, *Pantagruel*, prologue to Bk III [1552]; André Winandy, 'Rabelais' barrel', in *Intoxication and literature*, ed. Enid Rhodes Peschel (New Haven, 1974), pp. 8–25.

48. 'A descriptive catalogue [1809]', *The complete writings of William Blake*, ed. Keynes, pp. 565–66; Curtius, 'The muses', *European literature and the Latin Middle Ages*, trans. Trask, pp. 228–46.

49. Courtland D. Baker, 'Certain religious elements in the English doctrine of the inspired poet during the Renaissance', *ELH*, 6 (1939), 300–23.

50. *Life and letters of Harriet Beecher Stowe*, ed. Annie Fields (London, 1897), p. 377.

51. Allan Pritchard, 'George Wither: the poet as prophet', *SP*, 59 (1962), 211–30.
52. Letter dated 25 April 1803, *Complete writings of William Blake*, ed. Keynes, p. 823.
53. Letter dated 6 July 1803, *ib.*, p. 825.
54. 'Poems from the note-book 1800–03.', *ib.*, p. 419.
55. Peter Fleming, 'Take over', *Sunday times* (London) (18 July 1971), 21; Rosemary Brown, *Unfinished symphonies* (London, 1971).
56. Edward Young, *Conjectures on original composition* (London, 1759), p. 31.
57. Wellek, *A history of modern criticism: 1750–1950*, vol. 2, p. 140.
58. Herbert Read, 'The poet and his muse', *BJA*, 4 (1964), 103; 'A defence of poetry [1821]', *Shelley*, ed. Glover, p. 1027.
59. Albert Rothenberg, 'Inspiration, insight and the creative process', *CE*, 32 (1970), 176.
60. Valéry, 'Poetry and abstract thought [1939]', *The art of poetry*, trans. Folliot, p. 80; Eliot, 'The music of poetry [1942]', *On poetry and poets* (London, 1957), p. 38.
61. Rogers, *Shelley at work*, p. 204.
62. 'Far-far-away [1889]', *The poems of Tennyson*, ed. Christopher Ricks (London, 1969), p. 1405.

Notes to chapter 5

1. *Astrophil and Stella* [1582], LXXIV, *The poems of Sir Philip Sidney*, ed. William A. Ringler (Oxford, 1962), p. 203; Persius, 'Prologue', *Satires*.
2. 'New notes on Edgar Poe [1857]', *Baudelaire as a literary critic*, trans. Lois Boe Hyslop & Francis E. Hyslop (University Park, Penn., 1964), p. 134.
3. Valéry, 'On literary technique [1899]', *The art of poetry*, trans. Folliot, pp. 319, 321, 315.
4. Valéry, *ib.*, p. xix.
5. Eliot, 'Four Elizabethan dramatists [1924]', *Selected essays*, p. 114.
6. Valéry, 'Poetry and abstract thought [1939]', *The art of poetry*, trans. Folliot, p. 79.
7. '*Romeo and Juliet*', *Coleridge's literary criticism*, ed. Mackail, p. 225.
8. Conversation dated 20 June 1831, Johann Peter Eckermann, *Conversations with Goethe*, trans. John Oxenford, ed. J. K. Moorhead (London & New York, 1970), p. 415.
9. 'A receit [i.e. "recipe"] to make an epic poem [1713]', in *Pope, The rape of the lock. A casebook*, ed. John Dixon Hunt (Macmillan, 1968), pp. 25–29.
10. *John Webster*, ed. G. K. & S. K. Hunter (Harmondsworth, 1969), p. 30.

11. 'Biography [1832]', *The works of Thomas Carlyle* (30 vols., London, 1896–99), vol. 28, p. 49.

12. Stravinsky quoted by Saul Bellow, 'Ideas and the novel: an interview', *Dialogue*, 2, iii (1969), 58.

13. Sidney, *An apologie for poetry*, ed. Shepherd, p. 99.

14. 'Of a dance in the Quenis chalmer', *The poems of William Dunbar*, ed. W. Mackay Mackenzie (Edinburgh, 1932), p. 61; 'Lament for the makaris', *ib.*, p. 20; George Puttenham, *The arte of English poesie* [1589], ed. Gladys Doidge Willcock & Alice Walker (Cambridge, 1936), p. 60; John S. P. Tatlock, 'The epilogue of Chaucer's *Troilus*', *MP*, 18 (1920–21), 119–20; Sidney, *An apologie for poetry*, ed. Shepherd, p. 153.

15. 'A defence of poetry [1821]', *Shelley*, ed. Glover, pp. 1050–51.

16. 'October', *Spenser's minor poems*, ed. De Sélincourt, pp. 100, 96.

17. Edward John Trelawney, *Recollections of the last days of Shelley and Byron* [1858], in *The life of Percy Bysshe Shelley*, intro. Humbert Wolfe (2 vols., London, 1933), vol. 2, p. 197.

18. Robert Graves, *Poetic unreason* (London, 1925), pp. 100–01; Sigmund Freud, *Totem and taboo* [1913], trans. James Strachey (London, 1960), p. 95.

19. Graves, *Poetic unreason*, p. 28.

20. 'Preface to the *Fables* [1700]', *Essays of John Dryden*, ed. Ker, vol. 2, p. 252.

21. E. H. Gombrich, *Art and illusion* (London, 1960), p. 99.

22. Valéry, 'Poetry and abstract thought [1939]', *The art of poetry*, trans. Folliot, p. 63.

23. Ezra Pound, 'Madox Ford at Rapallo [1947]', *Pavannes and divagations* (London, 1960), p. 155.

24. Eliot, 'A brief treatise on the criticism of poetry', *Chapbook*, 2 (March 1920), 4.

25. Milman Parry, *L'épithète traditionelle dans Homère* (Paris, 1928); *The making of Homeric verse*, ed. Adam Parry (New York, 1971).

26. Huppé, *The web of words*.

27. Aristophanes, *Frogs*, 877; Roland Barthes, *S/Z* (Paris, 1970), p. 166.

28. J. W. Mackail, *The life of William Morris* (2 vols., London, 1901), vol. 1, p. 186.

29. Letter dated 16 December 1816, *Jane Austen's letters*, ed. R. W. Chapman (London, 1952), p. 469.

30. Théophile Gautier, *Poésies diverses: Émaux et camées*, ed. Ferdinand Gohin & Roger Tisserand (Paris, 1929), p. 24; James K. Robinson, 'A neglected phase of the Aesthetic movement: English Parnassianism', *PMLA*, 68 (1953), 733–54.

31. Riding quoted in Robert Graves, *The white goddess* (London, 1967), p. 444.

32. Horace, *Satires*, I 10 72–73, *Ars poetica*, 388.

33. Suetonius, *Life of Virgil*, 22; Sir Thomas Browne, *Pseudodoxia epidemica* (1646), Bk III, ch. 6.

34. Joachim du Bellay, *La deffence et illustration de la langue françoyse*, ed. Henri Chamard (Paris, 1904), pp. 301–02; William Rawley, *The life of the right honorable Francis Bacon* [1657], *The works of Francis Bacon*, ed. James Spedding *et al.* (14 vols., London, 1862–1901), vol. 1, p. 11.

35. I. A. Richards, '"How does a poem know when it is finished?"' in *Parts and wholes*, ed. Daniel Lerner (New York & London, 1963), pp. 163–74.

36. Valéry, 'Concerning "Le cimetière marin" [1933]', *The art of poetry*, trans. Folliot, pp. 140–41.

37. *The essayes of Michael Lord of Montaigne* [1580–95], trans. John Florio [1603], intro. A. R. Waller, Everyman's library (3 vols., London & New York, n.d.), vol. 3, p. 205.

38. *The variorum edition of the poems of W. B. Yeats*, ed. Peter Allt & Russell K. Alspach (New York, 1957); Joseph Warren Beach, *The making of the Auden canon* (Minneapolis, 1957).

39. 'A parallel of poetry and painting [1695]', *Essays of John Dryden*, ed. Ker, vol. 2, p. 152.

40. Wallace Hildick, *Word for word* (London, 1965); A. F. Scott, *The poet's craft* (Cambridge, 1957).

41. Ralph Maud, *Entrances to Dylan Thomas' poetry* (Lowestoft, 1963), p. 108; Dylan Thomas, *Letters to Vernon Watkins*, ed. Vernon Watkins (London, 1957), p. 104.

42. Maisie Ward, *Robert Browning and his world* (2 vols., London, 1968–69), vol. 2, p. 15.

43. Harvey Peter Sucksmith, *The narrative art of Charles Dickens* (Oxford, 1970), pp. 9–13.

44. Johnson, 'John Milton', *Lives of the English poets*, intro. Archer-Hind, vol. 1, p. 76.

45. 'Oxford in the vacation [1820]', *The works of Charles and Mary Lamb*, ed. E. V. Lucas (5 vols., London, 1903), vol. 2, p. 311.

46. Charlton, *Castelvetro's theory of poetry*, p. 22; Hugh Kenner, 'Subways to Parnassus', *Poetry*, 84 (1954), 43.

47. Charlton, *Castelvetro's theory of poetry*, pp. 22–23; *Literary essays of Ezra Pound*, ed. Eliot, p. 7.

48. 'Preface to *An evening's love* [1671]', *Essays of John Dryden*, ed. Ker, vol. 1, p. 147.

49. Milton C. Nahm, 'The theological background of the theory of the artist as creator', *JHI*, 8 (1947), 363–72.

50. Milton C. Nahm, *The artist as creator* (Baltimore, 1956).

51. Gustave Flaubert, letter dated 18 March 1857, *Correspondance* (8 vols., Paris, 1926–30), vol. 4, p. 164.

52. Ficino quoted in E. N. Tigerstedt, 'The poet as creator: origins of a metaphor', *Comparative literature studies*, 5 (1968), 471.

53. Landino quoted in Tigerstedt, *ib.*, p. 458.

54. Scaliger quoted in Tigerstedt, *ib.*, pp. 456, 477; Puttenham, *The arte of English poesy*, ed. Willcock & Walker, p. 4.

55. Abraham Cowley, 'Davideis [1668]', I, *Poems*, ed. Waller, p. 253.

56. Sir Thomas Browne, *Religio medici* [1643], ed. James Winny (Cambridge, 1963), p. 18; Shakespeare, *As you like it*, II vii 139.

57. 'Preface to *Troilus and Cressida* [1679]', *Essays of John Dryden*, ed. Ker, vol. I, p. 219; Logan Pearsall Smith, *Words and idioms*, 5th edn (London, 1943), pp. 91–95.

58. Coleridge, *Biographia literaria*, ed. Shawcross, vol. I, p. 272; E. M. W. Tillyard & C. S. Lewis, *The personal heresy* (London, 1939), p. 148.

59. Sidney, *An apologie for poetry*, ed. Shepherd, p. 101.

60. Terry Eagleton, *Marxism and literary criticism* (London, 1976), pp. 68–69.

61. Trollope, *An autobiography* [1883], intro. Morgan, pp. 241–42.

62. Valéry, 'Concerning "Le cimetière marin" [1933]', *The art of poetry*, trans. Folliot, pp. 140–41; 'A poet's notebook [1928]', *ib.*, p. 177.

63. Joseph Conrad, *A personal record* (London, 1925), pp. 98, 100.

64. Roland Barthes, *Writing degree zero*, trans. Annette Lavers & Colin Smith (London, 1967), pp. 72, 69.

65. Petronius, *Satyricon*, 118; Suetonius, *Life of Virgil*, 22.

66. Sir William Davenant, 'Preface to *Gondibert* [1650]', in *Critical essays of the seventeenth century*, ed. Spingarn, vol. 2, p. 24.

67. Constantine FitzGibbon, *The life of Dylan Thomas* (London, 1965), p. 371; Maud, *Entrances to Dylan Thomas' poetry*, p. 107.

68. Frank Kermode, 'Eliot's dream', *New statesman*, 69 (19 February 1965), 280.

69. 'The choice [1933]', *The collected poems of W. B. Yeats*, p. 278.

70. Hermann Hesse, 'The poet', trans. S. Leonard Rubinstein, *Accent*, 12 (1952), 183–88.

71. T. S. Eliot, *The use of poetry and the use of criticism* (London, 1933), p. 154; Dylan Thomas, 'Especially when the October wind [1934]', *Collected poems 1934–1952* (London, 1952), p. 16; George Barker, 'Holy poems', iii, *Collected poems 1930–1955* (London, 1957), p. 80.

72. Benn quoted in John Berryman, *77 dream songs* (London, 1964), p. 60.

Notes to chapter 6

1. Conversation dated 14 March 1830, Eckermann, *Conversations with Goethe*, trans. Oxenford, p. 361.

2. *Astrophil and Stella* [1582], I, *The poems of Sir Philip Sidney*, ed. Ringler, pp. 165, 459; 'Stanzas from the Grande Chartreuse [1867]',

The poems of Matthew Arnold, ed. Kenneth Allott (London, 1965), p. 291.

3. Letter dated 1885, quoted in Esther Salaman, *The great confession* (London, 1973), p. xi; *The essayes of...Montaigne*, trans. Florio, vol. 1, p. 15.

4. *The essayes of...Montaigne*, trans. Florio, vol. 2, p. 392.

5. Walt Whitman, 'A backward glance o'er travelled roads', *Prose works 1892*, ed. Floyd Stovall (2 vols., New York, 1963–64), vol. 2, p. 731; 'So long [1860]', *Leaves of grass*, ed. Blodgett & Bradley, p. 505.

6. 'Meditations in time of civil war [1923]', III, *The collected poems of W. B. Yeats*, p. 228.

7. Freud, 'Dostoevsky and parricide [1928]', *Complete psychological works*, ed. James Strachey *et al.* (24 vols., London, 1953–), vol. 21, p. 177; C. G. Jung, *Modern man in search of a soul* (London, 1933), p. 177.

8. Fernando Pessoa, 'Autopsychography', quoted in Michael Hamburger, *The truth of poetry* (London, 1969), p. 142.

9. Untitled poem [1908], *The variorum edition of the poems of W. B. Yeats*, ed. Allt & Alspach, p. 778.

10. Conversation dated 29 January 1826, Eckermann, *Conversations with Goethe*, trans. Oxenford, p. 124; James E. Miller, 'The masks of Whitman', *Walt Whitman* (New York, 1962), pp. 15–37; Wayne C. Booth, 'The author's voice in fiction', *The rhetoric of fiction* (Chicago & London, 1961), Part 2.

11. *The essayes of...Montaigne*, trans. Florio, vol. 2, p. 392.

12. William R. Crawford, *Bibliography of Chaucer 1954–63* (Seattle & London, 1967), pp. xxiv–xxviii; Samuel Butler, *The authoress of 'The odyssey'* (London, 1922); Heinrich Mutschmann, *Milton und das Licht* (Halle, 1920).

13. Ernest Hemingway, *Death in the afternoon* (London, 1932), p. 261.

14. Carlos Baker, *Ernest Hemingway* (New York, 1969), pp. 22, 26, 29, 59, 227.

15. Auguste Strindberg, *A madman's defence*, trans. Ellie Schleussner, rev. & ed. Evert Sprinchorn (London, 1968), p. 13.

16. Mario Jacoby, 'The muse and literary creativity', in *Anagogic qualities of literature*, ed. Joseph P. Strelka (University Park & London, 1971), p. 45.

17. W. H. Auden, *Forewords and afterwords* (London, 1973), p. 247.

18. Tillyard & Lewis, *The personal heresy*; René Wellek & Austin Warren, 'Literature and biography', *Theory of literature* (Harmondsworth, 1963), ch. 7.

19. D. J. Palmer, *The rise of English studies* (London, 1965), p. 96; William H. Gass, *Fiction and the figures of life* (New York, 1970), p. 165.

20. Sainte-Beuve, 'Chateaubriand jugé par un ami intime en 1803 [1862]', *Selected essays*, trans. Francis Steegmuller & Norbert Guterman (London, 1965), p. 281; Frank H. Ellis, 'Gray's *Elegy*: the biographical problem in literary criticism', *PMLA*, 66 (1951), 1006.

21. Matthew Arnold, 'Shelley [1888]', *The last word*, ed. R. H. Super (Ann Arbor, 1977), p. 320; 'The study of poetry [1880]', *English literature and Irish politics*, ed. R. H. Super (Ann Arbor, 1973), p. 182.

22. C. J. Sisson, 'The mythical sorrows of Shakespeare', *Proceedings of the British Academy*, 20 (1934), 45–70.

23. Edward Dowden, *Shakespeare* (London, 1877).

24. Letter dated 18 November 1782, *Letters of William Cowper*, ed. J. G. Frazer (2 vols., London, 1912), vol. 1, pp. 218–19.

25. Northrop Frye, *Fearful symmetry* (Princeton, 1947), p. 4.

26. Louis A. Landa, 'Jonathan Swift', in *English Institute essays, 1946* (New York, 1947), p. 28.

27. Conversation dated 6 July 1763, *Boswell's life of Johnson*, ed. George Birkbeck Hill, rev. L. F. Powell (6 vols., Oxford, 1934–50), vol. 1, p. 425.

28. Extract from Thomas Sprat, 'An account of the life and writings of Mr Abraham Cowley [1668]', in *Biography as an art*, ed. James L. Clifford (London, 1962), p. 12.

29. Conversation dated 19 September 1773, *Boswell's life of Johnson*, ed. Hill & Powell, vol. 5, p. 227.

30. George Wilbur Meyer, *Wordsworth's formative years* (Ann Arbor, 1943), pp. 4–5; Philip Collins, '*David Copperfield*: "a very complicated interweaving of truth and fiction"', in *Essays and studies 1970* (London, 1970), pp. 71–86.

31. Carlos Baker, 'Shelley's Ferrarese maniac', in *English Institute essays, 1946*, p. 51.

32. *The autobiography of Thomas Whythorne* [written 1576], ed. James M. Osborn (Oxford, 1961), pp. 42–43; Rudolf Gottfried, 'Autobiography and art: an Elizabethan borderland', in *Literary criticism and historical understanding*, ed. Phillip Damon (New York, 1967), pp. 113–14.

33. René Wellek, *Discriminations* (New Haven & London, 1970), p. 252.

34. Douglas Chambers, '"A speaking picture"', in *Encounters*, ed. Hunt, pp. 29, 56.

35. Anthony J. Podlecki, 'The Peripatetics as literary critics', *Phoenix*, 23 (1969), 123.

36. 'The marriage of heaven and hell [1790–93]', *The complete writings of William Blake*, ed. Keynes, p. 150; 'A defence of poetry [1821]', *Shelley*, ed. Glover, p. 1044.

37. Valéry, 'Poetry and abstract thought [1939]', *The art of poetry*, trans. Folliot, pp. 60, 79.

38. Walsh, *Literature and knowledge*, p. 105.

39. Letters dated 5 September 1933 and 27 September 1921, *The letters of A. E. Housman*, ed. Henry Maas (London, 1971), pp. 328, 187.

40. Conny Nelson, 'Two unpublished letters of Charles Dickens', *Research studies*, 38 (1970), 155.

41. Horace, *Ars poetica*, 102–03; Niall Rudd, *Lines of inquiry* (Cambridge, 1976), p. 171.

42. Yeats, 'Discoveries [1906]', *Essays and introductions* (London, 1961), p. 270; Johnson, 'John Milton', *Lives of the English poets*, intro. Archer-Hind, vol. 1, p. 96.

43. Wellek, *A history of modern criticism: 1750–1950*, vol. 2, p. 137.

44. 'Essay upon epitaphs [1810]', *The prose works of William Wordsworth*, ed. Owen & Smyser, vol. 2, pp. 58–59.

45. Donald Davie, 'On sincerity from Wordsworth to Ginsberg', *Encounter*, 31 (October 1968), 62.

46. Lionel Trilling, *Sincerity and authenticity* (London, 1972), p. 9.

47. Geoffrey Whitney, *A choice of emblems* (Leyden, 1586), p. 126; Patricia M. Ball, 'Sincerity: the rise and fall of a critical term', *MLR*, 59 (1964), 1–11.

48. 'Upon Julia's fall [1648]', *The poetical works of Robert Herrick*, ed. Martin, p. 12.

49. 'Burns [1828]', *The works of Thomas Carlyle*, vol. 26, p. 267; George Henry Lewes, 'The principle of sincerity', *The principles of success in literature* [1865], intro. Geoffrey Tillotson (Westmead, 1969), ch. 4.

50. Johnson, 'James Hammond', *Lives of the English poets*, intro. Archer-Hind, vol. 2, p. 62; Leon Guilhamet, *The sincere ideal* (Montreal & London, 1974).

51. 'The laws of Fesole [1879]', *The works of John Ruskin*, ed. E. T. Cook & Alexander Wedderburn (39 vols., London & New York, 1903–12), vol. 15, p. 359.

52. Edouard Roditi, *Oscar Wilde* (New York, 1947), p. 133.

53. 'To –, after reading a life and letters [1849]', *The poems of Tennyson*, ed. Ricks, p. 847.

54. Letter dated 19 December 1879, *The George Eliot letters*, ed. Gordon S. Haight (7 vols., London, 1954–56), vol. 7, p. 230.

55. Eliot, 'Shakespeare and the stoicism of Seneca [1927]', *Selected essays*, p. 127.

56. Forster, 'Anonymity: an inquiry [1925]', *Two cheers for democracy*, pp. 96, 92.

57. Sir Arthur Quiller-Couch, 'On style [1914]', *On the art of writing* (Cambridge, 1916), p. 213.

58. Valéry, 'Reflections on art [1935]', *Aesthetics*, trans. Manheim, p. 141.

59. Valéry, 'On the teaching of poetics at the College de France [1937]', *ib.*, pp. 83–84.

60. Arnold Hauser, *The philosophy of art history* (London, 1959), pp. 120, 124.

61. J. A. Burrow, 'The voice of them all', *TLS*, no. 3933 (29 July 1977), 937.

62. Alfred Owen Aldridge, 'Biography in the interpretation of poetry', *CE*, 25 (1963–64), 415.

63. Letter dated 27 October 1818, *The Letters of John Keats 1814–1821*, ed. Hyder Edward Rollins (2 vols., Cambridge, 1958), vol. 1, p. 387.

64. William K. Wimsatt & Cleanth Brooks, *Literary criticism: a short history* (London, 1957), p. 615; Wellek, *A history of modern criticism: 1750–1950*, vol. 2, p. 38.

65. Letter dated 3 November 1920, *The letters of Katherine Mansfield*, ed. J. Middleton Murry (2 vols., London, 1928), vol. 2, p. 72.

66. Letter dated 27 April 1818, *The letters of John Keats*, ed. Rollins, vol. 1, p. 273.

67. Letter dated 27 October 1818, *ib.*, p. 387.

68. Arthur Rimbaud, letter dated 13 May 1871, *Oeuvres complètes*, ed. Rolland de Reneville & Jules Monquet (Paris, 1963), p. 268; Wylie Sypher, *Loss of the self in modern literature and art* (New York, 1962).

69. Virginia Woolf, *A room of one's own* (London, 1929), p. 7; Norman Mailer, *The armies of the night* (New York, 1968); Henry Adams, *The education of Henry Adams* (Boston & New York, 1918).

70. Jorge Luis Borges, 'Borges and I', *Labyrinths*, ed. Donald A. Yates & James E. Irby (Harmondsworth, 1970), p. 282.

71. *The poetical works of William Wordsworth*, ed. De Sélincourt & Darbishire, vol. 4, p. 464.

72. Letter dated 27 October 1818, *The letters of John Keats*, ed. Rollins, vol. 1, p. 387.

73. 'Review of Swinburne's *Poems and ballads*, Third series [1889]', *Literary criticism of Oscar Wilde*, ed. Weintraub, p. 85.

74. Letter dated 27 December 1817, *The letters of John Keats*, ed. Rollins, vol. 1, p. 193.

75. Letter dated 24 September 1819, *The letters of John Keats*, ed. Rollins, vol. 2, p. 199.

76. Morse Peckham, *Victorian revolutionaries* (New York, 1970), p. 91.

77. Gamini Salgado, 'The rhetoric of sincerity: *The autobiography of Mark Rutherford* as fiction', in *Renaissance and modern essays*, ed. G. R. Hibbard (London, 1966), pp. 159–68.

78. Flaubert, letter dated 8 February 1852, *Correspondance*, vol. 2, p. 365.

79. Guy de Maupassant quoted in *Documents of modern literary realism*, ed. Becker, p. 89.

80. James Joyce, *A portrait of the artist as a young man* [1916], ed. Richard Ellmann (London, 1968), p. 219.

81. Eliot, 'Tradition and the individual talent [1919]', *Selected essays*, pp. 18–21.

82. Patrick Cruttwell, 'Makers and persons', *HudR*, 12 (1959–60), 487–507.

83. De Gourmont quoted in *Literary essays of Ezra Pound*, ed. Eliot, p. 353.

84. Lillian Hellman, *An unfinished woman* (London, 1969), p. 215.

85. Leon Edel, 'The poetics of biography', in *Contemporary approaches to English studies*, ed. Schiff, p. 43.

86. Leslie A. Fiedler, 'Archetype and signature: a study of the relationship between biography and poetry', *SR*, 60 (1952), 253.

87. Walter J. Ong, 'The jinnee in the well-wrought urn', *EIC*, 4 (1954), 309–20.

88. Donald Davie, *Articulate energy* (London, 1955), p. 165.

89. José Ortega y Gasset, *The dehumanisation of art* [1925] (Princeton, 1968).

90. Letter dated 5 June 1914, *The letters of D. H. Lawrence*, ed. Huxley, pp. 197–98.

91. Victor Erlich, 'Limits of the biographical approach', *CL*, 6 (1954), 131.

92. Puttenham, *The arte of English poesie*, ed. Willcock & Walker, p. 148; Stephen Ullmann, 'Style and personality', *Meaning and style* (Oxford, 1973), pp. 64–80.

93. G. Wilson Knight, *The crown of life* (London, 1947), p. 138; Brian Vickers, *Classical rhetoric in English poetry* (London, 1970), p. 96.

94. *Ancient literary criticism*, ed. Russell & Winterbottom, p. xv.

95. Wellek, *Discriminations*, p. 192.

96. Leo Spitzer, *Linguistics and literary history* (Princeton, 1948), pp. 11, 13.

97. Spitzer, *ib.*, p. 12.

98. D. Newton-De Molina, '"Nothing but –": a stylistic trait in Hobbes' *Leviathan*', *ES*, 53 (1972), 228–33.

99. Geoffrey N. Leech, *A linguistic guide to English poetry* (London, 1969), p. 171.

100. Eliot, *Collected poems 1909–1962*, pp. 14, 15, 24, 95, 98, 190, 192.

101. Tzvetan Todorov, 'The place of style in the structure of the text', in *Literary style*, ed. Seymour Chatman (London, 1971), p. 30.

102. Letter dated 5 June 1914, *The letters of D. H. Lawrence*, ed. Huxley, p. 198.

103. Sarah N. Lawall, *Critics of consciousness* (Cambridge, Mass., 1968), pp. 266–67.

Notes to chapter 7

1. 'The parliament of fowls', *The works of Geoffrey Chaucer*, ed. Robinson, p. 311.

2. John Calvin, *Institutes of the Christian religion* [1536], trans. Henry Beveridge (2 vols., London, 1962), vol. 1, p. 236.

3. Eliot, 'East Coker', v, *Collected poems 1909–1962*, p. 203.

4. John Barth, 'The literature of exhaustion', *New society*, 11 (1968), 718–19.

5. Cicero, *De oratore*, II 21 90–92; Quintilian, *Institutio oratoria*, X 2 26; Walter H. Bullock, 'The precept of plagiarism in the cinquecento', *MP*, 25 (1927–28), 293–312; Harold Ogden White, *Plagiarism and imitation during the English Renaissance* (Cambridge, Mass., 1935).

6. Robert Louis Stevenson, *Memories and portraits* (London, 1887), p. 59; 'Prolegomena [1912]', *Literary essays of Ezra Pound*, ed. Eliot, p. 10.

7. Sidney, *An apologie for poetry*, ed. Shepherd, pp. 138, 228.

8. Scaliger quoted in Charlton, *Castelvetro's theory of poetry*, p. 25.

9. Letter dated 28 October 1366, *Letters from Petrarch*, trans. Morris Bishop (Bloomington & London, 1966), p. 198.

10. Ezra Pound, 'French poets [1918]', *Make it new* (London, 1934), p. 166.

11. Pliny, *Natural history*, 'Preface', 21.

12. 'Ode to a nightingale [1819]', *The poems of John Keats*, ed. Miriam Allott (London, 1970), p. 528; 'The princess [1847]', vii, *The poems of Tennyson*, ed. Ricks, p. 836.

13. 'Annotations to "Poems" by William Wordsworth [1826]', *The complete writings of William Blake*, ed. Keynes, p. 783.

14. Edmund Gosse, 'In ancient Rome', *Yellow book*, 1 (1894), 153.

15. H. L. Levy, '"As myn auctor seyth"', *Medium aevum*, 12 (1943), 25–39; Alice C. Miskimin, *The Renaissance Chaucer* (New Haven & London, 1975), pp. 120–21, 133–34.

16. C. S. Lewis, *The discarded image* (Cambridge, 1964), p. 211.

17. 'To the pious memory of...Mrs Anne Killigrew...an ode [1686]', *The poems of John Dryden*, ed. Kinsley, vol. 1, p. 462.

18. Robert Burton, *The anatomy of melancholy* [6th edn, 1651–52], ed. A. R. Shilleto (3 vols., London, 1893), vol. 1, p. 23.

19. Jonathan Swift, 'The battle of the books [1710]', *A tale of a tub*, ed. Davis, p. 151; Matthew Arnold, *Culture and anarchy* [1869], ed. R. H. Super (Ann Arbor, 1965), p. 99; James W. Johnson, 'That neo-classical bee', *JHI*, 22 (1961), 262–66.

20. *The mirror of modestie* [1584], *The life and complete works in prose and verse of Robert Greene*, ed. Grosart, vol. 3, pp. 7–8.

21. 'Dedication of the *Aeneis* [1697]', *Essays of John Dryden*, ed. Ker, vol. 2, p. 197.

22. William Webbe, *A discourse of English poetrie* [1586], ed. Edward Arber (London, 1870), p. 87; Rudyard Kipling, *The seven seas* (London, 1896), p. 162.

23. John Donne, 'Satire ii', *The satires, epigrams and verse letters*, ed. Milgate, pp. 7–8.

24. Puttenham, *The arte of English poesie*, ed. Willcock & Walker, p. 253.

25. 'On criticism and plagiarism [1712]', *The critical works of John Dennis*, ed. Hooker, vol. 2, p. 27; James Smith, *Poems upon several occasions* (1713), quoted in James Sutherland, *A preface to eighteenth-century poetry* (Oxford, 1948), p. 135.

26. 'Verses on the death of Dr Swift [1739]', *The poems of Jonathan Swift*, ed. Harold Williams (3 vols., Oxford, 1937), vol. 2, p. 565.

27. 'On Mr Abraham Cowley [1668]', *The poetical works of Sir John Denham*, ed. Theodore Howard Banks (Newhaven, 1928), p. 150.

28. *Virgidemiarum*, Bk iv, sat. 1, *The collected poems of Joseph Hall*, ed. A. Davenport (Liverpool, 1949), pp. 57, 259–60.

29. White, *Plagiarism and imitation during the English Renaissance*, p. 16; Alex Lindey, *Plagiarism and originality* (New York, 1952), pp. 95–96.

30. Thomas McFarland, 'Coleridge's plagiarisms once more: a review essay', *YR*, 63 (1973–74), 272–73.

31. Christopher Ricks, 'The poet as heir', in *Studies in the eighteenth century III*, ed. R. F. Brissenden & J. C. Eade (Canberra, 1976), pp. 209–40.

32. 'Nil nisi bonum [1860]', *The Oxford Thackeray*, intro. Saintsbury, vol. 17, p. 363.

33. Herman Meyer, *The poetics of quotation in the European novel* (Princeton, 1968), p. 8.

34. R. W. Dent, *John Webster's borrowing* (Berkeley, 1960), pp. 18, 20.

35. Karl Marx & Frederick Engels, *The German ideology* [1845–46], *On literature and art*, ed. Lee Baxandall & Stefan Morawski (New York, 1974), p. 71.

36. 'An anatomy of the world [1611]', *John Donne: the anniversaries*, ed. Frank Manley (Baltimore, 1963), pp. 73–74.

37. Letter dated 1359, *Letters from Petrarch*, trans. Bishop, p. 183.

38. Alexander Gilchrist, *The life of William Blake* [1863], ed. W. Graham Robertson (London & New York, 1907), p. 317.

39. Young, *Conjectures on original composition*, p. 42.

40. Young, *ib.*

41. *The confessions of Jean-Jacques Rousseau* [completed 1765], trans. J. M. Cohen (Harmondsworth, 1953), p. 17.

42. Virginia Woolf, 'Mr Bennett and Mrs Brown [1924]', *Collected essays*, ed. Woolf, vol. 1, p. 320.

43. Timothy Leary, *The politics of ecstasy* (London, 1970), p. 135.

44. 'The new mutants [1965]', *The collected essays of Leslie Fiedler* (2 vols., New York, 1971), vol. 2, p. 383.

45. Pico quoted in Victor Angelescu, 'The concept of originality in English literary criticism' (unpub. Ph.D. dissertation, Wayne State University, 1968), p. 34.

46. Joseph Glanvill, *The vanity of dogmatising* (London, 1661), p. 137.

47. Giorgio Vasari, *The lives of the artists* [1550], trans. George Bull (Harmondsworth, 1965), p. 31.

48. A. A. Phillips, 'The cultural cringe', *Meanjin*, 9 (1950), 299–302.

49. Young, *Conjectures on original composition*, p. 65.

50. 'The American scholar [1837]', *The collected works of Ralph Waldo Emerson*, ed. Alfred R. Ferguson (Cambridge, Mass., 1971–), vol. 1, p. 69; Herman Melville, 'Hawthorne and his "Mosses" [1850]', in *Hawthorne: the critical heritage*, ed. J. Donald Crowley (London, 1970), p. 120.

51. William Carlos Williams, 'Prologue [1918]' to *Kora in Hell* [1920], *Imaginations*, ed. Webster Schott (New York, 1970), p. 24.

52. Conversation dated 29 April 1778, *Boswell's life of Johnson*, ed. Hill & Powell, vol. 3, p. 333.

53. D. H. Lawrence, *Apocalypse* [1931], intro. Richard Aldington (Harmondsworth, 1974), p. 126.

54. Guillaume Apollinaire, *Les peintres cubistes* [1913], quoted in Roger Shattuck, *The banquet years* (London, 1969), p. 322.

55. Antonin Artaud, 'Le théâtre et son double [1938]', *Oeuvres complètes* (14 vols., Paris, 1956–), vol. 4, p. 94.

56. 'The founding and manifesto of Futurism [1909]', *Marinetti: selected writings*, ed. R. W. Flint (New York, 1972), p. 42.

57. Marinetti, *ib.*, p. 43; 'Against past-loving Venice [1910]', *ib.*, p. 55.

58. 'Dada fragment [9 January 1917]', quoted in Robert Motherwell (ed.), *The Dada painters and poets* (New York, 1951), p. 53.

59. Janco quoted from an exhibition catalogue (1950) in Motherwell, *The Dada painters and poets*, p. 364.

60. George Santayana, *The life of reason*, rev. Daniel Cory (London, 1954), p. 82.

61. Letter dated 24 November 1781, *Letters of William Cowper*, ed. Frazer, vol. 1, p. 158.

62. Letter dated 10 March 1840, *The correspondence of Henry Crabb Robinson with the Wordsworth circle*, ed. Edith J. Morley (2 vols., Oxford, 1927), vol. 1, p. 401.

63. 'Preface [1802]', *Lyrical ballads*, ed. R. L. Brett & A. R. Jones (London, 1963), p. 251.

64. Letter dated 21 February 1818, *The letters of John Keats*, ed. Rollins, vol. 1, p. 237.

65. *Sir William Davenant's 'Gondibert'*, ed. David F. Gladish (Oxford, 1971), p. 269.

66. 'Le testament [written 1461–64]', *The poems of François Villon*, ed. Edward F. Chaney (Oxford, 1940), p. 44; 'The ballad of dead ladies

[1869]', *The works of Dante Gabriel Rossetti*, ed. William M. Rossetti (London, 1911), p. 541.

67. *Kant's critique of judgement* [1790], trans. J. H. Bernard (London, 1914), p. 189.

68. Letter dated 30 December 1918, *The letters of A. E. Housman*, ed. Maas, p. 158.

69. Wyndham Lewis, *The demon of progress in the arts* (London, 1954), p. 64.

70. Samuel Johnson, *Adventurer*, no. 137 (26 February 1754), ' *The idler* ' *and* ' *The adventurer*', ed. Bate, p. 491.

71. Homer, *Odyssey*, XXII 347; Pindar, *Olympian odes*, IX 47–48, *Isthmian odes*, V 63.

72. Quintilian, *Institutio oratoria*, X 2 5; Curtius, *European literature and the Latin Middle Ages*, trans. Trask, pp. 85–86.

73. Cicero, *De inventione*, I 7; Murry Wright Bundy, ' "Invention" and "imagination" in the Renaissance', *JEGP*, 29 (1930), 535–45.

74. 'A parallel of poetry and painting [1695]', *Essays of John Dryden*, ed. Ker, vol. 2, p. 138.

75. Alexander Gerard, *An essay on genius* [1774], ed. Bernhard Fabian (München, 1966), p. 27.

76. Eliot quoted in Wimsatt & Brooks, *Literary criticism: a short history*, p. 354.

77. Samuel Johnson, *Rambler*, no. 121 (14 May 1751), *The rambler*, ed. Bate & Strauss, vol. 2, p. 282.

78. Johnson, *The history of Rasselas*, ed. Tillotson & Jenkins, p. 27.

79. Young, *Conjectures on original composition*, p. 41.

80. Margaret Lee Wiley, 'Genius: a problem in definition', *Texas studies in English*, no. 16 (July 1936), 77–83; Elizabeth L. Mann, 'The problem of originality in English literary criticism', *PQ*, 18 (1939), 97–118.

81. Pope, 'The preface of the editor [to *The works of Shakespeare*, 1725]', in *Eighteenth-century critical essays*, ed. Scott Elledge (2 vols., Ithaca, 1961), vol. 1, p. 279.

82. William Ringler, ' *Poeta nascitur non fit*. Some notes on the history of an aphorism', *JHI*, 2 (1941), 497–504.

83. Johnson, *Rambler*, no. 154 (7 September 1751), *The rambler*, ed. Bate & Strauss, vol. 3, p. 55.

84. Young, *Conjectures on original composition*, p. 36.

85. Young, *ib.*, p. 12.

86. 'Preface [1800]', *Lyrical ballads*, ed. Brett & Jones, p. 240.

87. Benedetto Croce, *Aesthetic* [1900–09], trans. Douglas Ainslie (London, 1909), p. 24.

88. Anthony Storr, *The dynamics of creation* (London, 1972), pp. 31–32.

89. Alfred North Whitehead, *Science and the modern world* (New York, 1925), p. 75.

90. P. B. Medawar, *The art of the soluble* (Harmondsworth, 1969), p. 97; Forster, *Aspects of the novel*, p. 16.

91. Marie Boroff, 'Creativity, poetic language, and the computer', *YR*, 60 (1971), 481–513; Nemerov, 'Speculative equations: poems, poets, computers', *Reflexions on poetry & poetics*, pp. 177–95.

Notes to chapter 8

1. 'An essay of dramatic poesy [1668]', *Essays of John Dryden*, ed. Ker, vol. 1, p. 80.

2. Arthur Symons, *The symbolist movement in literature* [1899], intro. Richard Ellmann (New York, 1958), p. xv; Warren Ramsey, *Jules Laforgue and the ironic inheritance* (New York, 1953), pp. 192–204.

3. Eliot, 'Religion and literature [1935]', *Selected essays*, p. 394.

4. Conversation dated 25 December 1825, Eckermann, *Conversations with Goethe*, trans. Oxenford, p. 123.

5. Auden, 'Making, knowing and judging [1956]', *The dyer's hand* (London, 1963), p. 38.

6. Longinus, *On the sublime*, XIII 2.

7. 'A discourse concerning the original and progress of satire [1693]', *Essays of John Dryden*, ed. Ker, vol. 2, pp. 25–26.

8. Yeats, 'Pages from a diary written in nineteen hundred and thirty [1944]', *Explorations* (London, 1962), p. 310.

9. Eliot, 'Yeats [1940]', *On poetry and poets*, p. 252.

10. Johann Wolfgang von Goethe, *Elective affinities* [*Die Wahlverwandtschaften*, 1809], trans. R. J. Hollingdale (Harmondsworth, 1971), pp. 13–14, 50–57.

11. Baudelaire quoted in Enid Starkie, *Baudelaire* (London, 1957), p. 218.

12. Richard Ellmann, *Eminent domain* (New York, 1967), p. 3.

13. Eliot, 'Philip Massinger [1920]', *Selected essays*, p. 206.

14. Extract from James Howell, *Familiar letters* (1628), quoted in Tucker, *Enthusiasm*, p. 78.

15. 'An elegy upon the death of...Dr John Donne [1633]', *The poems of Thomas Carew*, ed. Rhodes Dunlap (Oxford, 1949), p. 72.

16. *Narrative and dramatic sources of Shakespeare*, ed. Geoffrey Bullough (8 vols., London & New York, 1957–75), vol. 1, p. 284.

17. Charles Muscatine, *Chaucer and the French tradition* (Berkeley & Los Angeles, 1957), p. 124.

18. 'Preface [1816]' to 'Christabel', *The poems of Samuel Taylor Coleridge*, ed. E. H. Coleridge, pp. 214–15.

19. *Aeneid*, VI 237–42; *Beowulf*, 1357–76; *Beowulf and the fight at Finnsburg*, ed. F. Klaeber, 3rd edn (Boston, 1950), p. 183.

20. 'The princess [1847]', IV, *The poems of Tennyson*, ed. Ricks, pp. 791–92; letter dated 21 November 1882, in Hallam Lord Tennyson, *Alfred Lord Tennyson* (2 vols., London, 1897), vol. 1, pp. 257–58.

21. Vladimir Nabokov, *Invitation to a beheading* (London, 1959), p. 6.
22. Jorge Luis Borges, 'Kafka and his precursors [1951]', *Labyrinths*, ed. Yates & Irby, p. 236.
23. Peckham, *Victorian revolutionaries*, p. 132.
24. *The complete works of Rabelais*, trans. Jacques Le Clercq [1936], The Modern Library (New York, n.d.).
25. Eliot, 'Tradition and the individual talent [1919]', *Selected essays*, p. 15.
26. Ezra Pound, *Selected poems* [1928], intro. T. S. Eliot (London, 1948), p. 14.
27. S. S. Prawer, *Comparative literary studies* (London, 1973), p. 64.
28. Lindey, *Plagiarism and originality*, p. 50.
29. J. Livingstone Lowes, *The road to Xanadu* [1927] (London, 1951), pp. 56, 62.
30. Robert Martin Adams, *Ikon: John Milton and modern critics* (Ithaca, 1955), p. 129.
31. Herbert Weisinger, 'Myth, method, and Shakespeare [1958]', *The agony and the triumph* (Michigan, 1964), p. 218.
32. George C. Taylor, 'Montaigne-Shakespeare and the deadly parallel', *PQ*, 22 (1943), 330–37; Richard D. Altick, *The art of literary research* (New York, 1975), pp. 90–113.
33. G. K. Hunter, 'Seneca and English tragedy', in *Seneca*, ed. C. D. N. Costa (London, 1974), p. 167.
34. Conversation dated April 1759, *Boswell's life of Johnson*, ed. Hill & Powell, vol. 1, p. 342.
35. Rosalie L. Colie, *The resources of kind*, ed. Barbara K. Lewalski (Berkeley, 1973), p. 77.
36. Don Cameron Allen, 'Pagan myth and Christian apologetics', *Mysteriously meant* (Baltimore & London, 1970), pp. 1–20.
37. W. B. C. Watkins, 'The plagiarist: Spenser or Marlowe?' *ELH*, 11 (1944), 249–65.
38. Eliot, 'Christopher Marlowe [1919]', *Selected essays*, pp. 120, 122.
39. Letter dated 16 August 1820, *The letters of John Keats*, ed. Rollins, vol. 2, p. 323; Spenser, *The faerie queene* (1590), II vii 28.
40. On 'the principle of disjunction' see Erwin Panofsky, *Renaissance and renascences in western art* (London, 1970), p. 84.
41. Jean H. Hagstrum, 'Kathleen Raine's Blake [i.e. *Blake and tradition* (2 vols., Princeton, 1962)]', *MP*, 68 (1970–71), 81.
42. Martin Nurmi, 'Negative sources in Blake', in *William Blake*, ed. Alvin H. Rosenfeld (Providence, 1969), pp. 303–18.
43. Yeats, *A vision*, p. 8; F. A. C. Wilson, *W. B. Yeats and tradition* (London, 1958).
44. 'Mr Pater's last volume [1890]', *Literary criticism of Oscar Wilde*, ed. Weintraub, p. 62.

45. W. H. Auden, 'Our bias [1940]', *Collected shorter poems 1930–1944* (London, 1950), p. 130.

46. 'Retirement [1782]', *The poetical works of William Cowper*, ed. Milford, p. 124.

47. George Steiner, 'Humane literacy [1963]', *Language and silence* (Harmondsworth, 1969), p. 27.

48. Leo Spitzer, 'History of ideas versus reading of poetry', *Southern review*, 6 (1940–41), 605.

49. Harold Cherniss, 'The biographical fashion in literary criticism', *University of California publications in classical philology*, 12 (1943), 287; Göran Hermerén, *Influence in art and literature* (Princeton, 1975); R. Primeau (ed.), *Influx* (Port Washington, 1977).

50. *Don Juan*, IV [1821], *Lord Byron: Don Juan*, ed. T. G. Steffan *et al.* (Harmondsworth, 1973), pp. 216, 631.

51. *Madoc* [1805], part I, canto 5, *Poems of Robert Southey*, ed. Maurice H. Fitzgerald (London, 1909), p. 477.

52. A. A. Prins, '"Unconscious borrowing" and the problem of inspiration', *ES*, 38 (1957), 67.

53. 'The princess [1847]', I, *The poems of Tennyson*, ed. Ricks, p. 754.

54. 'Prometheus unbound [1820]', II i, *Shelley*, ed. Glover, p. 468.

55. Hallam Lord Tennyson, *Alfred Lord Tennyson*, vol. 1, p. 258.

56. Johnson, *Adventurer*, no. 95 (2 October 1753), '*The idler*' and '*The adventurer*', ed. Bate, p. 425.

57. Peter Dronke, *Poetic individuality in the Middle Ages* (Oxford, 1970), ch. 1; F. P. Pickering, 'On coming to terms with Curtius', *German language and literature*, 11 (1958), 335–45; Arthur R. Evans, *On four modern humanists* (Princeton, 1970), pp. 85–145.

58. Dámaso Alonso, 'Tradition or polygenesis?' *Modern Humanities Research Association*, no. 32 (November 1960), 23.

59. V. Krishna Chari, 'Decorum as a critical concept in Indian and western poetics', *JAAC*, 26 (1967–68), 53–63.

60. Roland Barthes, *Le degré zéro de l'écriture* (Paris, 1953).

61. Letter dated 25 July 1920, *Letters of James Joyce*, ed. Stuart Gilbert & Richard Ellmann (3 vols., London, 1957–66), vol. 3, p. 10; George Boas, 'Il faut être de son temps', *JAAC*, 1 (1941–42), 52–65.

62. Basil Willey, *The seventeenth-century background* (London, 1949), pp. vii, 193.

63. 'An essay of dramatic poesy [1668]', *Essays of John Dryden*, ed. Ker, vol. 1, p. 99; René Wellek, *The rise of English literary history* (Chapel Hill, 1941), pp. 29–30.

64. 'Preface [1817]' to 'Laon and Cythna', *Shelley*, ed. Glover, p. 145.

65. Kingsmill quoted in Fraser Neiman, 'The *Zeitgeist* of Matthew Arnold', *PMLA*, 72 (1957), 977.

66. Matthew Arnold, 'Dr Stanley's lectures on the Jewish Church [1863]', *Lectures and essays in criticism*, ed. Super, p. 77; 'St Paul and

Protestantism [1870]', *Dissent and dogma*, ed. R. H. Super (Ann Arbor, 1968), p. 111; R. H. Super, *The time-spirit of Matthew Arnold* (Ann Arbor, 1970).

67. Yeats, *A vision*, pp. 18–19; Morton Irving Seiden, *William Butler Yeats* (Michigan, 1962), p. 113.

68. Pound, 'Hugh Selwyn Mauberley [1920]', II, *Personae* (New York, 1926), p. 188.

69. George Boas, *A primer for critics* (Baltimore, 1937), p. 49.

70. George Boas, 'In search of the age of reason', in *Aspects of the eighteenth century*, ed. Earl R. Wasserman (Baltimore, 1965), p. 18.

71. Anna Balakian, 'Influence and literary fortune: the equivocal junction of two methods', *YCGL*, 11 (1962), 28.

72. Dawn Ades, 'Freud and Surrealist painting', in *Freud*, ed. Jonathan Miller (London, 1972), p. 147.

73. Undated letter, W. H. Auden & Louis MacNeice, *Letters from Iceland* (London, 1937), p. 27; Walker Percy, 'Metaphor as mistake', *SR*, 66 (1958), 79–99.

74. Noel Stock, 'The serious artist', *X*, 1 (1960), 298.

75. Valéry quoted in Jean Hytier, *Poetics of Paul Valéry*, trans. Richard Howard (New York, 1966), p. 258.

76. Valéry, 'An after-dinner speech to the P.E.N. Club [1925]', *The art of poetry*, trans. Folliot, p. 277.

77. J. Bronowski, 'New concepts in the evolution of complexity', *American scholar*, 41 (1972), 577.

78. Harold Bloom, *The anxiety of influence* (New York, 1973), p. 95; *The ringers in the tower* (Chicago, 1971), dust-jacket.

79. Harold Bloom, *Yeats* (New York, 1970), p. 201.

Notes to chapter 9

1. Samuel Johnson, *Diaries, prayers, and annals*, ed. E. L. McAdam *et al.* (New Haven & London, 1958), p. 294; Burton, *The anatomy of melancholy*, ed. Shilleto, vol. 1, p. 18.

2. Sir John Hawkins, *The life of Samuel Johnson, LL.D.* [1787], ed. Bertram H. Davis (London, 1961), p. 151.

3. Milton, *Paradise lost*, I 26, 'The reason of Church government [1642]', *Complete poems and major prose*, ed. Merritt Y. Hughes (New York, 1957), pp. 212, 668.

4. *Kant's critique of judgement* [1790], trans. Bernard, p. 68.

5. 'The critic as artist [1891]', *Literary criticism of Oscar Wilde*, ed. Weintraub, p. 224.

6. Coleridge, *Biographia literaria*, ed. Shawcross, vol. 2, p. 9.

7. Benjamin Constant, *Journal intime*, 10 February 1804, quoted in John Wilcox, 'The beginnings of *l'art pour l'art*', *JAAC*, 11 (1952–53), 360.

8. F. R. Leavis, 'Henry James and the function of criticism', *Scrutiny*, 15 (1947–48), 99; Allan Rodway & Brian Lee, 'Coming to terms', *EIC*, 14 (1964), 112.

9. Helmut Hungerland, 'The concept of expressiveness in art history', *JAAC*, 3 (1944–45), 23.

10. J. L. Austin, *How to do things with words* [1962], ed. J. O. Urmson & Marina Sbisà (Oxford, 1975); John R. Searle, *Speech acts* (Cambridge, 1969); Mary Louise Pratt, *Toward a speech act theory of literature* (Bloomington, 1977).

11. Austin, *How to do things with words*, ed. Urmson & Sbisà, pp. 98ff.

12. Graham Hough, 'An eighth type of ambiguity', in *William Empson*, ed. Roma Gill (London, 1974), p. 82.

13. Hough, *ib.*

14. '[Introduction to] "The shortest way with dissenters" [1702]', *Selected writings of Daniel Defoe*, ed. James T. Boulton (Cambridge, 1975), pp. 86–87; Wayne C. Booth, 'Intentions once again', *A rhetoric of irony* (Chicago, 1974), pp. 120–34.

15. A. E. Dyson, 'Swift: the metamorphosis of irony', *Essays and studies 1958* (London, 1958), pp. 53–67.

16. Monroe C. Beardsley, *Aesthetics* (New York, 1958), p. 25.

17. '1887', *The collected poems of A. E. Housman* (London, 1939), 9–10.

18. Vaughan, 'Looking back [1678]', *Poetry and selected prose*, ed. Martin, p. 434.

19. Untitled poem written *c.* 1862, *The complete poems of Emily Dickinson*, ed. Thomas H. Johnson (Boston & Toronto, 1960), p. 276.

20. Hugh Kenner, *The counterfeiters* (Bloomington & London, 1968), pp. 30–31.

21. 'Laughing song [1789]', *The complete writings of William Blake*, ed. Keynes, p. 125.

22. George Watson, *The study of literature* (London, 1970), p. 70.

23. Hurd, *Letters on chivalry and romance*, pp. 61–62.

24. 'An essay on criticism [1711]', *The poems of Alexander Pope*, ed. Butt, p. 152.

25. Pope, 'The preface of the editor [to *The works of Shakespeare*, 1725]', in *Eighteenth-century critical essays*, ed. Elledge, vol. 1, p. 281.

26. Arnold Isenberg, '"Pretentious" as an aesthetic predicate [1952]', *Aesthetics and the theory of criticism* (Chicago, 1973), pp. 172–83.

27. 'Essay, supplementary to the preface [1815]', *The prose works of William Wordsworth*, ed. Owen & Smyser, vol. 3, pp. 80, 102; letter dated 2 August 1711, *The correspondence of Alexander Pope*, ed. George Sherburn (5 vols., Oxford, 1956), vol. 1, p. 132.

28. *Sir William Davenant's 'Gondibert'*, ed. Gladish, p. 273; Horace, *Ars poetica*, 139.

29. Homer Hogan, 'Hermeneutics and folk songs', *JAAC*, 28 (1969–70), 223–29.

30. E. D. Hirsch, 'Privileged criteria in literary evaluation', in *Problems of literary evaluation*, ed. Joseph Strelka (University Park & London, 1969), p. 29.

31. R. G. Collingwood, *The principles of art* (Oxford, 1938), p. 29.

32. Auden, 'Squares and oblongs', in *Poets at work*, intro. Abbott, p. 174.

33. Nemerov, *Reflexions on poetry & poetics*, p. 160.

34. Valéry, 'Concerning "Le cimetière marin" [1933]', *The art of poetry*, trans. Folliot, p. 148.

35. Martin K. Nurmi, 'Blake's revisions of "The tyger"', *PMLA*, 71 (1956), 669–85.

36. 'Ode to a nightingale [1819]', *The poems of John Keats*, ed. Allott, pp. 530–31.

37. *The notebooks for 'The brothers Karamazov'*, trans. Edward Wasiolek (Chicago & London, 1971), p. 16.

38. Plotinus, *The enneads*, trans. Stephen MacKenna, rev. B. S. Page (London, 1956), p. 422; Erwin Panofsky, *Idea*, trans. Joseph J. S. Peake (Columbia, 1968), pp. 25–32.

39. Geoffrey of Vinsauf, *Poetria nova* [1200–02], trans. Margaret F. Nims (Toronto, 1967), p. 17.

40. Wordsworth's comment quoted in *Lyrical ballads*, ed. Brett & Jones, p. 290; 'De finibus [1862]', *The Oxford Thackeray*, intro. Saintsbury, vol. 17, p. 596.

41. Entry for 12 February 1826, *The journal of Sir Walter Scott*, ed. W. E. K. Anderson (Oxford, 1972), p. 86.

42. C. Kerényi, *Prometheus* (New York, 1963), p. 36.

43. Josephine Waters Bennett, *The evolution of 'The faerie queene'* (Chicago, 1942), pp. 24–38.

44. 'Annotations to "Poems" by William Wordsworth [1826]', *The complete writings of William Blake*, ed. Keynes, p. 783.

45. Bernard Bergonzi, *T. S. Eliot* (London, 1972), pp. 91–92.

46. 'The circus animals' desertion [1939]', *The collected poems of W. B. Yeats*, pp. 391–92; *The cat and the moon* (Dublin, 1924), p. 37.

47. 'Interview with C. P. Snow', *Review of English literature*, 3 (July 1962), 95; 'The world of power and groups', *TLS*, no. 3582 (23 October 1970), 1223.

48. John Wain, *Preliminary essays* (London & New York, 1957), p. 104.

49. Letter written *c.* 1600, quoted in Evelyn M. Simpson, *A study of the prose works of John Donne* (Oxford, 1924), p. 298.

50. Ortensio Landi, *The defence of contraries* (1593), quoted in Brian Vickers, '*King Lear* and Renaissance paradoxes', *MLR*, 63 (1968), 308.

51. Twain, *The art of 'Huckleberry Finn'*, ed. Hamlin Hill & Walter Blair (San Francisco, 1962), p. 25.

52. Robert B. Heilman, 'Hardy's "Mayor" and the problem of intention', *Criticism*, 5 (1963), 208.

53. D. H. Lawrence, *Studies in classic American literature* [1923] (London, n.d.), p. 9.

54. Patrick Murray, '*Paradise lost*: Milton's intention and the reader's response', *Milton: the modern phase* (London, 1967), ch. 7.

55. W. K. Wimsatt & Monroe C. Beardsley, 'The intentional fallacy', *SR*, 54 (1946), 468–88; responses to this essay are collected in *On literary intention*, ed. David Newton-De Molina (Edinburgh, 1976).

56. Rosemarie Maier, '"The intentional fallacy" and the logic of literary criticism', *CE*, 32 (1970–71), 135–45.

57. Wimsatt, 'Genesis: a fallacy revisited', in *The disciplines of criticism*, ed. Demetz, p. 197.

58. Wimsatt, *ib.*, pp. 194–95.

59. A. D. Nuttall, 'Did Meursault mean to kill the Arab? – the intentional fallacy fallacy', *Critical quarterly*, 10 (1968), 95–106; Morse Peckham, 'The intentional? fallacy? [1969]', *The triumph of romanticism* (Columbia, S. Carolina, 1970), pp. 421–44; F. W. Bateson, *Essays in critical dissent* (London, 1972), p. 114.

60. Letter dated 4 January 1939, *The letters of W. B. Yeats*, ed. Allan Wade (London, 1954), p. 992.

61. Edmund Wilson, 'The ambiguity of Henry James', *The triple thinkers* [1938] (Harmondsworth, 1962), pp. 102–50.

62. *The notebooks of Henry James*, ed. F. O. Matthiessen & Kenneth B. Murdoch (New York, 1947), pp. 178–79; Frank Cioffi, 'Intention and interpretation in criticism', *Proceedings of the Aristotelian Society*, 64 (1963–64), 98.

63. Dorothea Krook, 'Intention and intentions. The problem of intention and Henry James's "The turn of the screw"', in *The theory of the novel*, ed. John Halperin (New York & London, 1974), p. 364; Russell M. Goldfarb, 'The problem of intention', *Sexual repression and Victorian literature* (Lewisburg, 1970), ch. 2.

64. Mark Kinkead-Weekes, *Samuel Richardson* (London, 1973), pp. 106–14.

65. Elias Schwartz, 'The meter of some poems of Wyatt', *SP*, 60 (1963), 155–65.

66. Letter dated 8 January 1852, *The letters of Herman Melville*, ed. Merrell R. Davis & William H. Gilman (New Haven, 1960), p. 146.

67. Virginia Tiger, *William Golding* (London, 1974), p. 38.

68. D. H. Lawrence, 'A propos of "Lady Chatterley's lover" [1930]', *Sex, literature and censorship*, ed. Harry T. Moore (New York, 1953), p. 120.

Notes to chapter 10

1. *Through the looking-glass* [1872], *The complete works of Lewis Carroll*, intro. Woollcott, p. 214.
2. Introductory note to the *Iliad*, I [1715], *The poems of Alexander Pope*, ed. John Butt (11 vols., London & New Haven, 1940–69), vol. 7, p. 82; Henry Fielding, *A journey from this world to the next* [1743], ed. George Saintsbury (London, 1902), p. 40.
3. Winters, *In defence of reason*, p. 11.
4. Robert Greer Cohn, *Toward the poems of Mallarmé* (Berkeley, 1965), p. 7.
5. E. D. Hirsch, *Validity in interpretation* (New Haven, 1967), p. 249.
6. Bridie quoted in Sheila Dawson, 'Infinite types of ambiguity', *BJA*, 5 (1965), 290.
7. Wilhelm Dilthey, 'The rise of hermeneutics [1900]', trans. Frederic Jameson, *NLH*, 3 (1971–72), 244.
8. Letter dated 11 April 1739, *The correspondence of Alexander Pope*, ed. Sherburn, vol. 4, pp. 171–72.
9. W. H. Auden, *Homage to Clio* (London, 1960), p. 90.
10. B. C. Southam, *A student's guide to selected poems of T. S. Eliot* (London, 1968), p. 112.
11. Henri Mondor, *Vie de Mallarmé* (Paris, 1941), p. 347.
12. 'The rose [1892]', *The collected poems of W. B. Yeats*, p. 35; *Autobiographies* (London, 1955), p. 255.
13. '[Note on] "The cap and bells" [1899]', *The collected poems of W. B. Yeats*, p. 526.
14. Hirsch, *Validity in interpretation*, p. 8.
15. Eliot, 'The music of poetry [1942]', *On poetry and poets*, p. 31.
16. 'Milton [1804–08]', *The complete writings of William Blake*, ed. Keynes, pp. 480–81.
17. John Wain & F. W. Bateson, '"Intention" and Blake's *Jerusalem*', *EIC*, 2 (1952), 105, 107.
18. 'The clod and the pebble [written 1793]', *The complete writings of William Blake*, ed. Keynes, pp. 162, 211.
19. Jean H. Hagstrum, 'William Blake's "The clod and the pebble"', in *Restoration and eighteenth-century literature*, ed. C. C. Camden (Chicago & London, 1963), p. 385.
20. Hirsch, *Validity in interpretation*, p. 10.
21. *The works of Thomas Nashe*, ed. Ronald McKerrow (5 vols., London, 1910), vol. 4, p. 440; Wesley Trimpi, 'The practice of historical interpretation and Nashe's "Brightnesse falls from the ayre"', *JEGP*, 66 (1967), 501–18; James Thorpe, 'The aesthetics of textual criticism [1965]', in *Bibliography and textual criticism*, ed. O. M. Brack & Warner Barnes (Chicago & London, 1969), pp. 102–38.

22. W. W. Greg, 'The function of bibliography in literary criticism illustrated in the study of the text of *King Lear*', *Neophilologus*, 18 (1933), 242.

23. Fredson Bowers, *Textual & literary criticism* (Cambridge, 1959), pp. 1–34; Morse Peckham, 'Reflections on the foundations of modern textual editing', *Proof*, 1 (1972), 122–55.

24. A. J. Smith, 'A John Donne poem in holograph', *TLS*, no. 3645 (7 January 1972), 19.

25. Geoffrey Tillotson, *Essays in criticism and research* (London, 1942), pp. xx, xxi.

26. Leo Spitzer, *Essays on English and American literature*, ed. Anna Hatcher (Princeton, 1962), p. 116.

27. *Astrophil and Stella* [1582], 1, *The poems of Sir Philip Sidney*, ed. Ringler, pp. 165, 459; 'Secrecy protested [1640]', *The poems of Thomas Carew*, ed. Dunlap, p. 11.

28. *The merchant of Venice*, III i 69; Boas, *A primer for critics*, p. 35.

29. F. W. Bateson, *English poetry* (London, 1950), p. 76.

30. Miskimin, *The Renaissance Chaucer*, p. 101; Walter J. Ong, 'The writer's audience is always a fiction', *PMLA*, 90 (1975), 9–21.

31. John M. Ellis, *The theory of literary criticism* (Berkeley, 1974), p. 139.

32. Letter dated 9 October 1908, *The letters of A. E. Housman*, ed. Maas, p. 271.

33. *Henry James and H. G. Wells*, ed. Leon Edel & Gordon N. Ray (London, 1958).

34. Theodore M. Gang, 'Intention', *EIC*, 7 (1957), 175–86.

35. Auden, 'In memory of W. B. Yeats [1939]', *Collected shorter poems 1930–1944*, p. 65.

36. Leech, *A linguistic guide to English poetry*, pp. 206–07.

37. John Locke, *An essay concerning human understanding* [1690], ed. Peter H. Nidditch (Oxford, 1975), p. 476; N. E. Collinge, 'Ambiguity in literature: some guidelines', *Arethusa*, 1 (1969), 13–29.

38. William Righter, *Logic and criticism* (London, 1963), pp. 100–07; Claes Schaar, 'Old texts and ambiguity', *ES*, 46 (1965), 157–65.

39. 'A defence of poetry [1821]', *Shelley*, ed. Glover, p. 1046.

40. Eliot, 'The frontiers of criticism [1956]', *On poetry and poets*, p. 113.

41. Wellek & Warren, *Theory of literature*, p. 42.

42. Beardsley, *Aesthetics*, p. 144.

43. Letter dated 23 September 1935, *The letters of W. B. Yeats*, ed. Wade, p. 840.

44. Valéry, 'Commentaries on "Charmes" [1929]', *The art of poetry*, trans. Folliot, p. 155; cf. pp. 141–43.

45. John Peter, 'A new interpretation of "The waste land"', *EIC*, 2 (1952), 242–66; F. W. Bateson, 'Editorial commentary', *EIC*, 19 (1969), 1–3.

46. Stuart Dodgson Collingwood, *The life and letters of Lewis Carroll* (London, 1898), p. 173.

47. William Empson, *Some versions of pastoral* (London, 1935), ch. 7.

48. Alberto Caeiro quoted in Michael Hamburger, *The truth of poetry*, p. 141.

49. Wolfgang Iser, 'The reading process: a phenomenological approach', *The implied reader* (Baltimore & London, 1974), pp. 274–94.

50. 'Gide', *The god that failed*, intro. Richard Crossman (London, 1950), p. 195.

51. A. C. Hamilton, *The structure of allegory in 'The faerie queene'* (Oxford, 1961), pp. 9–10.

52. Maurice Evans, *Spenser's anatomy of heroism* (Cambridge, 1970), pp. 90–91.

53. George Sandys, 'To the reader', *Ovid's metamorphosis Englished*, ed. Karl K. Hulley & Stanley T. Vandersall (Lincoln, Nebraska, 1970), p. 8; *Ludovico Ariosto's 'Orlando Furioso' translated...by Sir John Harington*, ed. Robert McNulty (Oxford, 1972), p. 8.

54. Geoffrey H. Hartman, 'The interpreter: a self-analysis', *NLH*, 4 (1972–73), 217.

55. Robert Johnson, *Essays, or rather imperfect offers* (London, 1601); William Mason, *A handful of essays, or imperfect offers* (London, 1621); *Henry V*, 'Prologue'.

56. Colie, *The resources of kind*, ed. Lewalski, p. 52.

57. Letter dated 9 February 1768, *Letters of Laurence Sterne*, ed. Lewis Perry Curtis (Oxford, 1935), p. 411.

58. Norman N. Holland, 'The new paradigm: subjective or transactive?' *NLH*, 7 (1975–76), 336.

59. Virginia Woolf, 'Character in fiction', *Criterion*, 2 (1923–24), 422.

60. Alain Robbe-Grillet, *Pour un nouveau roman* (Paris, 1963), p. 169.

61. Saul Bellow, [Keynote address before the inaugural session of the XXXIV International P.E.N. Congress, 13 June 1966], quoted in James Reeves, *The reputation and writings of Alexander Pope* (London & New York, 1976), p. 78.

62. Wimsatt, *The verbal icon*, p. 83.

63. I. A. Richards, *Practical criticism* (London, 1929), pp. 181–82.

64. 'Ideas and the novel. An interview with Saul Bellow', *Dialogue*, 2, iii (1969), 58.

65. Dawson, 'Infinite types of ambiguity', *BJA*, 5 (1965), 292.

66. Archibald MacLeish, 'Ars poetica [1926]', *New and collected poems, 1917–1976* (Boston, 1976), p. 107.

67. Leonard Forster, *The poet's tongues* (London, 1970), p. 83; Tom Stoppard, '"Orghast"', *TLS*, no. 3631 (1 October 1971), 1174.

68. Stevens, 'Adagia', *Opus posthumous*, ed. Morse, p. 177.

69. Stevens, 'The relations between poetry and painting [1951]', *The necessary angel*, p. 167.

70. Graham Hough, *An essay on criticism* (London, 1969), p. 133.

71. Maxine Greene, 'The whale's whiteness: meaning and meaninglessness', *Journal of aesthetic education*, 2 (1968), 51–72.

72. Robbe-Grillet, *Pour un nouveau roman*, p. 21.

73. Ronald Sukenick, 'The new tradition in fiction', in *Surfiction*, ed. Raymond Federman (Chicago, 1975), p. 43.

74. Paul West, 'Adam's alembic or imagination versus mc²', *NLH*, 1 (1969–70), 538.

75. Susan Sontag, *Against interpretation* (New York, 1967), p. 14.

76 Roland Barthes, 'What is criticism? [1963]', *Critical essays*, trans. Richard Howard (Evanston, 1972), p. 260.

77. Robert Scholes, *Structuralism in literature* (New Haven & London, 1974), p. 10; Jonathan Culler, 'Beyond interpretation: the prospects of contemporary criticism', *Contemporary literature*, 28 (1976), 244–56.

Notes to chapter 11

1. Solon, fr. 26, in Kathleen Freeman, *The work and life of Solon* (Cardiff & London, 1926), p. 213.

2. David Hume, *A treatise of human nature* [1739–40], ed. L. A. Selbye-Bigge (Oxford, 1960), p. 121.

3. 'Sir Eustace Grey [1807]', *The poetical works of George Crabbe*, ed. A. J. & R. M. Carlyle (London, 1908), p. 88.

4. *Convivio*, 3, *Literary criticism of Dante Alighieri*, ed. Robert S. Haller (Lincoln, Nebraska, 1973), p. 112.

5. *Boccaccio on poetry*, trans. Osgood, pp. 62–69.

6. Lucian, 'How to write history', 8, *Ancient literary criticism*, ed. Russell & Winterbottom, p. 537.

7. Pliny, *Letters*, VI 31; Mark Twain, *Adventures of Huckleberry Finn* (New York, 1885), p. 17.

8. J. M. Synge, *The playboy of the western world* [1907], Act 3, *Plays* (London, 1932), p. 267.

9. Cicero, *De oratore*, III 38 153; 'Preface to notes and observations on *The Empress of Morocco* [1674]', *The works of John Dryden*, ed. Scott, vol. 15, pp. 409–10; Ovid, *Amores*, II 12 41.

10. Leech, 'Honest deceptions', *A linguistic guide to English poetry*, pp. 166–82.

11. Joseph Spence, *Polymetis* (London, 1755), p. 300.

12. Quevedo quoted in J. Livingstone Lowes, *Convention and revolt in poetry* (London, 1919), p. 161.

13. Valéry quoted in Hytier, *Poetics of Paul Valéry*, trans. Howard, p. 77.

14. Laura Riding quoted in Martin Seymour Smith, 'Laura Riding's "rejection of poetry"', *The review*, no. 23 (September–November 1970), 11.

15. Laura Riding, *Selected poems* (London, 1970), p. 15.

16. Douglas Goldring, *The last Pre-Raphaelite* (London, 1948), p. 29.

17. C. S. Lewis, *English literature in the sixteenth century* (Oxford, 1954), p. 318.

18. Sir Walter Scott, *Peveril of the Peak* [1882], The illustrated Waverley novels (25 vols., London, 1877–79), vol. 15, pp. 34–35.

19. Bateson, *Essays in critical dissent*, pp. 245–46.

20. Kenner, *The counterfeiters*, p. 165.

21. Dorothy Knowles, 'The "document-play": Vilar, Kipphardt, Weiss', *Modern languages*, 52 (1971), 79–85.

22. Norman Mailer, *Marilyn* (London, 1974), p. 18; Frank Brady, 'Fact and factuality in literature', in *Directions in literary criticism*, ed. Stanley Weintraub & Philip Young (University Park & London, 1973), 93–111; *The literature of fact*, ed. Angus Fletcher (New York, 1976).

23. Leopoldo Alas, 'What naturalism is not [1891]', in *Documents of modern literary realism*, ed. Becker, p. 270.

24. Tolstoy quoted in Isaiah Berlin, *The hedgehog and the fox* (London, 1953), p. 13.

25. Robert Graves, 'The Persian version [1943]', *Poems selected by himself* (Harmondsworth, 1957), p. 162.

26. A. J. P. Taylor, 'Fiction in history', *TLS*, no. 3707 (23 March 1973), 327.

27. Haskell Fain, *Between philosophy and history* (Princeton, 1970), p. 107.

28. H. A. Taine, *History of English literature* [1863–64], trans. H. Van Laun (4 vols., Edinburgh, 1873–74), vol. 1, p. 34.

29. John Stuart Mill, 'Bentham [1838]', *Literary essays*, ed. Edward Alexander (Indianapolis, 1967), p. 203.

30. Letter dated 4 January 1939, *The letters of W. B. Yeats*, ed. Wade, p. 922.

31. 'The second coming [1920]', *The collected poems of W. B. Yeats*, p. 211.

32. Leo Tolstoy, *Anna Karenin* [1874–76], trans. Constance Garnett (London, 1911), p. 1; Vladimir Nabokov, *Ada* (London, 1969), p. 3; Jane Austen, *Pride and prejudice* [1813], ed. Tony Tanner (Harmondsworth, 1972), p. 51.

33. Walsh, *Literature and knowledge*, p. 47.

34. 'The tiger [1794]', *The complete writings of William Blake*, ed. Keynes, p. 214; 'God's grandeur [1877]', *Poems of Gerard Manley Hopkins*, ed. W. H. Gardner, 3rd edn (London, 1948), p. 70.

35. Marcia Eaton, 'The truth value of literary statements', *BJA*, 12 (1972), 170.

36. Housman quoted in Auden, *The dyer's hand*, p. 32.

37. Sidney, *An apologie for poetrie*, ed. Shepherd, pp. 123–24.

38. '[Second prologue to the 1616 folio of] *Epicoene*', *Ben Jonson's literary criticism*, ed. Redwine, p. 120; Northrop Frye, 'Myth as information', *HudR*, 7 (1954–55), 235.

39. Justus Buchler, *The main of light* (New York, 1974), pp. 97–98.

40. I. A. Richards, *Science and poetry* (London, 1926), pp. 62, 64.

41. John Hospers, 'Implied truths in literature', *JAAC*, 19 (1960–61), 37–64; Walsh, *Literature and knowledge*, p. 139.

42. 'Preface to Shakespeare [1765]', *Johnson on Shakespeare*, ed. Raleigh, p. 34.

43. Letter dated 16 October 1811, *The letters of Percy Bysshe Shelley*, ed. Jones, vol. 1, p. 117; letter dated 3 May 1818, *The letters of John Keats*, ed. Rollins, vol. 1, p. 279.

44. 'Character of Mr Burke [1807]', *The complete works of William Hazlitt*, ed. P. P. Howe (21 vols., London & Toronto, 1930–34), vol. 7, p. 308.

45. Forster, 'Anonymity: an inquiry [1925]', *Two cheers for democracy*, p. 91.

46. 'A primitive like an orb [1948]', *The collected poems of Wallace Stevens*, p. 441.

47. 'Ode on a Grecian urn [1819]', *The poems of John Keats*, ed. Allott, p. 537; letter dated 22 November 1817, *The letters of John Keats*, ed. Rollins, vol. 1, p. 184.

48. H. D. Aiken, 'The aesthetic relevance of belief', *JAAC*, 9 (1950–51), 314.

49. Francis Bacon, '*The advancement of learning' and 'New Atlantis*', ed. Thomas Case (London, 1951), p. 97.

50. Thomas Sprat, *A history of the Royal Society* (London, 1667), pp. 413–14.

51. 'Preface [1802]', *Lyrical ballads*, ed. Brett & Jones, p. 254.

52. Letter dated 1847, *Letters of Edward Fitzgerald*, ed. J. M. Cohen (London, 1960), p. 67.

53. Shakespeare, 'Sonnets', LIV, *The sonnets*, ed. Dover Wilson, p. 29.

54. Justin O'Brien, 'Proust confirmed by neurosurgery', *PMLA*, 85 (1970), 295–97.

55. Charles Dickens, *Bleak House* [1853], ed. Norman Page (Harmondsworth, 1971), pp. 42, 511–12; Gordon S. Haight, 'Dickens and Lewes on spontaneous combustion', *Nineteenth-century fiction*, 10 (1955–56), 53–62.

56. Manuel Bilsky, 'Truth, belief and the value of art', *PPR*, 16 (1955–56), 489.

57. F. H. Ludlam, 'The meteorology of Shelley's ode', *TLS*, no. 3679 (1 September 1972), 1015–16.

58. Henry James, 'The art of fiction [1884]', *The house of fiction*, ed. Leon Edel (London, 1957), p. 25.

59. 'Anacaona [1830]', *The poems of Tennyson*, ed. Ricks, pp. 283–86.

60. 'The vision of sin [1842]', *ib.*, p. 721; Kenner, *The counterfeiters*, p. 106.

61. Florence Moog, 'Gulliver was a bad biologist', *Scientific American*, 179 (1948), 52–55.

62. *The poems of John Keats*, ed. Allott, pp. 478, 62, 533.

63. Walter F. Cannon, 'Darwin's vision in *On the origin of species*', in *The art of Victorian prose*, ed. George Levine & William Madden (New York, 1968), p. 166.

64. 'The rime of the ancient mariner [1798]', *The poems of Samuel Taylor Coleridge*, ed. E. H. Coleridge, p. 190.

65. George Barker, 'The hippogryph and the water-pistol', *X*, 2 (1961), 91.

66. Shakespeare, *As you like it*, III iii 20; Laurence Lerner, *The truest poetry* (London, 1960), pp. 204–18.

67. Auden, *The dyer's hand*, p. 19.

68. Johnson, 'Gray', *Lives of the English poets*, intro. Archer-Hind, vol. 2, p. 390.

69. Graves, *Poetic unreason*, p. 189.

70. Eliot, 'Dante [1929]', *Selected essays*, pp. 270–71; M. H. Abrams, 'Belief and disbelief', *UTQ*, 27 (1958), 117–36; William J. Rooney, *The problem of 'poetry and belief' in contemporary criticism* (Washington, 1949).

71. 'Notes on Herbert's *Temple* and Harvey's *Synagogue*', *Coleridge's miscellaneous criticism*, ed. Raysor, p. 244.

72. Watson, *The study of literature*, p. 41.

73. A. E. Housman, *The name and nature of poetry* (Cambridge, 1933), p. 34.

74. 'The author's apology for heroic poetry and poetic licence [1677]', *Essays of John Dryden*, ed. Ker, vol. 1, p. 185.

75. Douglas Bush, 'Tradition and experience', in *Literature and belief*, ed. M. H. Abrams (New York, 1958), p. 43; Erich Heller, *The disinherited mind* [1952] (Harmondsworth, 1961), p. 139.

76. Trevor Eaton, *The semantics of literature* (The Hague, 1966), p. 28: 'A reference which is successfully communicated in the highest universe of discourse may be said to have affidence.'

77. Aristotle, *Rhetoric*, 1404a.

78. 'Tobias Smollett [1821]', *Sir Walter Scott on novelists and fiction*, ed. Ioan Williams (London, 1968), p. 68; James, 'The art of fiction [1884]', *The house of fiction*, ed. Edel, p. 26.

79. Ernest Hemingway, *The green hills of Africa* (New York, 1935), pp. 9–10.

80. Linda Dégh & Andrew Vázsonyi, 'Legend and belief', *Genre*, 4 (1971), 299.

81. E. C. Riley, 'The truth of the matter', *Cervantes' theory of the novel* (Oxford, 1962), ch. 5.

82. Eliot, 'Shakespeare and the stoicism of Seneca [1927]', *Selected essays*, pp. 135–36.

83. Harold Hobson, 'Samuel Beckett, dramatist of the year', *International theatre annual*, no. 1 (London, 1956), p. 153.

84. Burton, *The anatomy of melancholy*, ed. Shilleto, vol. 3, p. 81.

85. 'Timber, or discoveries [1640]', *Ben Jonson's literary criticism*, ed. Redwine, p. 26.

86. 'Preface to Shakespeare [1765]', *Johnson on Shakespeare*, ed. Raleigh, pp. 25–26.

87. Gottfried Lessing, *Hamburgische Dramaturgie* [1767], quoted in *Hamlet*, ed. Horace Howard Furness (2 vols., London & Philadelphia, 1877), vol. 2, p. 268.

88. Coleridge, *Biographia literaria* [1817], ed. Shawcross, vol. 2, p. 6.

89. George Barker, 'How to refuse a heavenly house', *X*, 1 (1960), 95; *The legend of good women*, Text F, 'Prologue', *The works of Geoffrey Chaucer*, ed. Robinson, p. 483.

90. Walter J. Ong, 'Voice as summons for belief', in *Literature and belief*, ed. Abrams, pp. 88–89.

91. Eliot, 'Dante [1929]', *Selected essays*, p. 257; Martin Jarrett-Kerr, *Studies in literature and belief* (London, 1954).

92. Richards, 'Doctrine in poetry', *Practical criticism*, p. 277; 'Poetry and beliefs', *Principles of literary criticism* (London, 1924), pp. 272–87.

93. Delmore Schwartz, 'Poetry and belief in Thomas Hardy [1940]', in *Critiques and essays in criticism*, ed. R. W. Stallman (New York, 1949), pp. 334–45.

94. Jeremy Hawthorne, *Identity and relationship* (London, 1973), p. 94; Eva Schaper, 'Fiction and the suspension of disbelief', *BJA*, 18 (1978), 31–44.

Notes to chapter 12

1. Allen Tate, 'Is literary criticism possible? [1951]', *Essays of four decades* (Chicago, 1968), p. 44; Sholom J. Kahn, 'Evaluation', in *Encyclopaedia of poetry and poetics*, ed. Alex Preminger (Princeton, 1965), pp. 259–64.

2. Alexander Gottlieb Baumgarten, *Aesthetica* (2 vols., Frankfurt, 1750–58).

3. *Kant's critique of judgement* [1790], trans. Bernard, p. 250.

4. 'Oscar Wilde on the witness stand', *The artist as critic*, ed. Richard Ellmann (London, 1970), p. 438.

5. '[Note on] *The merry wives of Windsor*, IV v 130', *Johnson on Shakespeare*, ed. Raleigh, p. 95.

6. Lawrence, *Studies in classic American literature*, p. 170; R. V. Johnson, *Aestheticism* (London, 1969), p. 13; Xenophanes of Colophon, fr. 11, in Kathleen Freeman, *Ancilla to the pre-Socratic philosophers* (Oxford, 1956), p. 22.

7. Lucretius, *De rerum natura*, 1 936–42.

8. 'The church porch [1633]', *The works of George Herbert*, ed. F. E. Hutchinson (Oxford, 1941), p. 6; *Milton's Areopagitica*, ed. H. B. Cotterill (London, 1904), p. 16.

9. 'Commentary', *TLS*, no. 3649 (4 February 1972), 126; E. Gilman, 'Literature and moral values', *EIC*, 21 (1971), 180–94; Vincent Buckley, *Poetry and morality* (London, 1959), pp. 14–15; John Casey, 'Art and morality', *The language of criticism* (London, 1966), ch. 9; T. J. Diffey, 'Morality and literary criticism', *JAAC*, 33 (1974–75), 443–54.

10. Jean-Paul Sartre, *What is literature?* trans. Bernard Frechtman (London, 1950), p. 46.

11. Strabo, *Geography*, 1 2 5, in *Ancient literary criticism*, ed. Russell & Winterbottom, p. 302; M. H. Abrams, 'Style and the man', *The mirror and the lamp*, pp. 229–35.

12. Cicero, *De oratore*, 1 18 83; Quintilian, *Institutio oratoria*, XII 1 1, in *Ancient literary criticism*, ed. Russell & Winterbottom, p. 417.

13. Q. D. Leavis, *Fiction and the reading public* (London, 1932), p. 233; F. R. Leavis, *The great tradition* (London, 1948), p. 8; Graham Hough, *The dream and the task* (London, 1963), pp. 32–33.

14. Lorrayne Yates Baird, 'The status of the poet in the Middle Ages and the problem of anonymity' (unpub. Ph.D. dissertation, University of Kentucky, 1969), pp. 45–46, 64–65.

15. W. H. Auden, 'September 1, 1939 [1939]', in *Poetry of the thirties*, ed. Robin Skelton (Harmondsworth, 1964), p. 283.

16. Ruskin quoted in Douglas Bush, *Mythology and the Renaissance tradition in English poetry* (Minneapolis, 1932), p. 28.

17. *Republic*, 392b, *The republic of Plato*, trans. Francis Macdonald Cornford (Oxford, 1941), p. 78.

18. '[Notes on] *King Lear*', *Johnson on Shakespeare*, ed. Raleigh, p. 161.

19. *Ib.*; Nahum Tate, *The history of King Lear* [1681], ed. James Black (London, 1976).

20. 'Preface to Shakespeare [1765]', *Johnson on Shakespeare*, ed. Raleigh, pp. 20–21; '[Note on] *Measure for measure*, v i 448', *ib.*, p. 80.

21. Charles Dickens, *Great expectations* [1860–61], ed. Angus Calder (Harmondsworth, 1965), appendix A: 'The end of the novel'; Addison, *Spectator*, no. 40 (16 April 1711), *The spectator*, ed. Donald F. Bond (5 vols., Oxford, 1965), vol. 1, p. 169.

22. *The usefulness of the stage* [1698], *The critical works of John Dennis*, ed. Hooker, vol. 1, p. 183; Richard H. Tyre, 'Versions of poetic justice in the early eighteenth century', *SP*, 54 (1957), 29–44.

23. Jean Seznec, 'The moral tradition', *The survival of the pagan gods*, trans. Barbara F. Sessions (New York, 1953), pp. 84–121.

24. *The trial of Lady Chatterley*, ed. C. H. Rolph (Harmondsworth, 1961).

25. 'Prologue to *Love triumphant* [1694]', *The prologues and epilogues of John Dryden*, ed. William Bradford Gardner (New York, 1951), p. 175.

26. Letter dated 30 January 1801, *The letters of Charles Lamb*, ed. E. V. Lucas (3 vols., London, 1935), vol. 1, p. 239.

27. Letter dated January or February 1808, *The letters of William and Dorothy Wordsworth: the middle years*, ed. Ernest De Sélincourt (2 vols., Oxford, 1937), vol. 1, p. 170.

28. 'Standard novels and romances [1815]', *The complete works of William Hazlitt*, ed. Howe, vol. 16, p. 6.

29. George Eliot quoted in Ian Gregor & Brian Nicholas, *The moral and the story* (London, 1962), p. 254.

30. 'Table talk', 31 May 1830, *The table talk and omniana of Samuel Taylor Coleridge*, ed. Ashe, p. 87.

31. 'The poetic principle [1850]', *The works of Edgar Allan Poe*, ed. Ingram, vol. 3, p. 201; 'New notes on Edgar Poe [1857]', *Baudelaire as a literary critic*, trans. Hyslop & Hyslop, p. 135.

32. *Republic*, 378d–e.

33. When the first authorised and unexpurgated edition of *Lady Chatterly's lover* (1928) was published by Penguin Books in 1960, the first printing consisted of 200 000 copies (Warren Roberts, *A bibliography of D. H. Lawrence* [London, 1963], pp. 96–97).

34. *The Oxford dictionary of nursery rhymes*, ed. Iona & Peter Opie (Oxford, 1951), p. 149.

35. Steiner, 'To civilise our gentlemen [1965]', *Language and silence*, p. 83.

36. Titus, 1:15; Sir John Harington, *A new discourse of a stale subject, called the metamorphosis of Ajax*, ed. Elizabeth Story Donno (London, 1962), p. 83; D. H. Lawrence, 'Introduction to *Pansies* [1929]', *Selected literary criticism*, ed. Beal, p. 28; Ludwig Marcuse, *Obscene* (London, 1965).

37. Stendhal, *Armance* [1827], ed. Henri Martineau (Paris, 1950), p. 3.

38. 'Preface to *The picture of Dorian Gray* [1891]', *Literary criticism of Oscar Wilde*, ed. Weintraub, p. 229.

39. George Orwell, 'Benefit of clergy. Some notes on Salvador Dali [1944]', *Collected essays* (London, 1961), p. 214.

40. Martial, *Epigrams*, 1 4 8; *The poetical works of Robert Herrick*, ed. Martin, p. 335; Rudd, *Lines of inquiry*, pp. 174–75.
174–75.

41. Théophile Gautier, *La préface de Mlle de Maupin* [1835], ed. G. Matoré (Paris, 1946), p. 25.

42. Leo Tolstoy, *What is art?* [1898], trans. Aylmer Maude (Oxford, 1930), p. 123; Oscar Wilde, *The picture of Dorian Gray* [1891], ed. Isobel Murray (London, 1974), p. 146.

43. Charles Rembar, *The end of obscenity* (London, 1969); C. H. Rolph, *Books in the dock* (London, 1969).

44. *Milton's Areopagitica*, ed. Cotterill, p. 3.

45. Richards, *Principles of literary criticism*, p. 32.

46. Palmer, *The rise of English studies*, p. 11; Frank Kermode, *The classic* (London, 1975).

47. Letters dated 22 and 27 January 1886, *The Swinburne letters*, ed. Cecil Y. Lang (6 vols., New Haven & London, 1959–62), vol. 5, pp. 131–36.

48. Joyce, *Finnegans wake*, p. 539; Aldous Huxley, *Crome yellow* [1921] (London, 1969), p. 65.

49. Johnson, 'Gray', *Lives of the English poets*, intro. Archer-Hind, vol. 2, p. 392.

50. 'Preface to Shakespeare [1765]', *Johnson on Shakespeare*, ed. Raleigh, p. 10.

51. Theognis, 'Immortality in poetry', in *Ancient literary criticism*, ed. Russell & Winterbottom, p. 3; Shakespeare, 'Sonnets', XVIII, *The sonnets*, ed. Dover Wilson, p. 11.

52. 'To the memory of my beloved...Mr William Shakespeare [1623]', *Poems of Ben Jonson*, ed. Johnston, p. 286.

53. '[Introductory sonnet to] *The house of life* [1881]', *The works of Dante Gabriel Rossetti*, ed. William M. Rossetti, p. 74; E. M. Forster, 'Cardan [1905]', *Abinger harvest* (London, 1936), p. 195.

54. 'Lycidas [1638]', *The poems of John Milton*, ed. Carey & Fowler, p. 245.

55. 'Epistle to posterity [1351]', *Letters from Petrarch*, trans. Bishop, pp. 5–12; Ovid, *Tristia*, IV 10 1–2.

56. 'Archdeacon Hare and Walter Landor [1853]', *The complete works of Walter Savage Landor*, ed. T. Earle Welby (16 vols., London, 1927–36), vol. 6, p. 37.

57. Denys Page, *Sappho and Alcaeus* (Oxford, 1955), p. 123.

58. Robert Escarpit, *The book revolution* (London & Paris, 1966), p. 34; Alfred Andersch, 'How trivial is the trivial novel?' *TLS*, no. 3632 (8 October 1971), 1219.

59. 'The first epistle of the second book of Horace imitated [1737]', *The poems of Alexander Pope*, ed. Butt, p. 637; Harry Levin, 'The judgement of posterity', *Grounds for comparison* (Cambridge, Mass., 1972), pp. 160–73.

60. George Boas, 'The *Mona Lisa* in the history of taste', *JHI*, 1 (1940), 224.

61. Miskimin, *The Renaissance Chaucer*, p. 30; Williàm R. Mueller, *Spenser's critics* (Syracuse, 1959).

62. Eliot, 'Tradition and the individual talent [1919]', *Selected essays*, p. 15; Kubler, *The shape of time*, p. 35.

63. Addison, *Spectator*, no 70 (21 May 1711), *The spectator*, ed. Bond, vol. 1, pp. 298–303; 'Preface to Shakespeare [1765]', *Johnson on Shakespeare*, ed. Raleigh, p. 16; Max Beerbohm, 'From a brother's standpoint [1920]', *The incomparable Max*, ed. S. C. Roberts, (London, 1962), p. 305.

64. Matthew Arnold, 'The study of poetry [1880]', *English literature and Irish politics*, ed. R. H. Super (Ann Arbor, 1973), pp. 168–70; John Shepard Eells, *The touchstones of Matthew Arnold* (New York, 1955).

65. F. R. Leavis, 'Arnold as critic', *Scrutiny*, 7 (1938–39), 328.

66. R. Brand's definition quoted in John D. Bailiff, 'Some comments on the "ideal observer"', *PPR*, 24 (1963–64), 423.

67. Joyce, *Finnegans wake*, p. 120; Lowry Nelson, 'The fictive reader and literary self-reflexiveness', in *The disciplines of criticism*, ed. Demetz, p. 175; Michael Riffaterre, 'Describing poetic structures', *Structuralism*, ed. Jacques Ehrmann (New Haven, 1966), p. 215; J. Kamerbeek, 'Le concept du *lecteur idéal*', *Neophilologus*, 61 (1977), 2–7; Robert DeMaria, 'The ideal reader: a critical fiction', *PMLA*, 93 (1978), 463–74.

68. L. F. Manheim, 'The problem of the normative fallacy', *Problems of literary evaluation*, ed. Strelka, p. 130.

69. Wladuslaw Tatarkiewicz, 'Objectivity and subjectivity in the history of aesthetics', *PPR*, 24 (1963–64), 157–73.

70. David Hume, 'Of the standard of taste [1757]', *Of the standard of taste and other essays*, ed. Lenz, p. 6.

71. Monroe C. Beardsley, 'Intrinsic value', *PPR*, 26 (1965–66), 1–17.

72. Letter dated 30 January 1818, *The letters of John Keats*, ed. Rollins, vol. 1, p. 218.

73. Hurd, *Letters on chivalry and romance*, pp. 61–62; Emerson R. Marks, *Relativist and absolutist* (New Brunswick, 1955).

74. Oscar Wilde, 'The critic as artist [1891]', *The artist as critic*, ed. Ellmann, p. 392; 'To read or not to read [1886]', *Literary criticism of Oscar Wilde*, ed. Weintraub, p. 4.

75. Sainte-Beuve, 'What is a classic? [1850]', *Selected essays*, trans. Steegmuller & Guterman, p. 8; André Malraux, 'Museum without walls', *Voices of silence* [1953], trans. Stuart Gilbert (London, 1954), part 1.

76. Wellek, *Discriminations*, p. 339; Wimsatt, *The verbal icon*, p. 81.

77. John Passmore, *The perfectibility of man* (London, 1970), p. 234; E. D. Hirsch, 'Faulty perspectives', *EIC*, 25 (1975), 154–68.

78. 'Annotations to Sir Joshua Reynolds' *Discourses* [1808]', *The complete writings of William Blake*, ed. Keynes, p. 451.

79. E. E. Kellett, *Reconsiderations* (Cambridge, 1928), p. 263; Jay B. Hubbell, *Who are the major American writers?* (Durham, N. C., 1972).

80. 'Locksley Hall [1842]', *The poems of Tennyson*, ed. Ricks, p. 699; Sydney Smith, '[Review of] *Statistical annals of the United States of America*, by Adam Seybert', *Edinburgh review*, 33 (January–May 1820), 79.

81. Lawrence Baigent, 'The poetry of Ursula Bethell', *Landfall*, 5 (1951), 24.

82. Nick Aaron Ford, 'Black literature and the problem of evaluation', *CE*, 32 (1970–71), 536–47; Cheri Register, 'The case against "phallic criticism"', in *Feminist literary criticism*, ed. Josephine Donovan (Lexington, 1975), pp. 8–11; Martha Vicinus, *The industrial muse* (London, 1974), p. 1.

83. Ellis, *The theory of literary criticism*, pp. 47, 102.

84. Boas, *A primer for critics*, p. 51.

85. James, 'The art of fiction [1884]', *The house of fiction*, ed. Edel, p. 37; Monica Lawlor, 'On knowing what you like', *BJA*, 4 (1964), 126–35.

86. Samuel Daniel, 'Musophilus [1599]', *Poems and a defence of rhyme*, ed. Arthur Colby Sprague (Cambridge, Mass., 1930), p. 70; Charles Tennyson, *Alfred Tennyson* (London, 1949), p. 490.

87. Aristotle, *Politics*, 1340b; 'Timber, or discoveries [1640]', *Ben Jonson's literary criticism*, ed. Redwine, p. 34.

88. Letter dated 4 May 1821, *The letters of Percy Bysshe Shelley*, ed. Jones, vol. 2, pp. 289–90.

89. Eliot, 'A brief treatise on the criticism of poetry', *Chapbook*, 2 (1920), 1–10; 'The perfect critic', *The sacred wood* (London, 1920), p. 7.

90. Steiner, 'Humane literacy [1963]', *Language and silence*, p. 21.

91. Letter dated 22 January 1758, *Correspondence of Thomas Gray*, ed. Paget Toynbee & Leonard Whibley (3 vols., Oxford, 1935), vol. 2, pp. 556–57.

92. 'A defence of poetry [1821]', *Shelley*, ed. Glover, p. 1031.

93. Henry Fielding, *The history of Tom Jones* [1749], ed. R. P. C. Mutter (Harmondsworth, 1966), p. 88; Williams, 'Prologue [1918]', *Imaginations*, ed. Schott, p. 13.

94. Barnett Newman quoted in Harold Rosenberg, *The anxious object* (London, 1965), p. 172.

95. Conversation dated 25 June 1763, *Boswell's life of Johnson*, ed. Hill & Powell, vol. 1, p. 409.

96. Francis Jeffrey, '[Review of] *The excursion*...by William Wordsworth', *Edinburgh review*, 24 (November 1814), 1.

97. Forster, 'The raison d'être of criticism in the arts [1947]', *Two cheers for democracy*, p. 129.

98. 'A few don'ts for Imagists [1913]', *Literary essays of Ezra Pound*, ed. Eliot, pp. 4–7.

99. Randall Jarrell, 'Introduction' to Christina Stead, *The man who loved children* [1940] (New York, 1965), p. xl.

100. 'An essay on criticism [1711]', *The poems of Alexander Pope*, ed. Butt, p. 144.

101. Arnold, 'The function of criticism at the present time [1864]', *Lectures and essays in criticism*, ed. Super, p. 270; *The poet as critic*, ed. Frederick P. W. McDowell (Evanston, 1967).

102. Hubbell, *Who are the major American writers?*, p. viii.

103. Manuscript note dated 12 November 1821, *The works of Lord Byron*, ed. Ernest Hartley Coleridge & Rowland E. Prothero (13 vols., London & New York, 1898–1901), vol. 11, p. 491; letter dated 18 September 1819, *The letters of John Keats*, ed. Rollins, vol. 2, p. 192; Myrick Land, *The fine art of literary mayhem* (London, 1963).

104. Auden, *The dyer's hand*, pp. 9–10 (and cf. p. 280).

105. Eliot, 'The perfect critic', *The sacred wood*, p. 15; 'The Metaphysical poets [1921]', *Selected essays*, p. 288; 'Milton II [1947]', *On poetry and poets*, p. 160.

106. Eliot, 'The frontiers of criticism [1956]', *On poetry and poets*, p. 107.

107. Eliot, 'The Metaphysical poets [1921]', *Selected essays*, pp. 287–88; Basil Willey, *The seventeenth century background* (London, 1934); Leavis, *Revaluation*.

108. Frank Kermode, *Romantic image* (London, 1957), pp. 138–66; Eliot, 'Hamlet [1919]', *Selected essays*, p. 145; 'The music of poetry [1942]', *On poetry and poets*, pp. 26–38.

109. 'Preface [1800]', *Lyrical ballads*, ed. Brett & Jones, pp. 246–47.

110. Helen Gardner, *The limits of literary criticism* (London, 1956), p. 62.

111. T. S. Eliot, *The waste land*, ed. Valerie Eliot (New York, 1971).

112. James, '*Middlemarch* [1873]', *The house of fiction*, ed. Edel, p. 261.

113. Untitled contribution by T. S. Eliot to *Revelation*, ed. John Baillie & Hugh Martin (London, 1937), p. 30; James, 'The younger generation', *TLS*, no. 635 (19 March 1914), 133; letter dated 23 November 1915, *The collected letters of D. H. Lawrence*, ed. Harry T. Moore (2 vols., London, 1962), vol. 1, p. 388.

114. Auden, 'Letter to Lord Byron', Part 2, Auden & MacNeice, *Letters from Iceland*, p. 54.

115. Malraux, *The voices of silence*, trans. Gilbert, p. 14.

116. 'Conversation with John Cage', in *John Cage*, ed. Richard Kostelanetz (London, 1971), p. 27.

Name index

Subject index

absolute values, the classics and, 190–94

aestheticist theories of value, 181, 182

aesthetics: disinterestedness in, 12; morally neutral, 185; organicist, 22, 24; quantitative, 17; use of word, 182; values of, seen by Marxists as class values, 50

affectivism: and criterion of belief, 175–76, 276–77; and theories of value, 181–82

allegory: moral meaning concealed in, 187; sometimes unintentional? 148

allusiveness, in literary imitation, 108–09

ambiguity: meaning of, for philosophers and for poets, 155–56

anonymity, attractions of, 93–95

antibiographism, 87–89, 99

anti-intentionalism, 146

antipast-ism, 112–13

architecture, as clue to form in writing, 17–19, 20

art: as ape of nature, 9; for art's sake, 12, 136, 184; of concealing art, 49–50; defence of errors in, as creative misunderstandings, 133–34; 'disorder' theories of, 6–8; form in, 4–6; not the expression of an age, but helps to make up an age, 132; as perfecting nature, 10; as product and as process, 28, 159; purposive without being purposeful, 136; as reflection or refraction of reality, 9–10; relation between life and, 86–87; as second nature, 2; as a storehouse of values, 190

artistic intent (*Kunstwollen*), 137

autarchies, literary, 11–13, 15

authors: confusion of books with, 90, implied by their books, 101, in their books, 83–87; as creators, 1–2, 77–79; as critics, 198–202; as liars, 164–66; passive under inspiration? 56–57; statements of, about intention, 135–36, 143–45; about literary influences, 119–20; about meaning, 150, 152; views about, change with time, 193

autobiographical element in books, 83–87; as irrelevance, 87–90; place for, and nature of, 90–91

axiologies (theories of value), 181–82, 202

beauty: measure and proportion as constituents of, 17; objective or subjective, 193; as product of aesthetic coherence, 171; as symbol of the morally good, 182

belief: affectivist criterion of (readers rate more highly something they believe in), 175–77; suspension of, 176

Beowulf, 62, 121

Book of Ballymote, 72

Book of Common Prayer, 49

Book of Kells, 18

books: hundred best, 191; as other worlds, *see* heterocosms; as raw materials for manufacture of critical discourse, 160

censorship, follows from ascribing moral values to literature, 189

chaos: as a law of nature, order as a dream of man, 4; 'man's rage for', 6–7; rearrangement of, into cosmos, 3, 16, 76

classics, the, and absolute values, 190–94

coherence, as criterion of truth (constituent parts of a work true to each other), 11, 171–73

collectivist theories of literary influences, 129, 130

commonplaces ('topics' of rhetoricians), transmitted by writers, 94, 129

complexity (obscurity) *v.* simplicity (clarity), in literary history and theory, ix–x; complexity of simplicity, 45

composition: difficulties of, not a criterion of value, 81

computers, simulation of poetic processes by, 118

consensus gentium, 191, 192; books selected by, 193

consistency: criterion of, as casualty of shift of interest from form as product to form as process, 29–30

consonance, theory of (true meaning of a poem is one that harmonises all interpretations), 150

history: separated from fiction only by the writer's intention, 166–67; as 'a version of events', 168

Holy Bible, 16, 30, 33, 43, 46, 49, 57, 59, 63, 76, 77, 87, 102, 106, 109, 127, 158, 165, 187, 189

humanism: defends literature as morally enlightening, 184; of Renaissance, and obscurity of great literature, 34–35

ignorance, as safeguard against being crushed by the burden of the past, 113

imagination in art, 10, 11

imitation: allusiveness as strength of, 108–09; of commonplaces, in literary continuity, 129; eclectic plagiarism as origin of, 106–08; as 'inferiority confessed', 112; literary theory of, 103–36; v. originality, in literary history and theory, ix–x, 102–03, 110

impersonalism, 91, 95; as doctrine of faith among anti-Romantic modernist writers, 97; influences critical theory more than critical practice, 99; interested less in the content than in the shape of ideas, 177–78; objections to, 97–99

incepts (inspirational moments), 57–59; bringing technical skill to bear on, 71

incredibility, 175–78

influences, literary: authors' statements about, 119–20; collectivist theories of, 129, 130; creative misunderstandings in, 132–34; hydrological metaphors for, 120; readers' discoveries of, 121; retroactive, 122; shortcomings of studies of, 123–27; theories of, not approved by authors, 121–22; unconscious borrowing and commonplaces in, 127–30; from the *Zeitgeist*, 130–32.

Information Theory, challenges traditional assumptions about ordered nature of aesthetic experience, 7–8

inspiration: as experience of involuntariness, 54–56; the incept in, 57–59; v. making of writings, in literary history and theory, ix–x, 17, 21–22; mantic or prophetic, 63; the miracle of fluency in, 51–54; passivity of author in, 56–57; psychic intervention in, 59–64; in theological sense, 59–60, 63; unconscious projections in, 64–66

intentionalism, literary scholarship committed to, 140

intentions of author: authors' statements on, 135–36, (too soon or too late) 143–44, (unacceptable) 144–45; discovered while

writing, 141–43; as feature of language used, 137–38; as guide to judgement, 140–41; as guide to meaning, 138–40; objections to consideration of, in assessing works of art, 141–47; purposeful and purposive, 136–37, (tensions between) 145, 146; separate history from fiction, 166; unconscious, 147–48

'interest' theories of value, 197

invention, change in meaning of word, 115–16

irony, 165

knowledge: conceived as the discovery of the new, 111; conceived as something to be recovered rather than discovered, 102, 111; inferior to genius, 117

language: denotative and connotative elements in, 40; as lens and as body or texture, 13–14, 161; ornamentalist and incarnational views of, 44; speech-act theory of, 137; tendency of, to desynonymise itself, 36; translocutionary, of poetry, 170; as utterance, perlocutionary or illocutionary, 137–38

liars, writers as, 164–66

lying, factual error and, 173–75

literature: as a communicative system, 41; as a non-communicative system, 42–43; texts made into, by the community, 197

madness, inspiration as a kind of, 56, 60–61

maker, word with same meaning as poet, in Greek, 69, and in Scots, 70

making of writings: can be studied in author's revisions, 75; as a craft, 62–70; v. inspiration, in literary history and theory, ix–x, 17, 21–22; as making something out of nothing, 76–79; ordeal of creation in, 79–82; prestige of revision in, 73–75; primacy of the word in, 70–73

Marxists: aim to liberate criticism from dogma that art organises the chaos of reality, 4; claim that aesthetic values are fundamentally class values, 50; see literary work as conditioned by historical moment, 79

masks or *personae*, in writing, 37, 95

meanings: authors' statements about, 150, 152; doctrine of indeterminacy of, 150; hierarchies of probable, 160; intended *see* intentions; intentions as a guide to, 138–40; irrelevance of? 161–63; monistic theory of, 149–50, 151–52, 153–54; permissible and impermissible, 157; plural